MURDER AND MADNESS ON TRIAL

INTERACTIONS
in the Early Modern Age

New religious expressions, technological advances, emerging cross-continental empires, environmental and social upheavals, and interactions among previously unconnected peoples and states both demanded and created a new world view, promoting change among some and retrenchment among others. Books in this series explore these changes, and their reception, from multiple perspectives. Topics covered include women and gender, race and ethnicity, religious expression and dissent, popular culture, technology, economics, politics and power, and war and military practice.

A previous version of this series was published as Early Modern Studies by Truman State University Press through 2018 and by The Pennsylvania State University Press through 2020.

MURDER AND MADNESS ON TRIAL

A Tale of True Crime from
Early Modern Bologna

Mònica Calabritto

The Pennsylvania State University Press
University Park, Pennsylvania

Library of Congress Cataloging-in-Publication Data

Names: Calabritto, Monica, author.
Title: Murder and madness on trial : a tale of true
    crime from early modern Bologna / Mònica
    Calabritto.
Other titles: Interactions in the early modern age.
Description: University Park, Pennsylvania : The
    Pennsylvania State University Press, [2023] |
    Series: Interactions in the early modern age |
    Includes bibliographical references and index.
Summary: "Explores the 1588 murder trial of Paolo
    Barbieri in Bologna, examining early modern
    violence, madness, criminal justice, medical
    and legal expertise, and the construction and
    circulation of news"—Provided by publisher.
Identifiers: LCCN 2022061467 | ISBN
    9780271095080 (hardback) | ISBN
    9780271095097 (paperback)
Subjects: LCSH: Barbieri, Paolo, 1563–1606—Trials,
    litigation, etc. | Trials (Murder)—Italy—Bologna.
    | Insanity (Law)—Italy—Bologna—History—
    16th century. | Bologna (Italy)—Social life and
    customs—16th century.
Classification: LCC KKH41.B39 C35 2023 | DDC
    344.454104/121—dc23/eng/20230303
LC record available at https://lccn.loc.gov
/2022061467

The Pennsylvania State University Press is a member
of the Association of University Presses.

It is the policy of The Pennsylvania State University
Press to use acid-free paper. Publications on
uncoated stock satisfy the minimum requirements
of American National Standard for Information
Sciences—Permanence of Paper for Printed Library
Material, ANSI Z39.48–1992.

This book is in memory of my mother, Rosa Orlando.
It is dedicated to my family and to
all the families affected by mental illness.

CONTENTS

ILLUSTRATIONS

THE BARBIERI FAMILY

ANTONIO MARIA BARBIERI († 1569): The pater familias.

IPPOLITA GESSI BARBIERI († February 1598): The matriarch.

AURELIO BARBIERI († between September 8 and 12, 1597): The oldest son, never married, trained as a lawyer.

PAOLO BARBIERI: Knight of the Order of Santo Stefano (1563–January 1606). He murdered his wife, Isabella Caccianemici, on October 24, 1588.

DIANA BARBIERI-RINIERI († 1607): One of Antonio Maria and Ippolita's daughters, married Valerio Rinieri.

EMILIO BARBIERI: Cousin of Aurelio, Paolo, and Diana, Knight of the Golden Spur.

THE CACCIANEMICI FAMILY

SCIPIONE CACCIANEMICI: Committed suicide in 1583.

ISABELLA CACCIANEMICI BARBIERI (ca. 1573–1588): The murdered wife, stabbed six times by her husband Paolo.

FRANCESCO MARIA BOLOGNETTI: Isabella's maternal uncle and business partner of the Barbieri family for almost twenty years.

THE COURT

ORAZIO ALAVOLINI: *Uditore* of the Torrone. He pronounced the final sentences in criminal trials.

FILIPPO VIOLANO: *Sotto-uditore* of the Torrone. He conducted the proceedings of the trials and worked under Alavolini's supervision.

DECIO CAMBIO: The notary who transcribed the proceeding of the Barbieri trial.

GIROLAMO LEONARDI: The *bargello*.

CAMILLO FERRARINI: The *cursore*.

THE PAPAL ADMINISTRATION

POPE SIXTUS V: Born Felice Peretti, he was pope from 1585 to 1590.

ALESSANDRO DAMASCENI PERETTI: Cardinal Montalto, Sixtus V's nephew, Bologna's *legato*.

CAMILLO BORGHESE: The future pope Paul V (1605–1621), Bologna's *vice-legato*.

THE TRIAL, ITS DEFENDANTS, AND THEIR LAWYERS

PAOLO BARBIERI: Because he was a fugitive, he did not have the right to a defense lawyer.

FRANCESCO (DI MENGOLI?): Paolo's servant, accused of helping Paolo flee Bologna. Because he was a fugitive, he did not have the right to a defense lawyer.

GIOVANNI FRANCESCO GRATO: Friend and defense lawyer of Aurelio Barbieri, accused of helping Paolo flee Bologna.

ERCOLE FONTANA: Defense lawyer of Carlo Ratta, a neighbor of the Barbieri, accused of helping Paolo flee Bologna.

MATTEO BURATTO: Defense lawyer of Ludovico Salani, a banker and an acquaintance of both Carlo Ratta and Aurelio Barbieri, accused of helping Paolo flee Bologna.

PAOLO SALAROLI: Defense lawyer of Leone Benini, a substitute notary of the tribunal of the Torrone and an acquaintance of both Carlo Ratta and Aurelio Barbieri, accused of helping Paolo flee Bologna.

THE PHYSICIANS INVOLVED IN THE TRIAL

GIROLAMO MERCURIALE: Renowned physician and university professor in Padua, Bologna, and Pisa. He cowrote a medical report on Paolo's health at the request of Aurelio Barbieri's defense lawyer Grato.

GASPARE TAGLIACOZZI: Surgeon famous for his innovative rhinoplasty procedure, university professor in Bologna. He cowrote a medical report on Paolo's health at the request of Aurelio Barbieri's defense lawyer Grato.

LUDOVICO LODI: Family physician of the Barbieri family and university professor in Bologna. He cowrote a medical report on Paolo's health at the request of Aurelio Barbieri's defense lawyer Grato.

ANGELO MICHELE SACCO: Surgeon and university professor in Bologna. He performed the autopsy on the body of Isabella Caccianemici Barbieri at the request of her uncle Bolognetti.

THE CHRONICLERS

VALERIO RINIERI (1547–1613): Brother-in-law of Paolo and Aurelio Barbieri.

PIRRO LEGNANI FERRI († 1622): Canon of the cathedral of San Pietro in Bologna from 1588 to 1618.

Member of the senatorial family Bianchini who wrote a chronicle of Bologna ranging from 1584 to 1638.

Anonymous Lateran canon of the church of San Giovanni in Monte in Bologna who wrote a chronicle of Bologna spanning the years 1588–95.

Francesco Ghiselli, cleric and canon of the basilica of San Petronio from 1685 to 1707, who wrote a chronicle in ninety-two volumes spanning the origins of Bologna to 1729.

ACKNOWLEDGMENTS

The saying "appearances can be deceiving" should be applied to this book: it took a long time to complete, even if it is not a voluminous text. Therefore, I owe debts of gratitude to several institutions and people. My first thanks go to the Harvard University Center at Villa I Tatti, Florence, which allowed me to conduct the initial part of my research for this project in 2004–5. The then director, Joseph Connor, and the interim director for the second part of my fellowship year, Katharine Park, the community of fellows, the librarians, and the administrative staff created an ideal environment for the initial phase of this project. A special thanks to Giovanna Benadusi, Maurizio Campanelli, Matteo Duni, Silvia Fiaschi, Giuseppe Gerbino, Allen Grieco, Machtelt Israels, Katharine Park, and Michael Wyatt, who listened to my rambling ideas during that time together.

I would also like to thank the office of the Dean and the Provost at Hunter College, City University of New York (CUNY), and its Research Foundation for the funding I received over the years in the form of Presidential Travel Awards and PSC-CUNY research awards. These funds were instrumental in financing my yearly summer trips to Italy to conduct my archival research. Course release time from teaching in Fall 2007 and Spring 2008 through the Andrew W. Mellon Foundation Program housed at the Center for the Humanities at the Graduate Center, CUNY, offered me the unique chance to discuss my research with colleagues from various CUNY campuses. During that year, I refined my ideas on how to narrate this complex historical narrative.

I spent many summers doing research in the high-vaulted reading room of the State Archive of Bologna. For weeks I would find nothing, only to be rewarded, when I least expected it, with a discovery that made my investigation proceed by leaps and bounds. The help I received from its archivists and staff has been extremely valuable. I would like to thank Diana Tura, Massimo Giansante, Tiziana Di Zio, and Giancarlo Brusati for their support and insightful suggestions. Anyone who has worked for a long time in an archive establishes professional connections with other scholars who work in the same space. Thank you, Giancarlo Angelozzi, Sarah Blanshei, Cesarina Casanova, Rita De Tata, Sherri Frank Johnson,

Andrea Gardi, David Lines, Domenico Medori, and Nicholas Terpstra. Thanks also to archivists and librarians of the Archiginnasio, the Archivio Arcivescovile, and the Biblioteca Universitaria of Bologna, whose assistance I always welcomed and appreciated. Thank you, Paolo Galimberti, director of the Fondazione IRCCS Ca' Granda Ospedale Maggiore Policlinico in Milan, who saw me jumping with joy when I found the name of Paolo Barbieri in the records held at the Archivio Storico of the Ospedale Maggiore. Thank you, Valentina Simonetta and Sergio Nelli at the State Archive in Lucca, who witnessed for two consecutive years my frustration in not finding a tangible shred of evidence about Paolo Barbieri in the criminal records of the city. Thank you, Carla Cerati, at the State Archive in Rome, who helped me recover a vast amount of documents related to the legal woes of Aurelio Barbieri in that city. And finally, thanks to the staff at the State Archive of Pisa, where I reconstructed Paolo's life as a young knight of the Order of Santo Stefano.

I relied on the kindness of many colleagues and friends, who commented on innumerable versions of the manuscript. First and foremost, Thomas Cohen, who never refused to read different permutations of this book and always gave me inspiring suggestions, no matter how messy and convoluted my prose was. Elizabeth Cohen led me to realize how vital orality is in interpreting the early modern period. Alessandro Pastore and Ottavia Niccoli were always available and willing to help me in my research. Their conversation at delicious dinners during some hot summer nights in Bologna never failed to restore my mood and fortify my body. Elizabeth Mellyn, whose work I admire so much and whose spirit of collegiality never stops surprising me, gave me insightful comments on my prose and how to make it less cumbersome and more jargon-free. Clare Carroll always believed in me and my scholarship from the time she was my advisor; with Sarah Covington, Clare gave me accurate and rigorous pointers on my book project. Clare also helped me find Olivia Spenser, who translated sections of Paolo Zacchia's *Quaestiones medico-legales* when I did not have the time or energy to do it myself. Robert Cowan organized and presided over in 2018–19 a writing group in which I received feedback that led me to a radical revision of the structure of my project. Special thanks go to Andrew Polsky, the Ruth and Harold Newman Dean of the School of Arts and Sciences at Hunter College, who was part of the writing group. Bettina Lerner always found time in her absurdly busy schedule to read portions of the manuscript and give me excellent ideas, even if (or perhap, because) her field is so far away from the early modern period. The anonymous readers gave insightful feedback that significantly improved the manuscript. Gerry Milligan helped me figure out where to send the manuscript. To all of you, thank you. Ellie Goodman, the executive editor at PSUP, has been encouraging and supportive of this book since our first meeting. Maddie Caso and John Morris were invaluable through the publication and editing process.

Various talks that I gave over the years helped me refine my ideas and understand where I was wrong. Gianna Pomata invited me to give a talk as part of the History of Science, Medicine, and Technology Colloquium at Johns Hopkins University in 2013. A few years later, Laura Di Bianco and Eugenio Refini invited me again to Johns Hopkins University, where I gave a lecture in the Department of Romance Languages. Andrea Malaguti and Roberto Ludovico asked me to give the third Elizabeth Mazzocco Lecture in Renaissance Studies at the University of Massachusetts at Amherst in 2018. At these lectures, colleagues and the audience became the sounding board for my developing project. They also rectified some of my preconceptions on subjects related to early modern medicine, crime, and insanity. Thanks also to Monica Azzolini and Nancy Siraisi for their scholarship in the history of medicine, from which I benefitted through their work in print and their conversations in person.

Colleagues and students in the Department of Romance Languages at Hunter College and the Comparative Literature Department at the Graduate Center supported me. I consider myself fortunate to have colleagues like Julie Van Peteghem and Paolo Fasoli, who are also dear friends and on whose support I can always count, no matter what. I am grateful to have them in my life. In the last few years, some conversations with Julie brought me to see the light at the end of the tunnel. Giancarlo Lombardi is a fantastic colleague and department chair of the Department of Comparative Literature at the Graduate Center. He let me teach the courses I wanted and always had faith in me and my capabilities as a teacher and scholar. He has also become a dear friend whose professional honesty and clarity I deeply respect. Paola Ureni's Florentine wit and contagious smile never failed to cheer me up in and out of the academic environment. Students in the seminars I taught at the Graduate Center in Fall 2013, 2018, Spring 2019, and Fall 2020 were a constant source of inspiration. Their innovative views on some of the material I had been toiling on for years allowed me to see my research and writing differently, pushing it towards more productive directions.

I had a stroke of genius in seeking the help of Monika Zaleska, whom I met as a student in a seminar I taught at the Graduate Center in Fall 2016, when I asked her if she wanted to work for me as editor of my manuscript. My conversations with her in the last two years and her editorial comments made this book's content and structure much better. Monika helped me to become a better writer. She also provided invaluable help with the index of this book.

I would not have been able to complete this book without the crucial help of some dear friends, who have become my family and my support network. Susanna Migli made it possible for me to live in a beautiful apartment when doing research in Bologna. She is an amazing woman whose strength and passion for life inspired me more than once not to give up on this project. Her loving support has been invaluable, and her friendship is a lifetime gift. When Susanna's apartment was unavailable, Bruno Persico was always willing to offer his. The dinners on his spacious terrace, permeated with the scent of jasmine, were the reward I envisioned after a long day in the archive. Shoshana Bulow contributed to keeping me balanced and optimistic when I felt everything but, and her sense of humor has never failed to bring me joy and laughter whenever I met her. The friendship of Elizabeth Cancelli, Valeria Finucci, Anja Grothe, Ikuyo Nakagawa, Ana Vicentini, and Katherine Volkmer made me realize that I was much more than a scholar writing a book. My cat GiuGiu offered me unconditional love that only a pet can give. Finally, the love, support, and quiet strength of Jorge Negrin, especially when, during the pandemic, it would have been easy to lose purpose and confidence, contributed to creating a calm and peaceful atmosphere, which allowed me to find pleasure in writing and to finish the manuscript.

ABBREVIATIONS

AAB   **Archivio Arcivescovile, Bologna**
Registri battesimali della Cattedrale

AOM   **Archivio dell' Ospedale Maggiore, Milan**
Amministrazione: visite, 1517–1640

Libro Mastro Entrate (1594–1598)

ASB   **Archivio di Stato, Bologna**
Assunteria di Torrone

Corporazioni religiose soppresse, Demaniale
S. Giacomo (Padri Agostiniani Eremitani)

Legato, Suppliche

Legato, Expeditiones

Tribunale del Torrone, Registri di atti processuali

ASLU   **Archivio di Stato, Lucca**
Potestà di Lucca, Inquisizioni

Sentenze e Bandi

ASPI   **Archivio di Stato, Pisa**
Fondo dei Cavalieri dell'Ordine di Santo Stefano

ASR   **Archivio di Stato, Rome**
Archivi dei 30 Notari Capitolini

Archivio del Collegio dei Notari Capitolini

Fondo Arcinconfraternita SS. Annunziata

BAB   **Biblioteca Comunale dell'Archiginnasio, Bologna**
Fondo Gozzadini

Fondo Malvezzi de' Medici

Fondo speciale Manoscritti B

BUB   **Biblioteca Universitaria, Bologna**

Introduction

When I first discovered the proceedings of Paolo Barbieri's criminal trial in the State Archive of Bologna, I had no idea that they would lead me on a fifteen-year journey researching the far-reaching reverberations of the 1588 murder of his wife, Isabella Caccianemici, whom Barbieri killed in a fit of madness. This book revolves around his criminal trial, which began after he fled Bologna the day of the murder, and traces the story of his insanity, exile, and confinement from 1583 until his death in 1606. Close relatives, servants, and everyday citizens of Bologna were implicated in his escape and became deeply involved in the trial that followed. Many believed that Paolo was crazy and could not be held responsible for the murder of his wife. During my research, I followed his story by combing through documents dispersed in four different Italian archives. In this book, I try to evoke the elusive world these documents represent by reconstructing fragments of Paolo's life, trial, and medical diagnoses through those involved in the proceedings. Though gaps and question marks remain, these documents bring together a picture of the social life of sixteenth-century Bologna, along with the medicolegal frameworks that dominated the age and led to the devastation of the Barbieri family following the verdict of Paolo's trial: guilty.

I tracked Barbieri's movements throughout Italy by digging up information from archives and libraries not only in Bologna, where the trial took place, but also in Pisa, Lucca, and Milan. From the end of 1588 to the beginning of 1590, Barbieri's trail grew cold. People said that before going to Milan, where he stayed for eight years, he was in Lucca for a while, but there is no evidence of this. Meanwhile, the financial problems caused by

Paolo's murder and escape plagued his older brother, Aurelio Barbieri, who became the unwilling protagonist of the trial after he was accused of having helped Paolo escape. Sometime after the trial concluded at the end of December 1588, Aurelio went to live in Rome, where his name emerged in legal documents between 1589 and 1590. Aurelio then lived in a two-bedroom apartment in the *rione* Campo Marzio until his death in September 1597, surrounded by Roman friends and acquaintances. None of his family was present, and their absence led me to think that after the 1588 trial, Aurelio's relationship with his family soured.

I followed Aurelio's traces to Rome, and through documents that I found in its State Archive, I reconstructed many of the legal actions that Aurelio pursued there from 1590 to 1597. These documents depict a man intent on disentangling himself from disputes with his business associate Francesco Maria Bolognetti, Isabella Caccianemici's maternal uncle, and with members of his family, among them his mother Ippolita and his sister Diana. Aurelio's last legal act consisted of writing a will leaving all his property to the powerful religious confraternity of the Santissima Annunziata in Rome. Aurelio's testament was a slap in the face of his family members in Bologna, who reacted by pursuing further legal actions to contest its validity. I followed the trail left by the supporting characters of this story, including Bolognetti, Ippolita Barbieri and her daughter Diana, Diana's husband Valerio Rinieri, and even Aurelio's defense lawyer, Giovanni Francesco Grato, in sources where their names appeared associated with those of Paolo and Aurelio.

During my year as a fellow at Villa I Tatti (2004–5), I conducted archival research in Bologna, looking for events reporting episodes of insanity. While perusing local chronicles at the Biblioteca dell'Archiginnasio in the early months of 2005, I found a short entry in an anonymous chronicle related to the tragic story of the nobleman Paolo Barbieri. On October 24, 1588, Paolo repeatedly stabbed his wife Isabella with his sword, leaving her wounded on the floor of their bedroom, and then escaped the city.[1] The killing must have shocked Bologna since the murderer and the victim belonged to two noble families: Isabella was very young, and the accused and his accomplices were noble and notable.

Paolo's story is exceptional and significant for three main reasons. The first is that it is a case study in the diagnosis of insanity in the early modern era, from its first symptoms to its tragic outcomes. There was no way to know whether Paolo was mad when he killed his wife, if his was a case of intermittent insanity, or if he feigned insanity to escape being caught.

In the narrative that I present, the notion of insanity is as much on trial as Paolo himself. The trial reveals discrepancies between medical and legal definitions and evaluations of a person's mental state and the diagnosis of insanity. However, something both early modern doctors and lawyers agreed on was that people tended to fake a myriad of illnesses, including madness, sometimes to escape punishment. The question of whether Paolo was insane was central to his trial: he was diagnosed with "hypochondriac melancholy," and his lawyer, Grato, defended his actions using the legal notion of "intermittent insanity," claiming that Paolo was not in his right mind at the time of the murder. However, doubts about Paolo's madness influenced the judge's final verdict: at issue, among other points, was why, if he was insane at the time of the crime, and therefore not guilty, he chose to flee.

This study intends to create a bridge between the microhistorical dimension of the murder case and macrohistorical perspectives on the legal and medical evidence used to identify intermittent madness, or its simulation, and the implications of medicine for legal argumentation. Through a microhistorical account of Paolo Barbieri's murder and of the fateful consequences of his actions on his life and on those of his family members, relatives, and the larger urban community of Bologna, it offers a case-specific analysis of macrotopics such as insanity, early modern criminal justice, the interaction between medicine and law in the courtroom, the coexistence of oral and written communication in legal documents and vernacular narrative, and the expression of emotions through legal actions. Scholars of legal, medical, and social history have discussed evidence and its affiliated terms, asking themselves, What is a fact? How does it become evidence? Can this evidence be fabricated or feigned? By the end of the sixteenth century, physicians and jurists started writing on the connection between evidence and imposture, reality and pretense. This study argues that the increased importance given to individual observation and experience in early modern medicine and law went hand in hand with an increasing concern for the dangers of deception in these fields. This concern assumed a central role in the case of Paolo Barbieri's insanity.

The second reason that Paolo's story is exceptional is that, in general, proceedings of early modern criminal trials contain only the initial charge and interrogations, in many cases because the two parties settled out of court or the plaintiff withdrew the charge.[2] This book focuses on a criminal trial recorded in its entirety, from the initial charge to the final verdict, including all the intermediate phases. At the State Archive of Bologna, an entire volume of more than three hundred fifty pages is dedicated to Paolo's case, spanning the years from the day of the murder to the final verdict released in December 1588. The volume also contains documents recording the aftermath of the murder and the trial until the year 1597. In this study, I intend to show that the trial's proceedings, especially its final verdict, express the papal curia's political involvement through Bologna's representatives, including the presiding criminal judge. The proceedings also manifest the curia's intent to exert power over the local aristocracy with penalties that affected the defendants' financial assets and properties. Besides the trial's proceedings, the State Archive of Bologna provided me with a vast array of documents held in the collection of the Augustinian Order of San Giacomo in Bologna, which expanded and further articulated the legal and medical dimensions of the story. Among the many documents related to the murder trial were two versions of the defense of Paolo's brother Aurelio, as well as a medical certificate written at the request of Aurelio's defense lawyer by three university physicians about their examination of Paolo's physical and mental state the summer before the murder. None of these documents were included in the trial's proceedings. Through them, I reconstructed the relationships between the judge presiding the trial and Aurelio's defense team and the connection between the legal and the medical assessments of Paolo's insanity.

The third reason for the importance of this story of madness is that it describes and interprets the economic and emotional consequences of Paolo's murderous insanity on his family and kin in the two decades after Isabella's killing shook the streets of Bologna. Paolo, his brother Aurelio, his mother Ippolita, his sister Diana, her husband Valerio Rinieri, business partners, lawyers, notaries, and judges in various Italian cities were all involved in and affected by the mess the Barbieri family found itself in after the trial. Archival sources in Pisa, Lucca, Milan, and Rome helped me flesh out Paolo's social background, his movements after the murder of his wife, and the fate of his estate. Legal documents that I found in Bologna and Rome also revealed that Paolo's family lost a vast amount of money as a result of the trial's various expenses in 1588 and its aftermath. Legal disputes erupted among family members, who also fought with former business partners and kin in various civil and criminal trials.

The richness of archival sources I used to reconstruct this exemplary story of insanity exposes not only how early modern medicine and law dealt with and treated cases of criminal insanity but the tension between legal and medical theory and their respective practices in the courtroom. It also illustrates a moment of transition in the administration of early modern justice in the Papal State, which moved slowly but inexorably toward a form of hegemonic justice at the expense of older forms of negotiated justice. That the pope's representatives also issued a verdict shows how central authority could interfere with the management of local justice and supports what scholars have argued in recent years regarding the management of justice in Bologna and the friction between the pope and the local nobility.

The abundance and variety of legal documents that I was able to find in various Italian archives—civil and criminal trials, wills, disputes about and renunciations of inheritance, evaluations of properties and land, restitution of dowries, and contestations of debts and credits—also made me keenly aware of the presence of a strong emotional component to these legal actions. As Daniel Smail argues in his writing on Marseille's thirteenth- and fourteenth-century criminal and civil justice, people in early modern Bologna conveyed their deep emotions by initiating and pursuing legal actions, regardless of the economic cost.[3] Contrary to the idea that medieval and early modern justice suppressed and negated emotions in the courtroom, Smail argues that it contributed to their open expression in the public arena. In early modern Bologna, Paolo's family and kin expressed hatred, anger, and revenge over people they perceived had trampled on their honor, trust, personal and family good repute, and *fama* through their legal actions.

This notion of *fama* was an important factor in the early modern legal and social sphere. *Fama* related to the "rumors" (*rumori*) that circulated from mouths to ears in the urban community of Bologna. Rumor had it that Paolo Barbieri killed his wife Isabella in a fit of madness, but was it instead anger or malice? Some suspected that he must have been violently angry with his wife and her servant, as he stabbed the former six times and wounded the latter on both hands and her face. In the vast number of chronicles that Bolognese citizens wrote in this period, I found four that reported the tragic event in slightly different ways. The variations exemplify the hybrid nature of early modern Italian society and culture, which oscillated between the spoken and written dimensions. The chroniclers, all citizens in good standing of Bologna, mixed what they heard on the street and their social circles with news from actors involved in the trial and eyewitness accounts of the immediate aftermath. The chroniclers were clerics, members of the nobility, and wealthy professionals, who narrated and interpreted this episode of criminal insanity in the context of

Bologna's political and social dynamics. Witnesses' depositions and chronicles make up the vernacular narrative of this tragic event. Both in and out of court, the narratives of Paolo's insanity and murder were presented in several modes—apology, lament, pleading, denial, moral positioning, and obfuscation. Like the criminal proceedings, the vernacular narrative in and out of the court revealed a binary view of insanity when discussing violent acts like homicide. Behavior that violated social and moral norms slowly sapped the community's willingness to extend its collective goodwill to a person deemed "a bit mad." In court depositions and chronicles, issues of morality, honor, shame, and fear intersected with the notions of rumor and *fama*. So did the legal disputes that followed Isabella's murder and the 1588 trial.

Michel Foucault's *Histoire de la folie à l'âge classique* (1961) was a seminal text for analyzing the notion of madness in its relation to reason, power, and culture in early modern Europe. Drawing on the reassessment of Foucault's homogenizing view of insanity in early modern Europe between the early 1980s and the mid-2000s, this book views early modern madness as a complex social, religious, political, and cultural phenomenon, the understanding of which was heterogeneous and internally divided.[4] Erik Midelfort and Angus Gowland have focused on the intellectual and cultural/religious notion of early modern madness and melancholy and proposed a vast time frame and scope for their investigation.[5] More recently, the essays in Wendy J. Turner's edited collection *Madness in Medieval Law and Custom* explore the theme of insanity in medieval Europe—England, mostly, but also France and Byzantium—from a legal and social point of view, while Elizabeth W. Mellyn's *Mad Tuscans and Their Families: A History of Mental Disorder in Early Modern Italy* focuses on the treatment and discussion of insanity in civil and criminal Tuscan courts between 1350 and 1670, and on its connections to and effects on the families of those deemed insane, the medical witnesses, and the urban communities where these cases occurred. While Turner's edited volume presents a rather wide and composite view of madness in common law and customs, and Mellyn's book explores insanity from a macrohistorical point of view and relies on the analysis of a large number of cases, my study focuses on the microhistorical account of Paolo Barbieri's murder.

There is a clear advantage to concentrating on one specific story of insanity from beginning to end: it allows the reader a close-up not only of the legal, social, and medical dimensions of such a story but also of the emotional ones—the shame, the anger, the fear that came with the notions of honor, and reputation—in and out of the court, in and outside hospitals, in and outside the city of Bologna. The research and work of Thomas Cohen in the Roman archives and that of the scholars who contributed to the issue of the *Journal of Medieval and Early Modern Studies* and the book by Sigurdur Gylfi Magnusson and Istvan Sijártó exemplify a renewed interest in microhistory, in the United States and Europe.[6] My study can provide details on the before and after that many microhistorians, who rely almost exclusively on court procedures, can only surmise. For almost two decades, my research has followed the main actors of the story outside of the court and to locales outside Bologna.

Starting in the early '90s, studies in early modern medical and legal history have shown a renewed interest in the early modern understanding of evidence. In two important books on these topics, *Interpretation and Meaning in the Renaissance: The Case of Law* (1992), and *Logic, Signs, and Nature in the Renaissance: The Case of Learned Medicine* (2002), Ian Maclean underlines the conjectural nature of medicine and law and then studies and interprets their nature, structure, and function. He also draws a complex map of early modern evidence in legal and medical theory that is extremely important for anyone interested in this topic and in these two disciplines. Unlike Maclean's work, which focuses on theory, my study looks at the interaction between theory and practice in medicine and law. It concentrates on how the notion of evidence is a key point of friction between the two disciplines.

My study also relies on the research that Italian scholars Leonardo Quaquarelli, Fulvio Pezzarossa, and Armando Antonelli conducted between the early '90s and the mid-2000s on Bologna's chronicles, composed between the fifteenth and the early eighteenth century.[7] In the United States, the collection of essays on medieval and early modern Italian chronicles *Chronicling History: Chroniclers and Historians in Medieval and Renaissance Italy* helped me formulate the relationship between the genre of chronicle and the fledgling discipline of history in the medieval and early modern periods, and to understand chronicles as hybrid documents, situated between writerly and oral traditions, defined as "any narrative work which recounts historical developments over a longer period of time in chronological order."[8] I view chronicles mainly as part of a larger vernacular narrative on murderous insanity, together with court depositions and other documents used for legal argument. Several recent studies have emphasized and zoomed in on the hybrid nature of early modern society and culture, where oral and written communication intersected with the manuscript and printed dimensions. These studies contributed significantly to elaborating my interpretation of the vernacular narratives related to Paolo Barbieri's story. Traces of orality and spoken performance, like hand gestures, sounds, and body movements, can also be detected in these reports. They can reveal the speakers' social and cultural background and the context in which they uttered them, as Elizabeth Cohen skillfully argued in several essays dedicated to the topic.[9] Finally, scholars of early modern legal history like Thomas Kuehn and Smail have shown that early modern civic and criminal disputes gave voice to strong emotions that people channeled by bringing a suit against someone, making or contesting a will, or claiming to be owed money by their opponents.[10] Emotions are also at the forefront of the work of Barbara Rosenwein, whose idea of "emotional communities" intersects with Pierre Bourdieu's notion of "habitus."[11]

The first chapter sets up the narrative of the murder and contextualizes the social and familial situation of the main actors in the story. It also underscores why Paolo's murder of his wife and the ensuing trial constitute a good example of the medical and legal issues concerning early modern insanity, introduces the book's guiding terminology, gives an account of Paolo's family and his marriage to the young Isabella Caccianemici, and describes how friends and family already knew or suspected for years that Paolo was violently mad. The examination of Paolo's murder and trial, which are discussed in further detail in the next two chapters, highlights early modern legal and medical language and norms regarding insanity and explains how these norms crept into the oral and written accounts of everyday people who analyzed the event based on their social status, on their belonging to cultural and emotional communities, and on Paolo's *fama*. Other stories of criminal insanity will be narrated and analyzed to emphasize these legal and medical norms and show the representative dimension of Paolo's story. They will also contribute to the discussion about early modern legal scholars' and physicians' fear regarding people pretending to be mad and about the lack of substantial evidence, both in the medical and legal field, which made it difficult to prosecute people appearing to suffer from insanity.

The second chapter focuses on the medical issues regarding insanity that arise from the relationship, at times contentious and hostile, between medical experts on the one hand and judge and defense lawyers on the other. The analysis starts with two medical reports. In one, written for the defense of Paolo's brother Aurelio, three physicians narrated an examination of Paolo's health that they conducted the summer before the murder. In the other, a surgeon explained the autopsy he conducted on Isabella's body to demonstrate whether the young woman was pregnant. If she were, Paolo would have been the murderer of his wife and his unborn child. The medical report narrating Paolo's distressing mental health is compared with the *consilium*, a popular genre among early modern physicians that bridged medical theory and practice and was centered on the relationship between patient and doctor. This comparison shows the similarities and the significant differences in the use of medical expertise at the service of an academic readership and for legal purposes. While the criminal judge admitted the report detailing Isabella's autopsy in the trial's proceedings, he excluded the medical consultation of the three doctors who diagnosed Paolo as insane before the murder. The judge's distrustful attitude toward the medical documents exemplifies the conflict between medical and legal opinion on criminal insanity in this era and in this particular trial. The chapter thoroughly discusses medical and legal questions of insanity, emphasizing the difficulty of diagnosing a person as insane. It also gives an overview of the stages of an early modern trial, which had no jury and gave ultimate authority to the judge's verdict. The conclusion offers a political explanation for why the judge rejected the medical report: a clash between papal and local politics might have been at the core of this dismissal.

The third chapter describes what happened in the aftermath of the crime and during the trial proceedings. It introduces Aurelio Barbieri, Paolo's brother, as the secondary main character of the story and the trial's unwilling protagonist, as well as the other defendants, Carlo Ratta, Leone Benini, and Ludovico Salani. The chapter builds on and exemplifies the legal and medical questions connected to Paolo's insanity in the first two chapters. It also follows in detail the stages of the trial, including the long defensive phase, where the lawyers of the four main defendants flaunted their legal skills to extricate their clients from the accusation of having helped Paolo escape. It discusses the investigation that the chief criminal judge of Bologna launched after Paolo's disappearance, the people whom he questioned in the inquisitorial and defensive phases of the trial, and the lawyers' justification of their clients' behavior during and after Paolo's escape. The problem was to establish whether Paolo was mad. On the one hand, contemporary treatises discussed in detail the probatory evidence that men of law should consider in establishing if a person was suffering from insanity. On the other, there was the bull issued by Pope Sixtus V in the summer of 1585, which called for those aiding and abetting criminals to be tried and their property confiscated: Paolo's status at the time of the murder affected not only the defendants but also their family properties.

The fourth chapter, through contemporary chronicles reporting the tragic event and its aftermath, explains how early modern laypeople viewed Paolo's murder of his wife Isabella inside and outside the institutional settings in which medical and legal questions were disputed: in the courtroom, through the witnesses' depositions, and outside the palace of justice. It shows how medical and legal knowledge was transmitted within the social groups of early modern society through the intertwined roles of oral and written accounts in the vernacular narrative, in contrast with the Latin used in official legal and medical documents. The discussion also expands on the notion of *fama*, discussed in the first chapter, and its role in shaping the opinions and biases expressed in vernacular narrative in and outside the courtroom. The chronicles' analysis takes a thematic and analytic view of the different ways their authors perceived the murder and why they came to different conclusions about Paolo and his diagnosis. It focuses on the causes and circumstances of the murder, the victim's identity and the killer's, and the trial's aftermath for Paolo's family and the other defendants. Considering Paolo's social position and *fama*, did the chroniclers find the violent crime he committed more justifiable? The chapter concludes with a discussion of a chronicle that reported the Barbieri murder. Written a century after the others, it emphasizes writing and reading as the predominant ways of communication and expression. It also exemplifies the stratification of information and news, *rumori* and *fama*, that settled over time around the event until its author organized it into a story.

The fifth chapter discusses the consequences of the trial and Paolo's madness for Paolo's family and kin and the citizens of Bologna and other Italian cities where Paolo went after he escaped from Bologna. The entwined network of legal quarrels over inheritance, dowries, and wills provides clues to understanding the hostile atmosphere engendered by Paolo's criminal madness, the fallout of which lasted almost twenty years, and the emotions that shaped and were shaped by medieval and early modern law and legal pursuits, emotions that communities as small as families and as big as neighborhoods and social groups considered appropriate and justified to be expressed in legal terms. The chapter begins by giving the trial's outcome for both the fugitive Paolo and servant Francesco and his accomplices. It discusses the verdict's long-term impact on the six defendants and their families, particularly on the Barbieri household. It follows Paolo's travels through various cities and his return to Bologna. Finally, it discusses the connection between emotions and law and how the interaction between the public and private spheres needs to be considered to understand the individual actors affected by Paolo's crime and the communities to which they belonged.

As far as I know, this study is unique in offering a detailed picture of how, in the early modern period, insanity and its devastating effects marked a man and his family for life. It shows how medical and legal experts tried to pigeonhole the illness into categories that fitted their theoretical frameworks. It exemplifies how rumor spread by word of mouth and created one's reputation and how difficult it was to dissociate a person from what family members, kin, neighbors, and fellow citizens thought of them. It represents how emotions manifested themselves through apparently unexciting and emotionless documents like testaments, civil disputes, debits and credits, and dowries. While other studies have centered on vast amounts of data to discuss and interpret early modern madness, mine brings to light the life of one person and his family as insanity ravaged their financial security, honor, and reputation, not to mention the lives lost and ruined, the hatred nurtured for decades among people who once were friends, and the permanent rifts among brothers, sons and mothers, and brothers and sisters. This is a tragic and gripping tale, a window "through a glass darkly" into early modern violence, madness, criminal justice, medical and legal expertise, and how news circulated and was narrativized.

My fifteen-year professional journey of research into the lives of Paolo Barbieri and his family paralleled and intersected with my personal journey in the world of mental illness. My life and the lives of my immediate family, relatives, and friends have been affected by the illness of my sister, an extremely intelligent and sensitive woman, for more than thirty years. The ravages that madness inflicted on Paolo reminded me of the devastating and long-lasting effects that manic depression has had on my sister's personal and professional life, the isolation she had to suffer, the many times she had to go, willingly or not, to the hospital, after she refused to take medication for long periods of time, and the humiliation she endured as others made decisions for her during these hospitalizations. The fear, frustration, anger, and desperation of Paolo's family, and in particular of his siblings Aurelio and Diana and his mother Ippolita, evoke in me the tangled web of feelings that my father and I have for my sister and for each other, desiring to help her, but also fearing to be swallowed by her pain, by her psychosis, by her anger. The distance Aurelio placed between himself and his family when he moved to Rome is parallel to the ocean of water and silence that I placed between myself and my family for many years. And even so, their pain, anger, animosity, and desperation reached me and affected me, no matter how distant I was. Writing about Paolo's insanity and its long-lasting effects on him and on his family allowed me, in the end, to exorcise my fears, my anger and desperation, when faced with my sister's illness and with my father's denial and desire not to suffer any longer for a daughter whom he desperately wanted to be sane and for another who, in his eyes, abandoned him, so that he had to take care of a mentally ill person all by himself. This book talks about a distant past. By writing it, I came to terms with my own past, and with my present.

CHAPTER 1

Prologue to a Murder

THE SCENE OF THE CRIME AND ITS ACTORS

"The day of October 24 a terrible act of violence occurred in this city."[1] October 24, 1588, around eight o'clock on a cold morning in Bologna: on the upper floor of a two-story house on Piazza Calderini, a gruesome crime was taking place.[2] Screams, quick footsteps on the stairs; then the young servant Maddalena Selani appeared downstairs with wounds on her face and hands. The owner of the house, "Signora" Ippolita Gessi Barbieri, and her two servants, Angelica Lenzanini and Cornelia Bolelli, stared in disbelief at the wounded Maddalena. She told them to go upstairs, that Ippolita's younger son, the *cavaliero* (knight) Paolo Barbieri, had injured her on the face and both hands with a sword that he had taken from the chest in the room on the upper floor where Maddalena slept, and was going to hurt his wife, Isabella Caccianemici.[3] Ippolita's servants and Andrea Ghirardi, the servant of Paolo's older brother Aurelio, were on the stairs when Paolo, a young and rather bulky man with a scant, reddish beard, ran down, holding a sword in his hands and screaming, "I have been killed! Oh, traitors, I will kill you all!"[4] Nobody dared to approach him. He rushed out into the cold morning air, barefoot and with nothing on but a thin nightgown—a pitiful and dishonorable spectacle, people later said.

Meanwhile, inside the house on Piazza Calderini, Ippolita's servant Angelica went upstairs into Paolo and Isabella's bedroom. Nobody had yet had a chance to open the curtains, and the room was dark. She heard Isabella moaning near the bed. She ran to her and saw that her nightgown

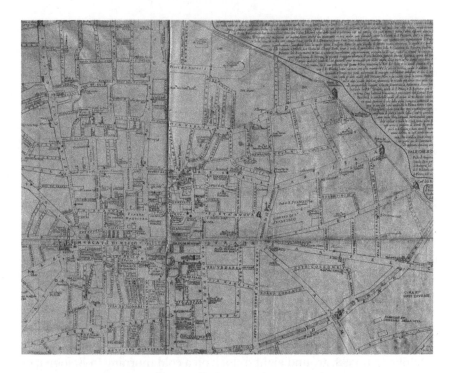

Agostino Mitelli, map of Bologna, mid-seventeenth century.
Biblioteca dell'Archiginnasio, Raccolta piante e vedute della città di Bologna,
Cartella 2, n. 18, detail.

was splattered with blood. Angela held her in her arms and whispered into her ear, "Pray to God and forgive your husband, that the devil blinded him!" The young wife said nothing.[5] When Cornelia entered the room, she saw Angelica holding the young woman's body and noticed the blood all over the nightgown. One can imagine how the two women felt as they held Isabella: there was nothing they could do to save her. To make her more comfortable, they lifted her from the cold floor and laid her on her bed with great care and Andrea's help. She was barely breathing. Like Angelica, Cornelia told the dying woman, "Forgive your husband!," and Isabella squeezed the servant's hand, as if to express that yes, she understood.[6] But she died without saying a word to anyone. When the criminal judge and the notary entered the bedroom and examined her corpse, they found six wounds; it was clear that she had been trying to escape as her husband pursued her, wounding her on her shoulder, under her armpit, on her head. Isabella's exact age was uncertain at the time of her death, but she was very young—between fifteen and eighteen years old.

Her brother-in-law, Valerio Rinieri, identified her.[7] She had been married for three years, but had not had any children. Later, the rumor spread that Isabella was five months pregnant when Paolo killed her.[8] If true, Paolo would be charged for killing two people—his wife and the fetus she was carrying.

When Ippolita arrived upstairs and saw what her son Paolo had done to his young wife—the wounds, all the blood on the floor and her nightgown—she beat herself and got out of control.[9] Again, screams echoed through the Barbieri house. From the marital bedroom Ippolita asked for a blessed candle, so that Isabella might at least die with a minimum of religious sacraments, and then called her son Aurelio upstairs. Aurelio replied, "What do you want me to do? I must send police officers to capture this traitor," and left, perhaps, the servant Maddalena stated, to go to the Torrone to report the crime.[10] Cornelia said that when she went downstairs, she met Aurelio on his way up to the bedroom. "What happened? How is she?" he asked her. "She is dead," Cornelia told him. "Oh dear, oh dear," Aurelio exclaimed and rushed out of the house.[11]

That day and for months to come, under porticos, in the streets, and at the market square, people of all classes gossiped and wrote of the alleged crime committed by Paolo Barbieri, of the details of the gruesome murder, and of Paolo's leaving the scene of the crime in a state of undress, brandishing a sword while his wife lay dying in their bed. Paolo was a nobleman and a member of a notable family of Bologna. His father, Antonio Maria Barbieri, had died in 1569, leaving behind his wife, Ippolita, and several children. Among them was Aurelio, a lawyer by training, never married, who lived off the money that the family properties generated, and Paolo, who was only six when Antonio Maria died.[12] On September 11, 1585, Paolo had married Isabella, of the old and noble Caccianemici family.[13] Francesco Bolognetti, Isabella's maternal uncle—Isabella's father, Scipione, had married Bolognetti's sister Angelica—was a long-term business partner in the banking enterprise that Antonio Maria Barbieri began in 1568 and that his sons Aurelio and Paolo inherited and continued until the year 1587. Bolognetti was also related to the Barbieri family through his blood ties with the Barbieri matriarch Ippolita, so his professional and personal connection to the Barbieri family might explain the marriage between Paolo and Isabella. According to some, Scipione Caccianemici had died by suicide at forty-six on April 24, 1583, because of his melancholic humors. Isabella, who was his only child, became the sole heir of the family's possessions.[14]

FIG. 1 Coats of arms of Paolo Barbieri's and Isabella
Caccianemici's parents. Archivio di Stato di Pisa, fondo
dell'Ordine di S. Stefano filza n. 41 inserto 47.

THE WARNING SIGNS, THE PRECEDENTS

Paolo was very proud of being a *cavaliero* of the Order of Santo Stefano,
which the duke of Tuscany, Cosimo I de' Medici, established in 1561, ostensibly to fight against heresy, and Pope Paul IV approved the same year.[15] For
Paolo, being a knight meant fighting with his sword those who attacked
him or his honor. It was a sign of his status as an aristocrat, a scion of a
noble family, a soldier.[16] To be accepted in the ranks of the Order, young
men from all over Italy had to submit proof that their paternal and maternal ancestors descended from noble and wealthy families, such as the Barbieri, the Gessi, the Fessii, and the Bolognetti. Paolo had no trouble proving

that his parents' families were related to the who's who of Bologna's ancient aristocratic families—the Ludovisi, Orsi, Gozzadini, Fantuzzi, Albergati, and Buoncompagni.[17] Their members were prelates, doctors, senators, and knights, and some even boasted a connection with Cardinal Guastavillani.[18] First Antonio Maria and then Aurelio and Paolo, after their father's death, were bankers, an activity that some considered beneath the dignity of a nobleman. However, it was reported that the Barbieri family members exercised it "in a noble way" and that agents performed all transaction on their behalf.[19]

As a *cavaliere milite* (military knight) of the Order,[20] Paolo had to go through three years of training that included two years of military service aboard a ship of the grand duke, and one year divided between a sojourn in the Order's "convent," the Palazzo of the Carovana in Pisa, and more military service.[21] Paolo was twenty when he was accepted into the Order's ranks on November 13, 1582.[22] Between 1583 and 1585, the year he married Isabella, he traveled aboard the grand duke of Tuscany's ships. While he was in training and later, when he was already married, Paolo was involved in trials for minor scuffles and manifested unreasonable and threatening behavior toward friends and strangers alike. In 1583 he got into a fight with a fellow knight, Cosimo Angiolini from Perugia, but at least this time he was not the instigator. They landed in Naples, and Cosimo, armed and ready to attack him, followed Paolo, whose sword, when he unsheathed it to defend himself, got caught up in his mantle and fell to the ground. Other knights intervened before Cosimo could strike him. A few months later, a trial, conducted within the Order, followed, before which a notary took Paolo's deposition. This is the only time that we "hear" Paolo's voice.[23] Initially, the young man denied that the confrontation ever happened. Then he declared that it was something of no importance. Only when the notary warned him that his repeated denials could worsen his situation considerably did Paolo relent and state how exactly things took place between him and Cosimo. During the trial other witnesses confirmed his account. When the notary of the Order asked him why he was so reluctant at first to tell exactly what happened and obfuscated the truth, Paolo declared that he was obeying the *uditore* of the ship: "Messer Auditore of the ships found me a few days ago and told me that the Cavaliere of the Chancellery [of the Order] would call me for the thing followed in Naples between Cavaliere Cosimo Angelini and me. He asked me to say that nothing happened between the two of us so that we don't hurt each other."[24] One can interpret Paolo's dogged resistance as the result of a knightly code of honor:

he had given his word, and an honorable man, a *cavaliero* of the Order of Santo Stefano, always kept his word, unless a higher authority compelled him to reveal the truth.

A fellow knight of the Order, Enea Rasi from Rimini, narrated a much more serious episode in Pisa a year later, in 1584, when both men were in training. This time Paolo was the perpetrator, and he tried to kill his comrade. Enea was in Paolo's room, writing a letter at a desk, when he heard a noise behind him. He turned and saw Paolo holding a hatchet over his head, ready to strike him down. Enea was able to escape only because Paolo bumped into a window. Showing admirably swift reflexes and presence of mind, Enea pushed Paolo onto a chest and away from him. Around the time of this incident, Paolo seemed "out of himself" (*fuori di se*) for a while. When he regained his senses, he apologized to Enea, saying that he had been suffering from melancholic humors for a while, which upset him greatly.[25] That same year or the year after, Paolo was involved in a fight in a public square. While in Pisa as part of the retinue of the grand duke of Tuscany, Francesco I, the nobleman Ulisse Bentivogli Manzoli[26] saw people running toward a "clamor" (*rumore*). He asked what was happening and was told that the *cavaliero* Paolo Barbieri had incited a duel with a comrade for no apparent reason. Bentivogli Manzoli did not state if the duel took place, but he did report that everybody "was surprised" (*restò maravigliato*) at Paolo's gratuitous act of violence.[27] A few years later, during the Carnival of 1587 in Bologna, Paolo was involved in another fight with Enea Rasi. Paolo accused Enea of having used a derogatory gesture to offend his honor—touching his beard while greeting him to insinuate that Paolo was a cuckold. From that day onward, every time Paolo saw Enea he complained that he was drawn to hurt people with his sword while walking around Bologna, to which Enea replied that maybe he should visit a doctor.[28] The incident at Carnival in 1587, and that in Pisa narrated by Bentivogli Manzoli a few years earlier, must have attracted the attention of many people, who might have recalled them when Paolo killed his wife Isabella. Communal spaces like squares, churches, and shops were the theaters in which violence caused by desperation or insanity played out. On June 16, 1564, a man unsheathed his sword for no apparent reason in a public square in Bologna and went on a rampage, wounding anybody he came across.[29] On April 20, 1592, a woman named Maddalena tried to commit suicide in the church of Vergato, a small village near Bologna.[30] In 1593 the barber Orazio Mazzetti cut a customer's throat while he was shaving him and then dragged him to a public square, alleging that his victim was a traitor and wanted to harm him.[31] These episodes were widely spoken about, recorded in proceedings of criminal trials, chronicles, and catalogues of capital punishments.

MEDICAL, LEGAL, AND LAY DEFINITIONS OF PAOLO'S MADNESS

Isabella and Paolo's family members knew about Paolo's erratic and aggressive behavior. Paolo and his wife lived on the upper floor of the house on Piazza Calderini, while Paolo's mother Ippolita and his older brother Aurelio occupied the ground floor along with several servants. The summer before Isabella's murder, three reputable physicians who taught at the University of Bologna—Girolamo Mercuriale, Gasparo Tagliacozzi, and Ludovico Lodi—had examined Paolo at his house, probably at the urging of his older brother Aurelio.[32] They concluded that his demeanor was provoked by melancholic humors—the same melancholic humors that Paolo had complained about to Enea Rasi in 1587. Later, during Paolo's criminal trial, family members, physicians, and the urban community of Bologna would claim that Paolo Barbieri was mad.

What caused Paolo's madness? Doctors claimed that burned juices formed in Paolo's hypochondrium (the portion of the body between the ribs and the innards) produced a specific category of melancholy, called hypochondriac melancholy, which was an object of study in early modern medical treatises and was said to affect many people in that period. The high number of people allegedly suffering from melancholy relates less to the real spread of this affliction than to people's conviction that they or others around them were troubled by it. In fact, the cause had to do with the increasing interaction between medical and theological/spiritual explanations of the notion of melancholy and the consequent "increased domain in which the concept of melancholy can be applied."[33] Nevertheless, doctors offered a possible prognosis and prescribed a cure tailored to the patient in consultations written in Latin and in the vernacular. Hypochondriac melancholy created obstructions in the intestines, distressed the stomach and liver, and then ascended to the brain. The fumes of these burned humors, the worst type, moved upward toward one's head, dehydrating the brain and causing violent rage and madness.[34] The three doctors who examined Paolo the summer of 1588 declared that it was this type of melancholy that afflicted him and that it could turn into insanity.

The trial against Paolo Barbieri and his presumed accomplices exemplifies how a medical diagnosis was used to recognize early modern criminal insanity and its main legal issues. What should be underlined here is the way medicine and law identified and categorized melancholy. Physicians held that melancholy could metamorphose into homicidal madness by virtue of an imbalance of the four humors in the human body, whose equilibrium was believed to be the critical factor for one's well-being. Early modern men of law and medicine evaluated insanity based on gathered evidence. Legal categories of conjectural evidence shaped the meaning of stories of melancholy and criminal insanity. Insane people showed lack of premeditation when performing a crime. However, according to both early medicine and law, mad people could regain their wits at times, thus becoming aware of their violent and criminal behavior. Did intermittent insanity afflict Paolo, or did he kill Isabella because he had a motive—jealousy, anger, or resentment at not yet having become a father? During the trial that followed the murder, insanity became the cornerstone of Paolo's defense. However, the judge seemed to believe that another motive, perhaps jealousy, had led to the crime, as evidenced by his line of questioning.[35]

Legal language coined the expression *lucida intervalla* (lucid intervals) to define a type of intermittent insanity whose outbursts corresponded to the violent manifestations of the melancholic furor identified by early modern physicians. Paolo's murder of his wife Isabella is an example of how early modern medical diagnosis and legal evidence categorized and interpreted episodic insanity. It also provides the reader with tools to examine legal and medical language and norms of the era regarding the notion of evidence, and to observe how both language and norms insinuated themselves into the oral and written accounts of everyday people, in public court depositions and personal chronicles.

Technical language, like that used in medicine and law, and its expressions were appropriated and applied to daily speech by a broad public, sometimes illiterate but knowledgeable enough to use these widespread terms.[36] For instance, Elizabeth Mellyn argues that the term "melancholy," initially part of a specialized medical vocabulary, became popularized in various types of documents and narratives. In the second half of the sixteenth century in Tuscany, says Mellyn, popularized medical expressions like "melancholic humors" surfaced in civil trials, instead of the more traditional *mentecaptus*, *furiosus*, and *insanus*, and their corresponding vernacular terms, to define erratic behavior that would prevent a person from managing the patrimony of his family. This change was due, Mellyn argues, to the popularization of a broad array of medical texts and religious and philosophical works that discussed melancholy and its effects on the body and soul and spread the language of the Hippocratic-Galenic humoral theory.[37]

Numerous episodes of violence in sixteenth-century Bologna were attributed to melancholic humors, but also to "diabolical inspiration." Pirro Legnani (?–1620), whose chronicle we will examine later in connection with the Barbieri murder, reported in his "Diario" on January 23, 1589, that Paolo Turchi threw himself naked into a well in the dead of night because of his melancholic humors.[38] Turchi was married with three children and was the administrator of the Monte di Pietà of San Pietro.[39] According to Legnani, he was a good man, whose suicide left everybody shocked.[40] The expressions "diabolical inspiration" and "diabolical spirit" appeared often in the depositions made by witnesses or defendants during proceedings of criminal trials. As reported at the beginning of this chapter, the servant Angela described Paolo's mortal wounding of Isabella as inspired by the devil. These and similar expressions were used to condemn violent actions, such as suicide, homicide, and verbal or physical assault, and suggested moral condemnation. In oral and written exchanges, in and out of the courts, terms like "melancholy" or "melancholic humors" coexisted with "diabolical spirits" or "diabolical inspiration." In traditional societies, the boundaries among law, morality, and customs were permeable; a criminal act affected the law and the rules established by communal customs.[41] While the perception of suicide and murder as egregiously sinful acts inspired by the devil was still active in the communal imagination, the medical notion that melancholy led to insanity was gaining ground.[42] People who took their own lives or committed murder were seen as also performing an act of violence against their families and communities. The action of killing oneself was equivalent to killing another person and created a rift in the city's social and moral order; like murder, suicide was condemned by the Catholic Church and by the community at large.

The probative signs identifying madness that jurists so thoroughly illustrated and discussed in their tracts were supposed to be applied to mad people's actions and behaviors. For instance, contemporary legal treatises listed as signs of insanity throwing stones, insulting people for no apparent reason, and not remembering things or remembering them in a disorganized way, as well as harassing people and disturbing the peace of the neighborhood. According to the list of signs formulated by contemporary jurists, the behavior of Tomaso de Rossi, aka Galetto della Mostarda, could be identified as that of a mad person. He threw stones against the windows and doors of private citizens' houses, disturbed the quiet of the community, and harassed people on the street. Lucia Marzocchi, who killed her two grandchildren and then tried to kill herself, did not remember why she rearranged the girls' bodies on the floor of their bedrooms after she had murdered them.[43] In their depositions several witnesses stated that Lucia killed the two girls because of her "bad thought" (*malpensiero*), namely, the belief that the children would die of hunger.[44] Lucia's concern for the scarcity of wheat was a real and dramatic problem in Bologna and the countryside around Bologna (*contado*) in those years. The harvest of 1671 had been dismal, and many anticipated a similar harvest in 1672.[45] Her double murder originated from justifiable fears; it was what she did with these fears that made her look unbalanced, perhaps, as Massimo Giansante suggests, a victim of "melancholic humors."[46] Lucia became obsessed by the thought of how much pain her grandchildren were destined to suffer, and, in a twisted act of altruism, decided to kill them before she killed herself. Lucia's actions and behavior resemble those of a victim of "melancholic humors," inducing her to violent murder. No word is given in the proceedings of the trial about her altered state of mind, but, after she killed her two grandchildren, Lucia was convinced that she did well in doing so.[47]

Galetto della Mostarda's erratic and violent behavior in the streets of Bologna recalls Paolo's outbursts in the years before the murder of his wife. Lucia Marzocchi's misplaced conviction and murderous behavior call to mind Paolo's conviction that he had to murder his wife Isabella to defend himself against those who wanted to kill him. The judge in Lucia Marzocchi's trial condemned the defendant to capital punishment, even though her behavior and actions fit the categories of probative evidence describing insanity that early modern jurists offered in their legal treatises.[48] To the judge, the perpetrator seemed to have volition and thus merited condemnation. When violent crimes were involved, conjectural evidence was trumped by the evidence produced by the suspects' actions—the murder.

NEGOTIATED AND HEGEMONIC JUSTICE, *RUMORE*, AND *FAMA*

Mario Sbriccoli writes about two types of justice coexisting in the early modern period: negotiated justice and hegemonic justice. Negotiated justice, typical of the medieval period, manifested itself mostly but not exclusively outside the courtroom, aimed at repairing an offense within a community, giving satisfaction to the offended party. It was frequently conducted through spoken conversations between the parties—a need for approval and belonging to the community guided these arbitrations.

The rise of hegemonic justice belonged to the court of law, was ultimately managed by the criminal judge, and had punishment as its ultimate goal. Legal norms that jurists established in written form in their treatises on legal practice regulated and formalized this type of justice.[49] Hegemonic justice became increasingly important between the end of the sixteenth and the beginning of the seventeenth century, as legislative apparatuses came to limit alternative spaces for settling justice outside of court. The Tribunale del Torrone (hereafter Torrone) embodied hegemonic justice in Bologna. This legal institution presided over Bologna's criminal trials from the first decades of the sixteenth century,[50] and was established and controlled by the papal curia. This type of justice coexisted and interacted with negotiated justice, which continued to act outside of the legal system as its alternative or complement, at least until the end of the sixteenth century.[51] In the early modern period, even if the community considered people like Lucia Marzocchi, Orazio Mazzetti, and Paolo Barbieri mad, and contemporary jurists listed many of their actions and behaviors as evidence of insanity, the judge, representing the power of the state and the hegemonic justice, had the authority to decide if they were acting out of madness and how those acts should be punished.

The story of Paolo's murder of his wife Isabella was narrated many times in court and informally, transmitted through the public space via conversation, adapted and manipulated in written chronicles, edicts, and legal documents. Scholars have emphasized that in early modern Italian urban society the oral and written media interacted continuously, and each of them was multilayered.[52] Written documents were either printed or in manuscript form, and even nonliterary texts contained various modes of communication and were inspired by different genres. Oral expressions were the product of the speakers' social, cultural, and economic status and gender and the contextual situation in which they were uttered. Elizabeth Cohen, who has written extensively on the indeterminate borderline between oral and written dimension in early modern urban societies, has coined the expression "situated oralities." According to Cohen, early modern criminal trials exemplified the tension interwoven in the hybrid nature of urban culture and society and the interaction between the oral testimonies of witnesses and defendants and the written transcription in vernacular and in Latin given by the notaries. Their transcriptions modified the oral messages performed by the people whom the judge interrogated, while keeping traces of orality in terms of words but also of "sound, gesture, and facial expression."[53] Also, often witnesses and defendants' testimonies were semiperformances, as spontaneous communication intersected with rehearsed scripts.[54] Chronicles, which constitute a source of information and narrative expression for the story of the murder committed by Paolo Barbieri, need to be recognized as the product of "the complex dynamics of interchange between oral and written culture," in which chroniclers "borrow[ed] from other literary genres and writing traditions."[55] Early modern manuscript chronicles could be shown, lent, and discussed,[56] and were in contact with oral performance and the printed world.[57] Adam Fox and Daniel Woolf emphasized how writing—and printing—"modified, marginalized or reinforced different aspects of oral culture."[58]

In the criminal trial that followed Paolo's murder of Isabèlla, defendants and witnesses narrated what they saw, but also what they inferred about Paolo's actions and circumstances before he killed his wife, using information they heard from neighbors, acquaintances, and the urban community—what could be called *rumore* or *fama*. Ottavia Niccoli writes that early modern rumor or gossip was the negative version of *fama* since it was an aggregate of true and false news.[59] One's *fama*, the common opinion of a person's behavior, became acquired legal status when it was accepted, "within disciplined limits, by communal legislators and by academically trained jurists and attorneys."[60] *Fama* was related to talk and reputation and was legitimized by the community and attached to nobles and commoners alike. Once one's *fama* was well known, it was extremely difficult to alter and became like a second skin. *Fama* could be good or bad, but either way it could have a decisive effect on the credit given to a person's word in the legal arena.[61] Fenster and Smail write that "public talk is, or creates, the *fama* that is useful in courts."[62] The notion of *fama* is fundamental in the theory and practice of justice in the medieval and early modern periods. For instance, several character witnesses labeled Galetto della Mostarda a man of "bad lifestyle" (*mala vita*) and *fama*, pointing out that he had been in jail several times for petty crimes; Galetto himself admitted to it when questioned about his criminal record.[63] Even before the trial, Paolo's *fama* was that of an unbalanced person, prone to bouts of melancholic despondency and violent aggression. Finally, at the junction where oral act met with written document, people in and out of court conveyed shame, fear, anger, pride, guilt, humiliation, and joy. These emotions intersected with honor-related violence and honor,[64] which was tied to the notions of "good repute" (*buona reputazione*) and *fama*.[65] During his trial Galetto della Mostarda stated that he had a reputation to defend, even if he realized that he "was a bit touched in the brain" (*pateva un poco di cervello*). After killing his wife, Paolo Barbieri did not want to part from his sword because he said it would be shameful for a knight of the Order of Santo Stefano to be seen without one.[66]

The notion of "habitus," which Pierre Bourdieu defines as "spontaneity without consciousness or will, opposed as much to the mechanical necessity of things without history in mechanistic theories as it is to the reflexive freedom of subjects 'without inertia' in rationalist theories," can explain how certain emotional responses could have been seen as "commonsense" behavior when people were faced with disputes, and how people's actions motivated by such emotions were not exceptional or aberrant but concordant with the embodied practices of the historical period in which they lived.[67] Since Bourdieu argues that habitus produces "reasonable" behavior, one can say that honor and the actions and emotions tied to it connected individuals to families as well as social, professional, and religious communities.[68] Emotions like shame and anger, and the value of honor, shaped and were shaped by the actors involved, directly or indirectly, in the trial for the murder of Isabella Caccianemici. They were all members of one or more of what Barbara Rosenwein calls "emotional communities." Rosenwein argues that scholars interested in this notion ought to investigate "systems of feeling" and "establish what these communities (and the individuals within them) define and assess as valuable or harmful to them (for it is about such things that people express emotions); the emotions that they value, devalue, or ignore; the nature of the affective bonds between people that they recognize; and the modes of emotional expression that they expect, encourage, tolerate, and deplore."[69]

THE NOTION OF EVIDENCE AND THE ANXIETY OF SIMULATION

Recent studies in early modern legal and medical history have shown a renewed interest in the concept of evidence.[70] They have emphasized the conjectural nature of evidence within the structure and function of law and medicine. Early modern medicine and law were applied arts that dealt with human nature's infinite variations and were based on the interpretation of signs, which are by nature ambiguous.[71] Both disciplines were rooted in logic and rhetoric, which were used to interpret and construct evidence. However, unlike medicine, early modern law tried to create a finite hierarchy of types of evidence, even though it was difficult for both disciplines to distinguish among the categories they created. Even if jurists and physicians devised complex and articulated sets of circumstantial evidence to identify symptoms related to insanity, its signs were confused and ambiguous. Paolo's story of criminal madness reflects the general concern that insanity could be feigned. This worry cast doubts on the validity of the signs that legal tracts listed as necessary to prove a person insane. Cases of simulated beggary, sanctity, pregnancy, identity—I am thinking here of the famous story of Martin Guerre, narrated by Natalie Zemon Davis—were discussed together with cases of pretended insanity, in and out of the court.[72] How did one gauge the evidence and weed out the deception? What brought people to fake various handicaps, illnesses, or psychological states? How did medicine and the law, the church, and the community separate the wheat of truth from the chaff of pretense?

The thought that Paolo, like other early modern men and women, could pretend to be mad to escape punishment was not far from the minds of judges, jurists, physicians, and members of the community. In this period, diagnosing or attributing insanity was problematic; the signs for recognizing madness were multiple and contradictory. The accusation of counterfeiting insanity, along with the necessity in a court of law to determine it through a multiplicity of signs—physical, verbal, behavioral—was part of a larger issue that manifested itself in many areas of early modern life. The shifting assessment of imposture has led some scholars to name this the "age of simulation."[73] However, it would be more correct to talk about an anxiety of simulation in fields as varied as politics, religion, philosophy, law, and medicine. Physicians and jurists entered this debate by agreeing that every illness could be feigned, and therefore that the physical and behavioral signs that pointed to evidence could deceive.[74] In early modern law and medicine, ascertaining the truth through signs also entailed reading the signs of disguise used by defendants, witnesses, and patients. Indeed, feigning insanity seems to have been quite common in this period. The physicians Giovan Battista Selvatico and Giovan Battista Codronchi wrote extensively about it at the end of the sixteenth century, as did the physician and legal adviser Paolo Zacchia in the first half of the seventeenth century. In Selvatico's *De iis, qui morbum simulant deprehendendis liber* (1595), he argued that patients tended to lie for three main reasons: fear, shame, and financial gain.[75] Codronchi devoted the first chapter of his *Methodus testificandi* (1597), a manual directed at both doctors and judges, to those who simulated illnesses to avoid prison or trial, including those who feigned madness.[76] Zacchia stated in his monumental legal-medical work *Quaestiones medico-legales* that "there is scarcely another disease more easily and more frequently feigned than insanity and no disease more difficult to discern."[77]

CONCLUSIONS

Criminal judges in Bologna tended to consider punishable by death even crimes committed by those whom the community considered insane. A doctrine of criminal responsibility emerged in which the fear of feigning insanity caused doctors and judges to cast aside the elaborate list of legal and medical signs that would give away a person as mad. Melancholy and insanity were tolerated as long they did not impact the social order of the city. Very few melancholic people were brought to trial, and when they were it was because they had committed violent acts against themselves or others and/or disturbed the city's social order by acting out their behavior in public spaces—the square, the church, the streets.

By the end of October 24, 1588, the day of the murder, Paolo had escaped, and Aurelio was placed in prison as soon as he arrived at the Torrone that morning, accused of helping his brother become a fugitive. An autopsy was then performed on the body of Isabella, requested by her uncle, Francesco Bolognetti, giving credit to the rumor that she had been pregnant and airing his resentments toward the Barbieri family. He also offered a bounty of five hundred golden scudi to whoever would bring Paolo back to Bologna, dead or alive.[78] Thus, after she was brutally murdered, Isabella's body was autopsied to satisfy her uncle's desire for vengeance.

CHAPTER 2

Medicine and Law on Trial

After having killed his wife Isabella, Paolo ran out of the house half naked with a sword in his hands and never went back. Two days after the murder, on October 26, 1588, the servant Francesco sent a letter to Aurelio Barbieri from Firenzuola, forty kilometers from Florence.[1] Francesco's letter was an anxious cry for help: the young man wrote to Aurelio that Paolo "was beside himself" (*è uscito di se stesso*), unable to do anything and stay put in one place for very long. They needed money badly, Francesco wrote, and soon: he had already had to pawn a ring, a cloak, and a collar to the innkeeper Battistino in Firenzuola, probably all belonging to Paolo, in exchange for food and lodging. They were told that they only had two days until Battistino stopped sheltering them, and then the pawned objects would be lost. The youth—let us remember that Francesco was described as being between sixteen and eighteen years of age[2]—concluded the letter by showing a deep understanding of Paolo's state: "I beg you, have compassion for the *cavaliero*'s fate; I also suggest to whoever comes not to scold him, either in person or by letter, so that he will not go further off the deep end."[3] From what Francesco wrote, Paolo clearly seemed unbalanced and unable to take care of himself. The question of Paolo's insanity hearkens back to the episodes of his aggressive and threatening behavior toward people that occurred between 1584 and 1587,[4] and to the examination that the physicians Mercuriale, Tagliacozzi, and Lodi performed on Paolo at his house in July 1588.

Three months before the murder the three doctors examined Paolo because of an illness of the head that had been plaguing him for many years, caused by "bad humors" (*humori cattivi*). After conducting a thorough assessment of the patient and questioning him and other people about his illness, they diagnosed Paolo as suffering from "a melancholic passion that [they] called hypochondriac," which had spread throughout the entire body.[5] This condition, which displayed itself during their examination, was very dangerous because the "very clear signs" (*manifestissimi segni*) they had detected in the patient could lead to violent fits of insanity. The three doctors also observed that Paolo consistently had dark thoughts, which often led to tears. This was why he avoided any sort of conversation and stayed at home most of the time, in a troubled state of mind. Paolo led such a solitary life because he was afraid of harming other people. One of his dominant thoughts was to "hurt people's feelings and in particular to injure them [physically]."[6]

The three doctors, trained in the humoral theory, believed that the melancholic humors that pervaded Paolo's entire body were burned, the worst type: it was common opinion among early modern physicians that the fumes produced by these humors moved upward toward the patient's head, thus dehydrating the brain and causing violent rage.[7] The doctors prescribed a general evacuation of the superfluous and noxious liquids in his body, the ingestion of sheep's whey, and baths in fresh water. These were the usual remedies prescribed to people affected by melancholic humors, as explained in detail by the medical texts of the time. Paolo started taking his medications, but after a few days he stopped. His situation rapidly deteriorated once the fall of 1588 arrived—the general belief was that any disturbance of the head worsened during this season, since the burned humors were more painful in the fall and led people to commit "horrendous and wild acts."[8]

The details of this examination were included in a legal certificate (*fede*) that the three doctors wrote after the murder at the urging of Aurelio's defense attorney, Giovanni Francesco Grato. Aurelio had become the unwilling substitute for his younger brother Paolo at the trial as well as the victim of a battle fought on the epistemological and political level. With his brother gone, he became the main defendant, accused of helping Paolo escape. An anonymous note, probably from Grato, asked the doctors to respond to a detailed guideline that asked them to state that Paolo committed the crime in a moment of madness and then regained control of himself when he escaped, as was expected of people suffering

FIG. 2 Lavinia Fontana, *Portrait of Girolamo Mercuriale*, 1588–89. Walters Art Museum, Mount Vernon–Belvedere, Baltimore, Maryland, USA. Photo: Wikimedia Commons / Badseed. Oil on canvas, 130.8 × 97.1 cm.

from this illness.[9] In other words, Grato asked the doctors to state in their expert opinion that Paolo was temporarily insane when he killed Isabella and then he returned to a state of lucidity after the murder. The medical experts wrote that they were not surprised at the news that Paolo killed his young wife for no reason. They maintained that Paolo's actions after he murdered Isabella exemplified insanity rather than conscious intent: "[His actions are] very clear signs of madness [*pazzia*] and extreme furor [*furore*]."[10] At the end of the document Mercuriale affirmed that he had held this opinion since he first learned of the murder. "Under oath I say what I said to many people immediately after I learned about the event, that is, that I do not have now nor have I ever had any other opinion": Paolo was insane at the time of his wife's homicide.[11] This certificate is the only extant medical opinion in which Paolo's physical and mental condition was spelled out.

The involvement of important university physicians like Mercuriale and Tagliacozzi underlined the privileged position of the Barbieri family in Bologna.[12] Girolamo Mercuriale (1530–1606) was the most famous of the three doctors involved in Paolo's story. At age fifty-seven, at the top of his career, he had moved to the University of Bologna in 1587 after

FIG. 3 Tiburzio Passarotti (attributed), *Portrait of Gaspare Tagliacozzi*, ca. 1575. Istituto Ortopedico of Bologna, Bologna, Italy. Photo: Science History Images / Alamy Stock Photo. Oil on canvas, 24.2 × 33.5 cm.

eighteen years at the University of Padua, lured by a more than generous yearly stipend.[13] At Bologna from 1587 to 1592, he taught at the most prestigious hour of the day, in the afternoon.[14]

Unlike Mercuriale, Gaspare Tagliacozzi (1545–99) never taught anywhere but at the University of Bologna. He started teaching surgery in 1570, and around 1590 he began teaching anatomy and the theory of medicine.[15] He was well known for his rhinoplasty procedures, on which he wrote a treatise dedicated to his patron Vincenzo Gonzaga, duke of Mantua.[16]

Very little is known about Ludovico Lodi (d. 1619). He had a very slow but steady career in the faculty of medicine in Bologna, but no printed work appeared under his name.[17] The end of the *fede* reflected the hierarchy among the three doctors at the university and in the city of Bologna. Mercuriale was the first to undersign the letter; then Tagliacozzi stated that he agreed with "everything that his Excellency [i.e., Mercuriale] wrote," and finally Lodi, who identified himself as the doctor of the Barbieri family and of Paolo for many years, affirmed that he had handwritten the document and that he supported what had been indicated in it.[18]

The night of October 24, near the Barbieri house, the surgeon Angelo Michele Sacco performed the autopsy on Isabella's body in the Sant' Andrea delle Scuole church in the presence of the parson.[19] Sacco was called by Isabella's uncle Bolognetti to find evidence of whether she was pregnant at the time of her death, following a rumor reported by the coachman Fantoni during the trial.[20] The Bolognetti and the Barbieri families had a tense relationship because of a failed banking enterprise between the men of the two families: Bolognetti was accused of having embezzled money from his business partners.[21]

The chief criminal judge of the tribunal of the Torrone, the *uditore* Orazio Alavolini, approved the autopsy.[22] Sacco was later questioned by the judge on November 4, 1588, and his deposition was the only testimony given by a doctor included in the official proceedings of the trial.[23] During his interrogation the surgeon reported that he found some "spermatic substance" as big as a "chestnut" in Isabella's uterus, which he concluded it to be "inanimate," as it had not yet attached itself (*annexa*) to the uterine wall.[24] Finally, with her autopsy, her body could be put to rest.

MEDICAL EXPERTISE ON CRIMINAL INSANITY IN THE COURT OF LAW: AN UNEASY COLLABORATION

The increasing institutionalization of sixteenth-century university professors like Mercuriale, Tagliacozzi, Lodi, and Sacco was one of the factors that confirmed and reinforced the presence of medical experts in court, which had been common practice in Italy since the beginning of the fourteenth century.[25] Physicians were called to give their professional opinion on cases of increasing complexity.[26] They were asked to evince corroborating proof for the argument put forward by the prosecution or defense in criminal issues such as pregnancy, loss of virginity, rape, infanticide, impotence, simulation of illness, poisoning, wounding, and drowning.[27] Tagliacozzi was called several times to give his expert medical opinion in criminal cases involving disfiguring wounds to the face.[28] Requests for medical expertise in cases of violent death went beyond their immediate practicality in the criminal court and appeared also in collections of medical consultations (*consilia*) that were used by medical students and by university physicians.

According to the fourteenth-century jurist Bartolo di Sassofferrato, the role of the medical expert could be compared to that of a judge.[29] However, very often the opinions of medieval and early modern Italian physicians in criminal and civil trials were not considered determinative or superior to those of other witnesses. At the end of the Middle Ages, medical expertise did not influence the judge's final decision. Physicians were considered privileged witnesses, but their opinion could not guarantee absolute certainty, which was what the judge expected and required in the court of law.[30] According to jurists Giovanni Battista De Luca and Antonio Maria Cospi, the maxim *credendum est peritis in arte* (people expert in their profession are to be believed) was debatable, and its validity and application ultimately rested on the judge presiding the trial. De Luca distinguished between *periti ad testificandum* and *periti ad iudicandum*, who corresponded more or less to the experts called by the defense and those called by the judge. The testimony of the experts called by the defense was considered at the same level as that of a lay witness, while that of the experts called by the judge was regarded as advice given by an expert in a specific field in which the judge was not an authority and who could help him reach the final verdict.[31] In practice, men of law did not welcome either type of expert, and this was particularly true when the experts were physicians, who were thought of as impinging on the judge's autonomy of decision.[32]

The opinion of the three doctors invited by the defense lawyer Grato was framed as that of *periti ad testificandum*. Sacco's opinion, even though initially requested by a relative of the victim, was considered the deposition of a witness who informed the judge of the evidence he found during his autopsy of Isabella's body. In neither case did Alavolini himself seek the doctor's expertise.

When the crime dealt with a situation as uncertain and ambiguous as a homicide committed by a person suffering from intermittent insanity, physicians had an important function in verifying defendants' mental—and juridical—status.[33] If defendants were mad while committing the act, they did not have a motive and therefore were innocent. If they were sane at the time of the act, they were culpable. Zacchia devoted the first section of the second volume of his *Quaestiones medico-legales* to insanity, which he organized and discussed from a medicolegal point of view, showing how complex and contradictory it was to determine whether a person was insane while committing a criminal act.[34] While medicine and law had a distinct set of categorizations to identify and treat insanity, in Paolo's story the two disciplines also established a sort of uneasy collaboration in which medical expertise was called to weigh in on a case of insanity by a defense lawyer who requested a medical opinion to benefit his client.

Besides fostering an interest in the study of ancient texts, the development of humanism in law and medicine offered a new approach to history and the past, which also manifested itself in a changing attitude toward the notion of evidence and proof in these disciplines.[35] Judges, lawyers, and physicians dealt with conjectural evidence, even when a wounded or dead body was involved. In the case of Isabella's body, witnesses stated that she was pregnant, but the truth was not known until Sacco performed the autopsy. In the case of Paolo's madness, Mercuriale, Tagliacozzi, and Lodi extrapolated and judged conjectural evidence based on signs that they saw in Paolo's behavior and actions when they examined him and learned of his history of past violence. Isabella and Paolo were mentioned on almost every page of the proceedings of the trial but were physically absent.[36] The notary could not record the judge's questions to them and their answers; the judge could not observe their behavior and way of talking. Their actions and behavior took shape through the words of witnesses, including the medical experts involved in the case, who constructed conjectural evidence related to both the victim and the perpetrator.

In their report, Mercuriale, Tagliacozzi, and Lodi alluded to the legal notion of intermittent insanity (*furor cum dilucida intervalla*), but without explicitly using the legal term. The fact that Paolo realized the gravity of his actions after he had committed the murder, the doctors wrote, was common to "many of these melancholic people, who, in a short period of time, commit very serious crimes when they reach a very high level of furor [*furore*] and then regain their previous way of being [i.e., before committing the murder]."[37] In that period of blind rage the fumes produced by the burned melancholic humors created "diabolical and wild images and thoughts" that induced Paolo to see in his wife somebody worthy of being punished, and even killed. After the fumes dissipated, the doctors claimed, he realized what he had done and chose to escape.[38] The statement quoted above exemplifies the legal doctrine of intermittent insanity, which was the core of Grato's defense for Paolo's brother Aurelio, the stand-in defendant. Sixteenth-century jurists Giacomo Menochio, Francesco Mantica, and Giuseppe Mascardi discussed the doctrine of intermittent insanity in their treatises on supporting evidence.[39] Mascardi and Menochio stated that when people who suffered from intermittent insanity committed a crime, they did it while insane, and the burden of proving otherwise fell on the prosecution. However, Mantica and Mascardi also voiced the contrary view, respectively in civil and criminal law. Mantica stated that if a person who suffered from intermittent insanity drew a will, he/she had to be presumed of sound mind, and whoever claimed that person insane while doing it had the responsibility of proving it. Mascardi argued the same thing for people suffering from intermittent insanity who committed a crime.[40] Zacchia justified Mascardi's apparently contradictory statements by explaining that people suffering from insanity "that result[s] from a fever, or from a different sickness that is accompanied by a fever, as in phrenitis, lethargy, and the like," should not be considered insane when they committed a criminal act, because when the fever stopped, so did their madness.[41] It is clear that the legal doctrine of intermittent insanity showed a level of ambiguity that the legal system had trouble applying to criminal cases like that of Paolo Barbieri: "The warnings and the alarm vis-à-vis the *furiosus* that has 'lucid intervals' show in jurists a component of intolerance for uncertain situations and therefore the tendency to a drastic solution that sets clearly the subject against the point of discrimination."[42] The association between law and medicine in the early modern court of law meant that at times medicine's epistemological nuances in relation to evidence created uneasiness in the court of law once they were expressed in medicolegal reports, as the courts tended to try to resolve uncertain situations like that created by the notion of intermittent insanity. Starting in the fourteenth and throughout the seventeenth century, when legal medicine was officially established with Paolo Zacchia's monumental work on the topic, medicine and law collaborated in the court of law, although in an increasingly argumentative manner. This uneasy collaboration, which often took shape in the medicolegal *consilium*, expressed the difference in register between the two disciplines, one based on plausibility and verisimilitude, the other aiming for absolute and univocal truth.[43]

MEDICAL EXPERTISE ON CRIMINAL INSANITY IN AND OUT OF THE COURT OF LAW: THE *FEDE* AND THE *CONSILIUM*

In medical literature physicians did not use the legal term "intermittent insanity" but described situations in which patients suffered from madness punctuated by periods of lucidity, particularly when they were affected by hypochondriac melancholy.[44] For many of the patients that Mercuriale diagnosed and treated as insane, the original cause was melancholy, either by itself (*per essentiam*) or together with other illnesses (*hypocondriaca*). Mercuriale defined melancholy as the condition of "corrupted imagination" or "corrupted discourse," or both,[45] and described how it could produce effects similar to those caused by mania, or be accompanied by mania, another illness of the head that was a form of delirium without fever, which affected the mind and one or more of the faculties of speech, memory, and imagination.[46] In Mercuriale's account of hypo-chondriac melancholy, burned juices formed in the hypochondrium—the upper regions of the abdomen—created obstructions in the intestines and affected first the stomach and the liver and then the brain. Mercuri-ale compared hypochondriac melancholy to a Trojan horse from which all the symptoms arose,[47] and stated that people throughout Italy suffering from this disease asked his advice every day.[48] In the report he cowrote for legal purposes, Mercuriale believed that Paolo suffered from hypochon-driac melancholy, which had led him to take leave of his senses several times, the last of which when he murdered his wife, Isabella.

The certificate's content and structure can be connected with the med-ical consultation (*consilium/consultatio*), an "epistemic genre" that early modern physicians, both in Italy and Europe, used extensively.[49] The genre of the medical consultation was codified in thirteenth-century Bologna, probably under the influence of the legal *consilium*, which appeared in the twelfth century and increased in number at the end of the thirteenth cen-tury.[50] Men of law used *consilia* to give advice about real or hypothetical cases in civil and criminal law, the result of which were measured against a set of existing rules, called *consilia sapientis*.[51] The genre of the medical *consilium* was largely developed in the fourteenth and fifteenth centuries, and in the sixteenth century it had a rather fixed structure.[52] It consisted of a written text in Latin, or more rarely in the vernacular, in which one doctor requested help about a specific patient from another doctor who identified the illness, gave a possible prognosis, and prescribed a cure tai-lored to the patient. In the fifteenth and especially sixteenth centuries, the *consilium* became the genre that mediated between the university course and the professional medical practice.[53] It allowed physicians to connect the mostly impersonal material found in the treatises with contemporary, individual cases treated in medical consultations.[54] Medical consultations done collectively, that is, in *collegio*, by two or three doctors at a patient's home were common in this period, and sometimes they were recorded in *consilia* printed for the medical readership.

Early modern physicians composed medical consultations not only at the request of colleagues inquiring about the health of wealthy patients,[55] but also for medical institutions and criminal courts. In medieval Bolo-gna, physicians composed medicolegal reports, which the notary called sometimes *consilia*, for the criminal court, invited by the judge or by the defense.[56] On the basis of their study of this type of *consilium*, which dif-fers from that written for therapeutic purposes, Marilyn Nicoud and Joël

Chandelier argue that the medieval medicolegal reports prepared the ground for the full development of the medicolegal discipline exemplified by Zacchia's *Quaestiones*.[57] At the beginning of the seventeenth century, Zacchia wrote a total of eighty-five *consilia* as a result of being asked to weigh in on sundry issues related to criminal and civil cases.[58] To bring an example that features a physician who treated Paolo Barbieri, Mercuriale wrote a *consilium* on behalf of the medical College of Padova in which he was asked to give his opinion on whether the death of a young man from Brescia had been caused by poison.[59]

The medical report written on Paolo's condition differs in terms of structure and readership from the many *consilia* that Mercuriale wrote on illnesses of the head and specifically on hypochondriac melancholy.[60] Writers of *consilia* like Mercuriale had a detached attitude toward the patients of whom they were writing. However, this approach was notably downplayed in the document that Mercuriale, Tagliacozzi, and Lodi wrote to support the argument that Paolo was mad when he killed Isabella and that he had been suffering from attacks of insanity for many years. The usual erudite allusions to the ancient medical authorities Galen, Hippocrates, and Avicenna found in Mercuriale's *consilia* on illnesses of the head are significantly absent in the document reporting Paolo's examination.[61] Usually, *consilia* did not record what happened to patients—whether they recovered, got worse, or died.[62] But the report written by the three doctors emphasized the tragic consequences of Paolo's illness and his refusal to follow the prescribed treatment. They adapted the style and language of their document to their readership. Readers of medical *consilia* consisted of colleagues and students and a restricted group of patients who could read Latin, while in the Barbieri trial they included the lawyer who invited the physicians to write the document, the notary, and the judge. Recognizing that it was intended for men of law, the doctors alluded in the last section of the letter to the legal doctrine of "insanity with lucid intervals" when they justified Paolo's actions after he committed the murder as those of a mad person. One of the main differences between reports written for a medical readership and those that physicians wrote for legal purposes is that the former had a therapeutic purpose, combined with an ethical concern, applied to a particular case, while the latter had a more practical and immediate purpose, and it was usually ancillary to the decision of the judge.[63]

One substantial similarity between a therapeutic *consilium* and a report written for legal purposes is the language with which the three doctors defined hypochondriac melancholy—very precise, corresponding at times to a literal translation of the explanations in Latin offered by Mercuriale in his medical consultations for therapeutic purposes. For instance, in one of his *consilia*, Mercuriale narrated the case of a twenty-year-old man who had lost his parents at an early age, had been verbally and physically abused by his tutor, and had been drinking wine since he was young. These factors led the youth to a debauched life, with the result that his faculties of imagination and speech were deeply affected and he started suffering from hypochondriac melancholy. He also had a strong desire to strike himself and others, a clear sign of a deranged mind. Mercuriale justified the young man's peculiar behavior by stating that burned humors upset the hypochondria and the liver, and consequently the brain. He recommended that the young man be treated with a regimen of regular sleep, a moderate life and diet, daily evacuation, bloodletting from the right arm and the hemorrhoids, and cauteries in both knees—physicians believed that, if followed, these remedies would restore a patient to a balanced state of mind.[64] Mercuriale and his colleagues had recommended that Paolo perform "general evacuations" (*evacuazioni universali*). However, they had noticed with disappointment that not only did he stop following the cure after a few days, but that he also made "many extremely serious mistakes in his lifestyle."[65] Vincenzo Carrari stated that when a sick person did not obey the doctor's prescription, he must be considered *furiosus*.[66] The jurist Mascardi also listed this behavior as a sign of "furor."[67]

Paolo's diagnosis of hypochondriac melancholy took shape through the signs that medical experts identified in his behavior and his words, which they used to formulate the conjectural evidence that Aurelio's defense lawyer Grato could exploit to his advantage. Because hypochondriac melancholy ultimately affected the brain and led people suffering from it to insanity, Grato could use it as the medical counterpart to the legal notion of intermittent insanity. A few decades later Zacchia made the connection between the legal doctrine of intermittent insanity and hypochondriac melancholy in a *quaestio* devoted to various categories of madness:

Next in this category [of intermittent insanity] come the melancholic hypochondriacs, who resemble the paraphrenetics in that their madness does not come from a fault of the brain, but from a sickness of the belly, and it is aggravated by excess. . . . Though hypochondriacs do have attacks and turns for the worse, they do not happen every day or every other day, or every few days, but rather monthly or

yearly, and they last for much longer; for instance, the sickness rup-
tures forth [literally, to become raw again, to dehisce like a stitched
wound] in certain times like spring or autumn, though other times
they are sound enough in mind.[68]

Both Paolo and the young man for whom Mercuriale wrote the medical
consultation discussed earlier suffered from hypochondriac melancholy,
which affected their faculties of imagination and speech and made them
desire to harm themselves and others. Unfortunately for Isabella, Paolo
acted on his desire and killed her, thinking in his deranged mind that she
was somebody who deserved to be harmed.[69]

CONCLUSIONS

Giuseppe Mascardi proposed a list of thirty-seven signs as a *vademecum*
for the legal expert when assessing if someone was insane: many of them
were related to the person's legal and medical status.[70] At the end of this
list Mascardi wrote a sort of warning: "Since insanity is nothing else but
an illness of the mind and the soul, and therefore hides inside [oneself]
and cannot appear under our senses, it must be proven through nothing
else but actions and signs."[71] On the other hand, early modern medicine
became increasingly interested in finding a method through which the
hidden causes of illnesses could be revealed after a careful examination
of all the accidental and substantial signs of an illness, so that the appropriate cure could be applied to the patient. The ability to find the hidden
causes revealed whether a physician was competent.[72]

Both law and medicine based their method of finding the truth, whether
in a trial or in a medical diagnosis, on probable evidence—this is why Aurelio's defense lawyer Grato and the three physicians who wrote the medical
certificate found common ground in defining and describing the causes of
Paolo's intermittent insanity.[73] It is also true that in the second half of the
sixteenth century *experientia* and *de visu* observation became central in
established medical genres like *consilia*, and in new ones like *observationes*.[74] In these genres, tangible evidence was increasingly important, even
though universal categories, inherited from Aristotelian natural philosophy, were not completely dismissed.[75]

In the legal report by Mercuriale, Tagliacozzi, and Lodi, evidence relied
both on direct observation and medical textual precepts. Grato used this
document to support his line of defense, which was based on the legal

notion of intermittent insanity and which relied not on tangible, but on conjectural evidence. The collaboration between medicine and law, which, as we described earlier, grew in the sixteenth century, underlined many similarities but also a fundamental difference. Medicine was based on accumulation and probability, for which clues to any form of illness were innumerable, as innumerable as the idiosyncrasies of the human body. Law tried to create a finite hierarchy of types of evidence, even if it was difficult to make a distinction among them, and even if, like medicine, it based its system of categorization on individual cases, which by their nature never repeated themselves.[76]

The relationship between the defense lawyer and the three physicians in relation to Paolo's madness showed the adaptation of the medical discourse for legal purposes, continuing the development of a tendency that had begun at least two centuries earlier.[77] The signs with which the physicians built their evidence, and the diagnosis they provided for Paolo Barbieri, were used to support the legal doctrine of intermittent insanity. While Mercuriale, Tagliacozzi, and Lodi did not lie in their diagnosis, the defense lawyer Grato deftly manipulated the "inartificial proofs"—that is, circumstantial evidence provided by the doctors—into "artificial proofs," which he used for the benefit of his client, Paolo's brother Aurelio.[78]

While the defense lawyer and the medical experts established a collaboration to describe Paolo as insane, Judge Alavolini did not accept this line of argumentation based on conjectural evidence. Alavolini's evaluation of Paolo's behavior rejected the expert medical opinion on which Grato built his defense and focused, instead, on Paolo's actions—he killed his wife, he got dressed, and then he escaped. A two-pronged explanation can be offered for the judge's stance. One is related to the tense relationship between judges and experts of any kind, and in particular physicians. In a legal system that aimed increasingly at centering the authority and autonomy of decision in the hands of the judge, Alavolini might have deeply resented the opinion of medical experts on the thorny issue of intermittent insanity, especially when it involved a murder. The second explanation is political and focuses on the peculiar situation of Bologna within the papal state. While judges were ultimately under the jurisdiction of papal authority, the men who offered or were hired for their legal services in a criminal or civil court of law, the so-called *procuratores*, were not. In the second half of the sixteenth century, members of the local nobility, who filled the seats of Bologna's municipal offices, stalled attempts by the papal authority to control who could represent a defendant in court.[79] The trial for the murder of Isabella, which went on for almost two months and whose aftermath lasted for almost nine years, was not only about Paolo's insanity, his escape, and the accusation of helping him leave Bologna produced against his brother Aurelio and several other men. It was also an expression of the conflict of power between centralized and local authorities in the papal state over criminal justice and an example of the controversial relation in this period between hegemonic and negotiated justice.

CHAPTER 3

Insanity on Trial

THE CIRCUMSTANCES OF THE TRIAL AND ITS DEFENDANTS

After he left his house, Paolo ran south on Strada Castiglioni. That much everybody who was questioned on the day of the murder, and later during the trial, could agree on. But as to what happened next, each had differing accounts. The proceedings of the trial retell differing accounts of that day, creating a substantial amount of ambiguity around the facts, and many questions aimed at ascertaining whether Paolo was mad and whether Aurelio was an accomplice. Did Paolo suffer from intermittent insanity? Would this condition, recognized as a legal and medical category, justify his actions? If Paolo was not mad, did the men who helped him become his accomplices? When did Paolo's brother Aurelio learn about the death of Isabella—before or after he rushed to see his friend, the lawyer Grato? Did Aurelio order the servant(s) to bring Paolo some clothes and pick up his sword? And if he did, was it before or after he learned that Isabella had died from her injuries?

The people who happened to be at Carlo Ratta's house, where Paolo found refuge, all agreed on the following narrative. On the morning of October 24, several men arrived at Ratta's house: Tomaso Brocchi, a friend of Ratta; Ludovico Salani, a banker; Leone Benini, a substitute notary of the criminal tribunal of the Torrone;[1] and Francesco, Paolo's seventeen-year-old servant. That morning Ratta, a notable and wealthy citizen of Bologna, had his house door open because there was a cargo of wood to unload.[2] Tomaso Brocchi was the first to arrive, and while he and

Ratta conversed standing in the doorway, they saw a young man coming toward them with a sword in his hands and wearing only his nightgown: he entered the house and asked for clothes. The banker Salani was the first to recognize who he was—Aurelio Barbieri's younger brother, the *cavaliero* Paolo Barbieri—and warned Ratta and the notary Benini that the young man suffered from melancholic humors.[3] When the judge interrogated him immediately after the murder, Benini said that Paolo "suffered a bit in the head, and just recently this humor has come back to him" (*pateva un poco di cervello, et che era poco che gl'era venuto un[′] altra volta l'humore così*).[4] Benini also remembered that his brother Aurelio had told him months earlier about a legal guarantee worth two hundred scudi that he submitted to the Torrone for his brother's erratic behavior, fearing that Paolo could hurt someone in their house or even him because of his "humors."[5] When questioned at his house immediately after the murder, Ratta said that he had no idea who Paolo was or that he had killed his wife but thought that he was *matto*: "He was shaking, holding that unsheathed sword in his hands like a madman."[6] Salani and Benini described Paolo's behavior the morning of the murder in detail. When they saw him running on the street, half naked, barefoot, and holding a sword, they thought that he was a young man who had run into some trouble at home, or a scholar caught with someone else's wife, scantily clothed as he fled danger.[7] When Paolo entered Ratta's house, he started kissing everybody; he trembled and claimed he had been wounded and was being followed by people who wanted to kill him.[8] Benini also said that Paolo did not want to part from his sword even after they convinced him to lie down but clutched it in his hands, saying, "I am a knight and it is shameful for me to be without a sword!"[9] Finally, persuaded by Salani to give up his sword, Paolo kept complaining that he had been wounded in his shoulder. When they told him that it was not true, he said, "Alas, Ludovico [Salani], I have been murdered, here is the court."[10] Because Paolo appeared to act and speak in an irrational way, and because they saw him half naked and shaking in the cold, Benini and Salani decided to go to his house to warn Aurelio so that he would send his brother clothes and shoes. Shortly after they left, Francesco arrived at Carlo Ratta's house with garments and a heavy cloak. Once Paolo got dressed, he went away with Francesco, leaving his sword behind.[11] After Benini learned from Aurelio that his brother Paolo had fatally wounded his wife, he hurried to report the tragic news to the Torrone, the palace where the *legato*, the pope's highest representative in Bologna, and the *uditore*, the chief criminal judge, resided and worked together with the *sotto-uditore*, a judge who responded to the *uditore*, and a contingent of notaries who recorded the complaints and lawsuits (*querele* and *denunce*).[12] Salani followed in Benini's footsteps, but when he arrived at the Torrone, he found that the notary had already told one of his colleagues to record the crime and had gone in person to Alavolini, who sent the *sotto-uditore* Filippo Violano, along with the notary Decio Cambio and the *cursore* Camillo Ferrarini, to the Barbieri house to examine Isabella's body.[13] Alerted by Benini, the *bargello* Girolamo Leonardi went with his men to the Ratta house and to the city gates of Bologna and had the alarm bells sound throughout the city to keep Paolo from escaping.[14] But it was too late; Paolo had already left the house of Carlo Ratta with his servant Francesco and fled Bologna through Porta Castiglioni, one of the city gates.

Another version of the events surrounding the murder was given during the trial by Lazaro dei Bernabo, a wool dyer, and his friend Domenico Cortesi, a shoemaker, and reveals the ambiguity caused by conflicting versions of the morning of the murder.[15] On October 29, in the presence of the notary Cambio, Lazaro and Domenico testified that on the morning of October 24 they saw a rather big young man, with a sparse reddish beard and a blue cloak, emerging on Strada Castiglioni from the path that divided the Barbieri house from that of the family Guidotti. A shorter, older man accompanied him, wearing a white apron and holding a set of keys. Lazaro and Domenico walked behind the two men all the way to Ratta's house on Strada Castiglioni; they saw that the younger man walked ahead of the older, who followed him closely. The young man carried under his cloak an empty scabbard and a bloodied piece of white cloth.[16] The young man and his companion were constantly turning to look behind themselves; Lazaro and Domenico even heard the older man telling his companion to pull up the bloody cloth, because everybody could see it. When the young man and his mate were in front of Carlo Ratta's house, they entered, and the owner followed them inside.

Later that morning, Lazaro and Domenico heard the news that the *cavaliero* Barbieri had killed his wife. Could the young man with the reddish beard they saw be the same man that they had heard was running down the streets with a sword in his hands? Was the rumor of his crime exaggerated?[17] Lazaro and Domenico went to the judge of the Torrone that morning to report what they had seen. No other witness came forward supporting their narrative. Perhaps their low social standing could explain why the judge Violano, who presided most of the trial, chose to disregard their version of the story and only the notary Cambio questioned the two men.[18]

THE TRIAL AND ITS PHASES

Immediately after Salani and Benini reported the news of Isabella's fatal stabbing at the Torrone,[19] the criminal trial began: that same day Violano questioned the men and the servants who were at Ratta's house when Paolo arrived, and all the servants of the Barbieri household in Piazza Calderini, where the judge had gone to examine the body of the murdered Isabella together with Cambio and the *cursore* Ferrarini.[20] In general, proceedings of early modern criminal trials contain only the initial charge and the inquisitorial part of the trial (*pro informatione curiae*), probably because very often the two parties settled out of court or the plaintiff withdrew the charge.[21] However, the trial against Paolo Barbieri and his supposed accomplices contains all the main phases of a criminal trial. The regular procedure included four main stages: the initial charge; the inquisitorial process, during which the judge, usually the *sotto-uditore*, could also order the torture of the defendant, if he deemed it necessary to extract the truth; the defensive process, during which the *sotto-uditore* examined the witnesses that the defense lawyers had chosen after they had a chance to read the proceedings of the inquisitorial process and to formulate objections to the judge's accusation and points (*articula*) on which the witnesses were questioned; and the pronouncement of the sentence by the *uditore*, who usually examined the proceedings led by the *sotto-uditore* and pronounced the final verdict.[22] The reason why the Barbieri trial went through all the four stages probably has to do not only with the seriousness of the crime and its vast resonance in the city, but also with the status of the people involved—notable and noble men with means and ties to some of the most powerful local families, and even to some members of the high clergy in Rome. Because the main defendants were high on the social scale, they were not subjected to torture; also, they could afford to pay for the examination of the witnesses by the judge during the defensive phase of the trial, the cost of which fell on the defendants.[23]

THE FIRST PHASE OF THE TRIAL: THE INQUISITORIAL PROCESS

The inquisitorial process lasted for five days, from October 24 to October 27. Only the *sotto-uditore* Violano and the notary Cambio, who was

Veduta della Dogana, e Carceri della Città di Bologna

FIG. 4 "Veduta della Dogana e Carceri della Città di Bologna,"
in *Diario Bolognese Ecclesiastico e Civile* (1774). Biblioteca
dell'Archiginnasio, BCABo GDS, Cartone Panfili, c. 46.

assigned to transcribe the judge's questions in Latin and the answers of
the witnesses in Italian, were privy to these depositions, as was customary in criminal trials in Bologna at that time. Witnesses and defendants
were interrogated behind closed doors, with just the judge and the notary
attending. Only when the trial reached the defensive phase did defendants
have the right to ask the judge for a copy of the witnesses' earlier depositions through their lawyers. By the end of October 24, it was clear to *sotto-uditore* Violano that Paolo had fled Bologna with his servant Francesco
and was not going to be caught. Carlo Ratta and the men who arrived at
his house—Tommaso Brocchi, Ludovico Salani, and Leone Benini—all
claimed that Paolo had acted and spoken like a crazy man. That was why
Benini and Salani went to the Barbieri house to alert his brother Aurelio,
urging him to have someone bring clothes to Paolo. With his questions,
Violano intended to establish, first, was Paolo really crazy? Second, what
did he do and where did he go after the murder? Third, who told Francesco to bring Paolo clothes and when? And fourth, did Aurelio know that
Isabella was dead when he left the house in a hurry?

Violano questioned many people on October 24. The person whom he did not question, that day or any other day of the trial, was the matriarch Ippolita Barbieri, whose voice was only heard through other depositions. Except for Tommaso Brocchi and the notary Leone Benini, who was jailed a few days later, on October 27, everybody else was put behind bars by the end of that day. In fact, Paolo's brother Aurelio was in prison from the morning of October 24, when he went to the Torrone to report his brother's crime with Giovanni Francesco Grato, who became his defense lawyer during the trial.[24] In Paolo's absence, Aurelio became the main defendant, together with Carlo Ratta, Ludovico Salani, and Leone Benini. It seems that Violano suspected that Paolo acted mad to escape, and that Aurelio, Ratta, Benini, and Salani had helped him.

Mad or Not? The Legal Dilemma About Paolo's Insanity

Paolo's legal status during the trial needs to be evaluated in relation to how early modern men of law viewed insane people, in the theory of the treatises they wrote and in the practice of the trials they presided. The reconstruction of this context will help us understand why Violano and Alavolini decided that Paolo was not crazy, thus making Aurelio, Ratta, Benini, and Salani guilty of abetting a criminal's flight.

In the Middle Ages and in the early modern period, civil and criminal jurists wrote articles describing the behavior of people presumed insane that developed from Justinian's *Institutes*, available since the sixth century,[25] while others were distilled from contemporary social behaviors and experiences.[26] Once these distilled social behaviors and experiences became normative legal models, judges were allowed to adopt, question, and, at times, disregard them during trials. According to the fourteenth-century jurist Baldo degli Ubaldi (1327–1400), insane people could not be considered guilty of crimes they had committed, and therefore could not be punished because they "[are] punished enough by [their] insanity" (*satis punitur suo furore*).[27] The terms *furor* and *furiosus*, which can be translated with "insanity" and "insane," defined a person who needed to be supervised and had several legal restrictions.[28] Sane people committed crimes with intent; if there was no intent, jurists stated, the authority to punish disappeared.[29] In the second half of the sixteenth century, several famous men of law devoted sections of their treatises on evidence of insanity and the way mad people could be identified. Menochio, Mantica, and Mascardi categorized corroborating evidence of madness in criminal and civil trials. The titles of their works contain the terms *probatio, praesumptio, coniectura*, and *indicium*, all referring to degrees of proof that could be used in a trial.[30] *Probatio* subsumed the tools that determined the judge's reasoning in resolving a case: documents, testimonies, the opinions of experts, and confessions.[31] *Praesumptio* denoted the logical consequence that derived from facts that had been proven.[32] *Coniectura* was a conjectural inference, therefore less important than *praesumptio*; beneath the *coniectura* were the *indicia* and the *signa*. *Indicia* implied *signa* and were foundations for a *praesumptio*, formed by a reasoning process based on probability, possibility, or correspondence, while *signa* were simple phenomena.[33] This seemingly precise hierarchy of probable evidence was in fact subject to different and sometimes discordant evaluations that depended on the judge who presided over the trial.[34] Full evidence was when the culprit was caught *in flagrante* (red-handed). Testimony was not considered very strong evidence, especially if only one witness delivered it. The most convincing partial evidence was given by the testimony of at least two witnesses. However, the importance of a deposition depended also on the witness's social status—let us remember, for instance, the value given to the testimonies of the wool dyer Lazaro dei Bernabo and the shoemaker Domenico Cortesi during the Barbieri trial. Finally, *fama* was considered important partial evidence but may or may not have been proof relevant enough for the judge.[35] According to Menochio, those who went half dressed and showed their private parts could be presumed insane.[36] Mascardi and Francesco Mantica warned that individuals affected by insanity might not remember their names or their actions, or might not answer pointed questions or any question at all.[37] Menochio considered it a sign of madness if a person answered a question with something completely unrelated.[38] Also, he argued that leaving the scene of a crime with a sword in hand proved that the suspect had committed a crime.[39]

If these signs sound familiar, it is because we have encountered them in the story of Paolo Barbieri as it was reconstructed by the judge through the witnesses' depositions. But they were not enough to convince Violano and Alavolini that Paolo was mad. In fact, Mascardi, Menochio, and Mantica admitted that it was very difficult to prove that a person was insane. Finding support in Degli Ubaldi, Menochio observed that someone could detect signs of insanity only if he or she lived for an extended time with a mad person, because madness was an invisible ailment that revealed itself not through sound or sight but through *iudicio rationis*, that is, through the logical evaluation of various types of evidence. This statement seemed to contradict the view, maintained by the medical discipline, that madness was the result of an imbalance of humors detectable in a patient's face, skin, and body. Degli Ubaldi and Menochio pointed to the inner nature of madness, and by doing so they offered not only a very modern perspective of insanity but also a link to the notion of simulation.[40] Menochio warned judges that they should have "full knowledge of the trial in which an individual claims to be mad, as many pretend to be as such."[41] If in doubt, one should presume the defendant *sanae mentis* (of sound mind); so, if a lawyer claimed that his client was insane, he should prove it by bringing convincing evidence. Early modern jurists supported this statement by claiming that the natural "default mode" of all human beings was mental sanity, and whoever stated otherwise had to shoulder the burden of proving it.[42] To complicate an already ambiguous and murky categorization, both civil and criminal law believed that madness could be intermittent, which meant that people could have periods of sanity before, during, or after the criminal act;[43] and, if they became mad after committing the crime, they could not be punished.[44] However, when reasonable doubt arose about a hidden motive or cover-up, the person was considered sane, and thus punishable by law.[45] After killing Isabella, Paolo fled the scene of the murder. According to Aurelio's lawyer Grato, Paolo was in the grip of insanity when he committed the crime, and then, realizing the enormity of his action, in a moment of lucidity he decided to escape; according to Violano, he knew what he had done all along and chose to play the role of madman when he arrived at Ratta's house.

The Papal Bull and Church Politics in Bologna

Even if fleeing the law did not necessarily lead to a conviction,[46] it was a damning sign, which, in the end, played a pivotal role in the way Violano, in agreement with Alavolini, decided to conduct the trial. Escaping justice could have serious legal repercussions on the family and property of the fugitive, especially for a wealthy nobleman. At the time of the Barbieri trial, Pope Sixtus V required that a bull he wrote in 1585 against rebellious aristocrats in the Papal State be applied to fugitives in criminal trials. Sixtus V's bull is the linchpin of the trial, and it must be kept in mind from now on to understand the trial's judicial praxis. Violano alluded to it several times at key points of his interrogations of Aurelio Barbieri and the other three defendants during the inquisitorial phase of the trial. At the time of Isabella's murder, Bologna was part of the Papal State, and under its authority. However, Bologna's local nobility, which expressed itself through the Senate, constantly strove for more independence from the central power; some of its members were restive, taking justice into their hands by performing acts of "transversal retaliation" (*vendetta trasversale*), abetting banditry or even becoming bandits themselves, plundering the lands around Bologna and in the Romagna. The relationship between Bologna and the central authority in Rome changed every time a new pope was elected. When Paolo killed Isabella, Sixtus V had been pope for more than three years, and he remained in power until the end of August 1590. A few months after becoming pope, Sixtus V launched a campaign to eradicate banditry throughout the papal state; he also issued an edict (July 1, 1585) in which those who helped criminals escape, or offered them refuge, would see their properties confiscated and their relatives heavily fined.[47] Sixtus V's sanction was not new, but, unlike his predecessors, the pope asked his emissaries to enact it. Also, the bull gave to the Apostolic Chamber the profits of the monetary penalties that had remained at the disposal of the city of Bologna for extraordinary expenses.[48]

Sixtus V's edict is significant in the Barbieri trial for two important reasons. If Paolo murdered his wife deliberately and not in a moment of melancholic fury, he was a fugitive murderer, to be treated with the same harsh punishment inflicted on fugitive bandits who infested the northern regions of the Papal State: thus, Paolo's properties, which he shared with his brother Aurelio, were liable of confiscation. Also, if Paolo was not afflicted by intermittent insanity, Aurelio and the other three defendants were accomplices in helping him escape, and therefore they needed to be tried.

The conduct of the *uditore* Alavolini and the *sotto-uditore* Violano during the trial was in line with the politics of Sixtus V and his functionaries, in particular the *legato* and the *vice-legato*.[49] Alavolini was from Macerata in the Marche, the same region where the pope was born, and was probably his protégé. Violano, from Modigliana in Romagna, worked at the service of papal criminal justice all his life.[50] The *legato* was a high prelate, chosen by the pope, who represented papal authority in Bologna and controlled the functioning of criminal justice, to the dismay of Bologna's government and Senate, which were in the hands of the local nobility. In this period cardinal Alessandro Peretti, Sixtus V's nephew, was the *legato* of Bologna, but he resided almost exclusively in Rome, so the *vice-legato*, Camillo Borghese—the future Pope Paul V (1605–1621)—fulfilled the responsibilities of the *legato*. Borghese started his tenure barely a month before the beginning of the Barbieri trial, during a turbulent period in Bologna caused, among other things, by a prolonged period of famine in the city and in its *contado*. Borghese had the task of establishing a viable relationship with the leading classes in the city, while showing that, in the end, the curia had the final word. All main characters in the administration of justice in Bologna at the time of the Barbieri trial were loyal subjects of the pope, who chose them, directly or indirectly, to play important roles in the city's political, economic, and legal affairs. Since coming to power in May 1585, Sixtus V had pursued a robust politics against opposed factions of bandits, whose leaders were often members of noble and wealthy Bolognese families. Hence the very harsh papal bull of July 1585. In June of 1589, persuaded by the cardinal nephew, Borghese, and Alavolini, the pope suspended from then forward the enforcement of the bull.[51]

The Questioning of the Defendants

During the inquisitorial phase of the trial, Violano questioned the main defendant, Aurelio Barbieri, three times. From the way he spoke and behaved, Aurelio, who, we should remember, had been trained as a lawyer, came across as shifty, more interested in concealing than revealing the truth, focused on portraying himself as a man shocked and not in control of his actions after Paolo's flight, but also as a brother concerned about his younger sibling's mental and physical state, which was why he had sent the servant Francesco to Ratta's house with clothes for Paolo. When questioned for the first time on October 25, Aurelio claimed that his brother had been overcome by "furor" the day of the murder, as it had happened other times before, confirming the opinion of those who encountered him the day of the murder: Paolo was insane.[52] Asked why his brother had murdered his wife, Aurelio answered, "I believe that this act was caused by insanity, because I know that he did not have any reason to do so; he would have this humor sometimes and would stay at home three or four days without saying a word."[53] During his second interrogatory on October 26, Aurelio added disturbing details about his brother's behavior at home. Every day at mealtime Paolo would sit at the table, silent like a stone, with his head down; out of frustration, Aurelio would leave after eating to shun his brother, "who always had the humor, and nobody knew what he had."[54] Paolo was in this state the day before the murder. To avoid him, Aurelio returned home toward midnight.

Aurelio seemed genuinely scared of his brother. He claimed that when the servant Maddalena came knocking at his door asking for help, he first locked the room and got dressed and then opened the door to face the servant.[55] Aurelio stated that the morning of the murder he was unable to think straight (*ero fora di me*).[56] When his mother urged him upstairs to the room where Isabella had been stabbed, Aurelio instead asked a neighbor to rush to summon his friend the physician Tagliacozzi. When the doctor arrived and went upstairs to see Isabella, Aurelio did not wait for him but rushed out of the house to talk with Grato, whom he then accompanied to the Torrone.[57] Aurelio said that he knew that Paolo had gone to a house in Strada Castiglioni, because Benini and Salani told him to send clothes for his brother there; only then, Aurelio said, did he order the servant Francesco to bring his brother garments and a coat.[58] Violano found inconsistencies in Aurelio's answers, so he pressed him with more questions. He noticed that Aurelio first said he did not remember the name of the person whose house Paolo entered, but later he mentioned the name Carlo Ratta. Aurelio also denied repeatedly that he knew that Isabella had died before he sent Francesco to Ratta's house and ran out of the house to see Grato, thus contradicting what several servants had stated during their depositions the day before.[59] From his answers, Aurelio appeared to blur, not clarify, the sequence of events. He repeated that he was beside himself when Tagliacozzi returned downstairs after a very short visit to Isabella and did not understand what the doctor told him. But hadn't he claimed that he left before Tagliacozzi returned downstairs? And when a servant told him that Isabella was dead (è spedita), Aurelio, "beside [himself]" (fora di [se] stesso), could not believe that his brother would kill his wife. Aurelio did not know for sure that Isabella was dead, because he never went upstairs to see her. When defendants Salani and Benini were questioned on October 27, they contradicted Aurelio's statement and said that he had known of Isabella's death. According to Benini, Aurelio knew that Paolo had mortally wounded Isabella, but only when Salani arrived did Aurelio blurt out, while pounding his head with his fists, that she might be dead: "It gets worse, [Paolo] wounded his wife and I believe she is dead."[60]

When Violano referred for the first time to Sixtus V's edict against criminals and murderers and their accomplices during his first interrogation, Aurelio seemed short of excuses: ostensibly exasperated, he said, "Your Honor, now I have to suffer for this!"[61] However, at the end of the second interrogation, Aurelio, without being prompted by Violano, told him that he did not know about Sixtus V's bull before his brother escaped, and that anyway, he did not contravene it, since he first reported the tragic event to a representative of the Torrone, the notary Benini, and then came to the Torrone. Aurelio's claim, uttered as a sort of afterthought, reveals the craftiness of his answers. When Violano resumed the interrogation and showed the flaws in his argument—why didn't he go to Ratta's house when he learned from Benini that his brother was behaving in a strange way, and in somebody else's house?—Aurelio responded, "Your Lordship, I was in a daze and did not know what I was doing, and it made no difference to me whether I went there [to Ratta's house] or came here [to the Torrone]; however, if your Lordship consents, I say that my lawyer will answer this question at this trial."[62] When Ratta was asked the same question about the papal bull against fugitive criminals and his accomplices, he replied that yes, he had heard of its existence but was unaware that one was supposed to pursue actively the fugitive criminals—perhaps one can detect a trace of sarcasm in his final sentence.[63] Like Aurelio and Carlo Ratta before him, Benini defended himself against the accusation of not complying with the papal edict, claiming that once he learned that Paolo had killed his wife, he did everything in his power, and nothing less, to help justice apprehend the fugitive.[64] When it was Salani's turn to answer the question, he begged the judge to forgive him: "Your Lordship, I throw myself on your mercy, if I failed in anything, if I made any mistake, it was out of ignorance, and I ask your forgiveness; here I am, do what you want, and this is the truth."[65] Things did not look good for the four main defendants, who seemed to have obfuscated the truth regarding their knowledge of Sixtus V's bull in one way or another. Violano's repeated allusions to the bull are evidence that he considered these men accomplices in a murder and in the murderer's escape. If found guilty, the threat of imprisonment and confiscation hung over them and their families' properties.

When questioned, Carlo Ratta sounded like a detached spectator who had had the misfortune of having left the door of his house open the day of the murder when Paolo, a stranger to him, barged in without permission. After Benini and Salani left his house to warn Aurelio, Paolo got dressed with the servant Francesco's help and asked for water. Ratta sent his servant Sante Tacconi to get it and then left Paolo and Francesco in the room. After what he believed was a short time, Ratta went out on Strada Castiglioni, where he glimpsed Paolo walking away with Francesco. That was, Ratta claimed, the last time he saw the two men. Brocchi, who was still at Ratta's house when the master and his servant left, said that when he saw the two men walking toward Porta Castiglioni, he commented that they were going the opposite way to where the Barbieri family lived, but he did not receive any answer.[66] Ratta realized that something was amiss only when he learned that the *bargello* Leonardi and his men were looking for Paolo at the house of his cousin Ludovico Ratta, a knight and a count palatine and the father of Dionisio, whose ecclesiastical career brought him in contact with cardinals and the pope in Rome.[67] Ludovico also lived on Strada Castiglioni, more or less across from Carlo, who had an image of the Virgin Mary on the outside wall of his house. This image, it became clear later, was the reason why the *bargello* went to the wrong house. Carlo ran to his cousin's house and only then found out that Paolo had hurt his wife.[68]

By the end of October 25, Grato and Ercole Fontana had been hired by Aurelio Barbieri and Carlo Ratta as their respective defense lawyers—officers of the tribunal had gone to Ratta's house and told him that the *uditore* wanted to talk with him at the Torrone the evening of October 25. Instead, he was put in jail with his servants Sante Tacconi and Giovan Battista Massilli, who had accompanied him.[69] Grato and Fontana asked the judge to release their clients on bail, but their requests fell on deaf ears.[70] Violano examined Ratta again the day after he was placed under arrest, with the intent of understanding why and how Paolo Barbieri could leave Ratta's house without being stopped. Ratta brushed off the judge's objections as to why he did not say that Paolo had been in his house when he went to that of his cousin Ludovico, where the *bargello* was sent by mistake to take hold of Paolo: "Your Lordship, I did not say that the *cavaliero* had been in my house and that he had left in the direction of the gate of Strada Castiglioni to the city officials or to anyone else because I did not think of it."[71] Violano continued the interrogation. Did Paolo talk with his servant Francesco while getting dressed?—"No, they did not exchange a word"—Did Ratta speak with the servant—"No, I did not"—Did the same servant who left with Paolo also take his sword? To this question, Ratta answered that another servant came to pick up Paolo's sword. Who was this other servant? Ratta did not know. Implicit in Violano's query about the identity of the second servant were the following questions: Where did this man bring the sword? Where was the sword now? Finally, Violano asked Ratta if he saw blood on Paolo's clothes or sword when he came to his house; No, he did not. Ratta was dismissed and brought back to jail. He was questioned for the last time on October 31, in reference to the deposition of Lazaro and Domenico. He denied everything they said but stated again that besides Francesco, who brought Paolo's clothes, another servant from the Barbieri household came to the house to take away Paolo's sword. Would Ratta be able to recognize him? No, because he really did not pay attention to him: "A man does not mind that much those matters for which he thinks himself not accountable, and the door of my house is always open, and people always come, and I do not ask who is this and who is that."[72] The detail of the second servant taking away Paolo's sword was never brought up again during the trial, and the sword was never found.

During his interrogations, Benini said he realized that Paolo "was doing a lot of crazy stuff," and so he decided to go to the Barbieri house to inform Aurelio.[73] After learning from Aurelio that Paolo had gravely wounded his wife, Benini went immediately to the *bargello* and urged him to go at once to Ratta's house. Then he rushed to inform the *uditore* of the Torrone—as a notary, Benini knew the criminal procedures to be followed after a murder.[74] When asked why he had not gone back to Ratta's house to make sure that Paolo was still there after he learned that a crime had been committed, Benini said, "It did not come to my mind" or "I didn't think of it,"[75] while he thought that when he went to the Torrone to report the case, the captain of justice and his men would have found Paolo still in bed there.[76] Was Benini speaking in good faith? Salani decided to visit Aurelio too: there he met Benini, who had arrived shortly before him, and the physician Tagliacozzi. Salani walked to the Torrone to report the incident, but there he realized that Benini, once again, had preceded him.[77]

By the end of the inquisitorial phase of the trial, each of the main defendants chose to play a certain role in the story of Paolo's flight. Aurelio portrayed himself as the caring brother who sent clothes to Paolo thinking that he had fallen prey to one of his usual attacks of melancholic insanity, and as a dutiful citizen who reported the crime immediately to the Torrone. Ratta played the part of the detached spectator who was involved only because the door of his house was open. Salani and Benini played the roles of concerned acquaintances who meant to help a man suffering from insanity by asking his brother to send clothes to Ratta's house, and of diligent subjects of the Papal State, who did everything they could to bring Paolo to jail once they learned that he had mortally wounded his wife. To emphasize his client's diligence, on October 31 Benini's lawyer Salaroli asked and received permission from the *uditore* Alavolini for the *bargello* Girolamo Leonardi to be questioned on how the events unfolded after his client approached him the day of the murder. With Leonardi's deposition, Salaroli intended to demonstrate that it was not because his client lacked diligence or zeal that the murderer fled Bologna. On November 1 Leonardi was questioned. According to his account, when Benini was finally able to talk after he ran toward Leonardi, sweaty and out of breath, he told him that the *cavaliero* Paolo Barbieri had killed his wife and that somebody should go and arrest him at Ratta's house in Strada Castiglioni, where Paolo was resting in bed in a room on the ground floor. Leonardi gathered some of his men to make the arrest, but he was given the wrong directions and ended up at the house of Ludovico Ratta, which was across the street from that of Carlo, his cousin. Leonardi even went toward Porta San Mamolo and sent officials outside the city walls to check if anyone had seen men on the run. On his way back, he met Violano, Benini, and the chief notary with other officials of the Torrone, who told him that they had already gone to Carlo Ratta's house and found no one. Not satisfied, Leonardi also searched Carlo's house, probably frustrated that a man identified as "Angelo delle bollette" had given him the wrong directions: "This is the truth and in short, I went to the other house of the Ratta family that I told you about because I understood that that was the house since . . . there is an image of the Virgin Mary in the wall."[78]

THE SECOND PHASE OF THE TRIAL: THE DEFENSIVE PROCESS

After a one-day break, the trial resumed on October 29, and the defensive process began. The chief criminal judge, the *uditore* Alavolini, who, until then, had Violano preside over the trial, ordered Aurelio Barbieri, Carlo Ratta, Ludovico Salani, Leone Benini and four male servants of the Barbieri and Ratta families—Giovanni Fantoni, Andrea Ghirardi, Sante Tacconi, and Giovan Battista Massilli—to be placed *alla larga*, that is, to be transferred from cells in absolute isolation to jails where the defendants were given permission to communicate with the external world and to consult the lawyers who drafted their defense.[79] Alavolini gave them three days to prepare the defenses, but the lawyers objected that that was too short. Ratta's lawyer Fontana and Salani's lawyer Matteo Buratto immediately asked for a copy of the inquisitorial process. On October 31 copies were given directly to Aurelio Barbieri, Carlo Ratta and Ludovico Salani. By November 1 all defense lawyers had obtained a copy of the inquisitorial phase of the trial.[80] From November 3 until November 24 the judge interrogated witnesses *pro parte* following a list of questions each lawyer had prepared and that the judge had amended in advance. From then on, the proceedings consisted of requests and objections from the lawyers of the four main defendants and of the depositions of their witnesses.

The questioning of the witnesses during the defensive phase of the trial followed thus: the judge first asked why the witness had come to depose in favor of the defendant, then asked his questions and those based on the points (*articula*) prepared and submitted by the defense lawyer, some of which were meant to emphasize the defendant's good reputation in the community (*fama*).[81] Buratto and Salaroli produced similar strategies: they depicted their clients as having done everything in their power to help authorities capture Paolo and his servant Francesco. Fontana and Grato had a harder time convincing the judge that their clients were oblivious to Paolo's intention to escape, but they used all the legal and rhetorical tools at their disposal.

Diligentia and *Fama* as Defense Strategies for Salani, Benini, and Ratta

Buratto and Salaroli argued that their clients did not deserve to be punished; instead, they should be commended for their diligence. Buratto presented in writing to Violano the formal objections (*exceptiones*) to the accusations against Salani and the points on which the witnesses for the defense were to be questioned.[82] Buratto argued that his client should be rewarded for his "absolute diligence" (*exactissima diligentia*) in helping the authorities capture Paolo.[83] Salani could not have predicted that Paolo, whom he left in bed and half naked, would leave Ratta's house so quickly. Finally, it was not Salani's fault if the *bargello* went to the wrong house.[84] Buratto concluded his rebuttal by stating that, for all these reasons, his client did not contravene Sixtus V's edict. Buratto listed five points that Violano later used to question the witnesses called to vouch for Salani. The first point regarded his client's good reputation and behavior as a citizen of Bologna and a good Christian, who had always obeyed the edicts and orders of the papal authorities. This point was common to all the other defenses and meant to determine the good *fama* of the defendant. The defense lawyer Giulio Cesare Abbati confirmed Benini's good reputation at the Torrone over the ten years he had known him.[85] The point on which the three witnesses in favor of Ratta—all noblemen—were questioned concerned Fontana's client's *fama* as "an honest and obedient man, of good standing, character and repute."[86] Grato portrayed Aurelio as a "good, gentle, calm, and peaceful man" (*vir bonus, placidus, quietus et pacificus*). The social dimension of one's *fama* translated into legal *fama*, even though the two notions did not overlap.[87]

After having established his client's impeccable reputation, Buratto focused on Salani's actions the day of the murder, which he had already described in his objections, except for one: why didn't Salani try to gather people who could help him keep Paolo at Ratta's house after he left the Barbieri house? Because, Buratto claimed, it was very early in the morning and almost no one was around between Strada Castiglioni and Piazza Calderini, where the Barbieri lived. Later the lawyer Salaroli similarly argued that his client Benini would not have found help to keep guard of Paolo because nobody was around: it was way too early for the noblemen who lived in that neighborhood, who usually got up much later in the day.

The witnesses proposed by Buratto were men whom Salani encountered the day of the murder on his way to the Torrone and after he arrived there—a used-clothes seller (*strazzarolo*)[88] and several notaries, along with notable and noble citizens of Bologna, who testified in favor of his diligence and sense of duty in general and the day of the murder.[89] Buratto's strategy was to establish Salani's good *fama*—his reputation as a good Christian, a good family man, and an honest, law-abiding citizen of Bologna—and his movements after he left the Barbieri house. The notary Giovan Battista Tursoni, a longtime friend of Salani, echoed—he said—the opinion of all citizens and noblemen of Bologna, who knew the defendant as "a good, truthful, trustworthy man, a man of excellent conduct, *fama*, status, and judgment."[90] Tursoni added that Salani's respect for the law was manifest in his refusal to help criminals and assassins in the past, in his making every effort to bring them to justice, and in his respecting and obeying to the decrees emanated by the authorities.[91] Ercole Fantuzzi and Giacomo Leonori were noblemen brought to bolster Salani's good name and social standing. They both stated that Buratto asked them to give the judge their "opinion" (*giudizio*) on the events of October 24 and on Salani's involvement, and to vouch for the defendant's good character and *fama*.[92] The two men thought that the banker performed his duty, and that he could not have fought Paolo, who was armed. They also shifted the blame for the failed capture onto the *bargello*.[93] Fantuzzi made no secret that his opinion was based on what he learned from the defendant when he went to visit him[94]—a rather biased source, Violano could say. Leonori claimed that his *giudizio* on the actions of his friend of many years on October 24 was grounded on the *publica fama* that circulated in the city.[95]

The term *diligentia* also took center stage in Salaroli's objections to the judge's accusations against his client Benini. Salaroli intended to prove that his client's actions the day of the murder manifested nothing less than *exactissima diligentia*, and not negligence, which was the accusation the judge brought up against him. *Diligentia* implies effort and dedicated care, qualities lacking in those who are negligent. *Diligentia*, *negligentia*, and *culpa* were tightly connected in early modern law: if the first was missing, the other two resulted.[96] The witnesses were interrogated on Benini's actions the day of the murder. Moved by concern and sympathy (*compassio*) for Paolo and his family, Benini went to warn Aurelio, but at the news that

Paolo had wounded his wife, he ran to the *bargello* Leonardi to inform him about Paolo's whereabouts and urge him to do all that was necessary to apprehend the man. Benini's conscientiousness was a consistent feature of his character and his behavior at work: the assistant notary of the Torrone, Curzio Rumuli, stated that "he has always complied with the orders of his superiors; as a matter of fact, the *auditori* who had been here for a time kept him and liked him, and they made use of his service without reservation, and he obeyed them and served them faithfully and with the utmost diligence."[97]

According to the *cursore* Ferrarini, whom Benini ordered to run to the city gates, have them locked, and sound the alarm with church bells, the notary would have been negligent if he had not come directly to the Torrone to denounce Paolo's crime.[98] Cesare de Rossi, who worked with the *bargello* Leonardi and met Benini on his way to the Torrone, described the notary as "diligente," while he seemed to criticize Leonardi for the time he wasted in gathering his men and going to the wrong house: "They stalled quite a bit before the officers were assembled; and more or less fifteen more minutes passed before the captain [Leonardi] brought them all to Strada Castiglione in the house of Monsignor Ratta."[99]

Fontana presented only one long objection to the judge's accusation against his client, Carlo Ratta, who should be released without delay. Using the legal technical language associated with evidence, Fontana rebutted the accusations against his client by stating that there was no "full evidence" (*probatio*) or even "circumstantial evidence" (*indicium*) that Ratta committed any "crime" (*crimen*) or "offense" (*delictum*). Also, no "malicious intent" (*dolus*) or "negligence" (*culpa*) could be attributed to Ratta, because when he first met Paolo, his aspect and attire, the way he ran at such an early time of the day on the street, and the words and actions he said and performed while at Ratta's house showed that he was "out of his mind and completely insane" (*demens et furiosus*).[100] The rest of Fontana's objections echoed what Ratta had claimed when questioned by Violano—he did not know that Paolo was a criminal when he barged into his house, and he did not contravene the papal bull by not reporting that Paolo had stayed in his house after the latter had escaped. Fontana seemed confident that Ratta's social status and connections in high places sufficed to exonerate him; perhaps this is why his line of defense was the most succinct of the four. Probably Fontana wrote his defense after perusing legal treatises on probative evidence, and after reading Sixtus V's edict with care: he must find a justification for Ratta's seemingly careless behavior. On November

4 and 5 Violano questioned the witnesses for Ratta: the noblemen Rodolfo Seccadinari, Bartolomeo Accursi, and Antonio Volta.[101] The three men had known Ratta for decades and were his neighbors on Strada Castiglioni. They emphasized Ratta's good reputation in the city and among the local noble families. He was a reserved man, focused on his family and his property and abiding by the laws established by the authorities of Bologna and the Papal State. Carlo Ratta's reputation was that of "a gentleman of good virtue, respectful conscience and good repute and status," one "used to living as a good Christian."[102]

The Three Defense Strategies for Aurelio Barbieri

Grato was on friendly terms with Aurelio Barbieri: he was the person to whom Aurelio ran the morning of October 24, and he remained on good terms with him even when Aurelio moved to Rome, a few years later.[103] Grato tried his best to show Aurelio as a victim, unaware of the gravity of the crime and of his brother's intention to escape. Between November 4 and November 22, Grato wrote three different versions of his defense for Aurelio, but only one was transcribed in the proceedings of the trial. Violano refused the other two defenses, which I found buried among a vast pile of documents belonging to the family of Valerio Rinieri, Paolo and Aurelio's brother-in-law.[104] This important discovery emphasizes substantial differences in Grato's three lines of argument, and the lawyer's ability to manipulate the evidence at his disposal and construct different narratives to defend his client. The three defenses also exemplify the tension between Grato's interpretation of the notion of evidence and that given by the judges Alavolini and Violano. These differences show how from the evaluation of the same facts the three men of law constructed two separate sets of evidence. Facts, as Lorraine Daston writes, are inert; they are mercenaries in the service of evidence.[105] Daston's sentence is exemplified by Grato's three versions of Aurelio's defense, in which the lawyer arranged and manipulated the facts that happened on October 24 to build different types of evidence that could exculpate his client. By constructing evidence in this trial, Grato also constructed the truth(s) of what happened.

On November 4, Grato presented his first defense, the same day that Alavolini began the inquisitorial phase of the trial against Paolo and his servant Francesco. The two men were supposed to present and defend themselves to the court against the accusations within six days from the beginning of the inquisition.[106] Grato claimed that the trial against his client should not continue because Aurelio did not help his brother escape by sending him clothes, and thus he did not contravene Sixtus V's papal edict. Grato claimed that his client was in good faith when he sent Francesco with garments to protect Paolo from the frigid winter cold, since he ignored that Isabella had died from the wounds his brother inflicted on her. Paolo did not commit the crime intentionally, but while "in a semi-irrational state" (*simistultus*) and oppressed by a "very violent insanity" (*furore maximo*) caused by bodily humors. If Paolo could not be considered a murderer because of his mental state, Aurelio did not contravene Sixtus V's edict because he did not help a fugitive killer but a mad person.

Grato intended to dispel in Violano's mind any doubt or suspicion of infidelity or mundane domestic violence. The lawyer portrayed Paolo's relationship with Isabella as harmonious: according to witnesses, he loved and respected Isabella, who loved him in return. Paolo showed affection for his wife by hugging and caressing her, and by spending time with her. On the other hand, Isabella was a model obedient wife, "judicious, peaceful, gentle, and wise."[107] Grato reported that the night before the murder Paolo, who was "seized by his humor" (*oppressus humore*), went to bed early, and Isabella followed him. The servants in the house heard and saw no sign of altercation or fight. Grato described in great detail how Paolo's "hypochondriac melancholy," from which he had been suffering for at least the last three years, would cause him "bad" images in the brain and in the head and make him act in a way both dangerous and offensive toward other people.[108] Grato's description was probably inspired by the medical terminology that the physicians Mercuriale, Tagliacozzi, and Lodi used when they narrated their examination of Paolo during the summer of 1588, and by the signs of insanity listed by early modern jurists in their treatises on evidence.[109] Jurists also stated that a person vexed by melancholy was presumably mad.[110]

Grato stated that Paolo's behavior was known to the entire city and described it by employing signs listed in legal treatises to explain melancholic madness. The common opinion—*rumor* or *fama*—was that Paolo was "raging mad" (*furios[us], et insan[us]*). When he was not oppressed by melancholic humors, Paolo complained to priests and religious figures about his state and would say publicly that when bad images and illusions came to his head, they pushed and almost forced him to hurt, torment, and hit friends, his wife's servants (but not his wife!), and other people. Paolo would try to resist these images and temptations, but sometimes he did not even try, and would hurt others. This was why he would not talk with anyone and would stay by himself. After wounding—note, Grato writes "wounding" instead of "killing" here—and striking his wife and her servant, Paolo ran out half naked with no undergarments, brandishing his sword. His face was dark, which was a well-known sign of melancholy, and he was running with a dangerous weapon. If he had had his wits, Grato astutely observed, Paolo could have gotten dressed and no one would have prevented him from doing it, since in the house the day of the murder there were only women, scared to death of being wounded. Paolo's behavior and actions constituted evidence of insanity—Grato strategically left out the fact that Aurelio and his servant Andrea were also at the house at the time of Isabella's murder.[111] Grato concluded that when people suffering from this form of madness realized what they had done during their frenzy, they became greatly distressed, and this state of mind made them even more inclined to bouts of madness and unable to exercise their free will.[112] The original list of witnesses appended to this defense included, among others, the three physicians who wrote the *fede* that I discussed in the previous chapter, Enea Rasi, the knight of the Order of Santo Stefano whom Paolo tried to kill in 1584, and Paolo and Aurelio's cousin from their father's side, Emilio Barbieri. Grato also announced that his defense was limited to Aurelio—a preemptive move, perhaps, since in fact the bulk of his argument was to demonstrate that Paolo was insane.[113]

There is no written document reporting how Violano reacted, but on November 7 Grato submitted again his objections and points and declared that he did not intend to say a word to defend Paolo. A week went by, and none of the witnesses in favor of Aurelio were questioned. In the meantime, five days had passed since Alavolini's first issue of the inquisition against Paolo Barbieri and Francesco on November 4, and there was no trace of the two defendants, so Alavolini renewed the convocation on November 11, 1588. On November 14, Grato repeated to Violano that he intended to defend only Aurelio, and that the judge should question the witnesses in favor of his client only on some of the points presented in a revised version of his defense.[114] In this new defense Grato shifts his attention to Aurelio's character and behavior before and after the murder. He no longer mentions the legal doctrine of intermittent insanity, seemingly having given up in his attempt to include Paolo in his defense. Still, several articles describe and define Paolo's madness from a medical point of view; the effect that Paolo's chronic bouts of lunacy had on his family, servants and even the citizens of Bologna, and Paolo's own reaction to his "extreme trouble of the mind" (*maxim[um] gravam[en] mentis*). Grato portrays Aurelio as the good brother who was so worried about Paolo's state that he asked for the expert opinion of Mercuriale, Tagliacozzi, and Lodi months before the murder. Then the lawyer conjures up the image of Aurelio as the desperate brother, cursing Paolo for the wounds he inflicted on his wife and shouting that his actions would bring destruction on him and on their family. Finally, he invokes the image of Aurelio the concerned citizen, who could not wait to go to the Torrone to alert the *bargello* so that his brother, for whom Aurelio felt hatred, could be brought to justice. Grato is eager to stress two main issues: one was that nobody in his/her sane mind would dare to try to face a man armed with a sword and who had already wounded several people in the house. The other was that an honorable person, possessing good judgment, would understand that Aurelio sent clothes to Paolo to defend the reputation (*honor*) of the Barbieri family in Bologna and out of *pietas*—a combination of familial duty, piety, and pity—for his mad brother:

> Rather, he did it to protect the honor of his own family, which is also recognized as noble in the city of Bologna, so that Paolo would not go around naked, and would not be seen wearing only his nightgown, forced to show exposed parts of his body of which one should be ashamed, and others part of the body as well; and it was also a duty of piety (*officium pietatis*) because Aurelio himself was told that [Paolo] was exposed and was shaking because of the cold weather; then Sir Aurelio ordered that clothes be sent to Sir Paolo, to help him, especially when he heard that his head, feet, and back were bare except for the nightgown, and that he was running on the street with his sword unsheathed, like a raging madman.[115]

All honorable men kept in high regard their reputation and that of their families. Aurelio, an honorable man, was no different and thus could not tolerate that his brother ran throughout the city missing almost all his clothes. The feeling of *pietas* comes second. The expression "duty of piety" (*pietas*) is different from the feeling of pity as compassion. It appeared in Roman law to define the dictates of natural affection that an individual should respect when drawing, for instance, a testament.[116] So it makes sense that Aurelio, being of sane mind and wanting to protect his family's reputation, sent clothes to his brother because he, like everybody else in the city, was aware that Paolo was insane. One of the few references to Aurelio and Paolo's mother Ippolita appeared almost at the end of this document, never to be included in other defenses. Aurelio and Ippolita had a friendly, loving, and respectful relationship with Isabella. Perhaps Grato meant to convince Violano that no member of the Barbieri family nurtured animosity or hatred against Isabella. In the end, Paolo was able to escape not because of an orchestrated effort led by Aurelio, but by sheer luck and "divine concession" (*indulgentia divina*).[117]

Judging by its absence from the trial's proceedings, Grato's new strategy seemed to have failed, just like the first. Presumably Alavolini did not allow either the first nor the second defense because he intended to keep Grato from using Paolo's insanity while defending Aurelio; in fact, both defenses seemed to excuse Paolo's murderous actions. On November 21, Grato contested Aurelio's summons to appear in court to hear the *uditore*'s sentence against him, arguing that the judge had first to accept and question the witnesses listed in his third line of defense, which he presented between November 21 and November 22, and which is the only one included in the proceedings of the trial. The difference between this brief and those described earlier is startling: almost no mention is made of Paolo's insanity, while the focus is on describing Aurelio as a good, law-abiding Christian citizen who went almost out of his mind when he learned of Isabella's killing and ran immediately to Grato and then to the *uditore*, who arrested him and put him in jail.[118] References to Paolo were made only to emphasize that Aurelio was appalled at what his brother had done, but he was not aware that Isabella, whom he loved with a brotherly love, was dead.[119] On the day of the murder Aurelio did not hear the commotion in the house because his bedroom and that of the two spouses were separate and far away. Finally, Aurelio did not try to keep Paolo from leaving the house because he was afraid that his brother could wound him, even kill him, with his sword.

Grato wrote in his third defense about the feelings of *pietas* and *honor* as the motives that pushed Aurelio to send clothes to his brother. This time, though, Aurelio is depicted as feeling first a sense of brotherly pity and thinking in a second moment of the family's honor, when he imagined his brother, a knight, being without shoes and hat and showing his nakedness for everybody to see. Aurelio's first emotion was a "fellow feeling" for what Paolo might have felt, while the second emotion was related to the shame that Aurelio and his family might have experienced at the thought that other people could see the private parts and the naked flesh (*pudibunda, carnes et caetera nuda*) of a member of their family, an ordained knight of the Order of Santo Stefano. Also, Aurelio had not sent his brother a hat, without which Paolo could not have escaped. It may sound strange to a modern reader, but Grato seemed to suggest that not sending head-gear was the proof that Aurelio did not intend to help his brother escape; he simply wished that he be protected from the cold.[120]

On November 24 Violano and the notary went to the house of Emilio Barbieri to question him on the new articles prepared by Grato. Of the long list of witnesses *de parte* that appeared in Grato's first defense, only the name of Emilio was left, while Filippo Ghisleri and a member of the Marescotti family were added simply to vouch for the "bona fama Domini Aurelij."[121] Emilio's testimony added a few new details about the aftermath of the murder. Emilio was a notable figure within the aristocratic com-munity of Bologna: a "count palatine" and a "knight of the Golden Spur," he was married to a noblewoman of the Orsi family of Bologna.[122] Viola-no's questions to Emilio were those that the *auditore* Alavolini approved "in actis ultimo loco productis."[123] He first inquired as to the nobleman's whereabouts the morning of the murder. Emilio stated that on his way back from his villa in the countryside he passed by Aurelio's house. As soon as Aurelio saw Emilio, he started crying, saying that he was ruined because Paolo had wounded his wife. Aurelio urged Emilio to go upstairs to visit Ippolita. When he saw her, Emilio felt compassion for the old woman's distress and decided to bring her in his carriage to the house of her sister. When he returned downstairs, he was told that Aurelio had gone to the Torrone to report the crime. Afterward, Emilio got home to change his clothes, went to Mass, and then he again visited Aurelio's house, where he found Violano.[124] Asked about his cousin's reputation in the city, Emilio emphasized Aurelio's status as a good citizen and a good Christian and concluded that everybody in Bologna shared his opinion: "And I believe that my opinion and consideration of Sir Aurelio is the same as that held by everybody else, and on this matter I do not think that there is need of evidence, since in Bologna it is known who Sir Aurelio is."[125] Emilio also confirmed that Aurelio had a cordial relationship with Isabella, who was "a decent, virtuous, and calm young woman, and of excellent conversation."[126] He claimed that after approaching the carriage, Aurelio, beside himself, told him that Paolo had committed a crime, but not that he killed his wife. Emilio was convinced that Aurelio sent clothes to his brother "out of com-passion and to protect the honor of his own family,"[127] and that he would not have done it if he had realized that Paolo had committed a murder, because he knew very well of the punishment for those who helped crim-inals escape. Did Emilio's deposition help Aurelio's case? From what hap-pened later, it does not seem so. Even if Emilio was an influential figure in

Bologna, he was not powerful enough to sway the judge's opinion in favor of his cousin Aurelio.

The story of Paolo's murder and escape led to several conflicting "truths" in court. The "truths" constructed by the judge, the physicians, the witnesses, and the defense lawyers during the trial for the murder of Isabella Caccianemici were made of signs, proofs, and conjectures that witnesses and codefendants had presented while questioned during the trial. These "truths" were also made by rules illustrated in legal treatises describing and categorizing the elements admissible in court for criminal and civil trials. Also, in the reconstruction and interpretation of Paolo's murder and escape, the incoherent words he uttered while leaving his house after the murder and when he arrived at Carlo Ratta's house could be established only on the basis of other people's words, which the judge and the defense lawyers of Paolo's alleged accomplices constructed as evidence (or lack thereof) of Paolo's madness. Would Paolo's presence have affected the result of the trial? If we accept that he was mad when he killed his wife, he might not have helped very much, since people like him would not remember their names or their actions, or would not answer pointed questions, or any question at all.

CONCLUSIONS

The defense strategies of the four lawyers revolved around two main legal notions: one was the *diligentia*—or lack thereof—with which Salani and Benini followed the edict of Sixtus V against fugitive criminals; the other was the alleged intermittent insanity that afflicted the murderer. Buratto and Salaroli countered the judge's allegation that their clients were negligent in obeying to the edict of Sixtus V against fugitive criminals by blaming the *bargello* Leonardi and his men, who were too slow in getting together and who went to the wrong house. Fontana and Grato centered their defenses around the presumed lack of definitive corroborating evidence that would make their clients guilty of helping a fugitive escape, and on the legal doctrine of intermittent insanity. Fontana adopted language filled with legal jargon and relied on two elements to exculpate his client: one was that Ratta believed that Paolo was insane; the other was Ratta's *fama*, his reputation as a notable citizen of Bologna and as a member of a very important local family. Grato attempted various lines of defense for Aurelio, first focusing on Paolo's presumed insanity with lucid intervals, caused by his long-standing melancholy, and then, when this strategy did not work, on Aurelio's sense of *pietas* toward his brother and honor toward his family.

The conclusion that Alavolini reached excluded all the medical and legal evidence on Paolo's insanity that Grato had put forward in his first two briefs and indirectly rebutted similar points that Fontana made in Ratta's defense.[128] Was it because he thought that Paolo's insanity was a charade? As we saw in the first chapter, jurists and physicians alike shared Alavolini's concern about the possibility of feigning madness. Alavolini's decision to reject Grato's argument about Paolo's madness was acceptable and reasonable since contemporary legal theory justified doubts about simulated insanity. His construction of a procedural truth based on the elements that were brought to the court by witnesses, defendants, and defense lawyers was not unfair. The judge on one side and the defense lawyers on the other transformed the facts into evidence that could be used to support contrasting arguments. And yet, if the main issue appears to be whether Paolo was aware of what he was doing when he killed his wife, whether he had intent, whether he feigned madness, another possible explanation, of a political nature, can be formulated. Alavolini probably consulted the *legato* Peretti or the *vice-legato* Borghese before expressing the final verdict in trials that involved notable people. In the old regime "the power to judge was not at all autonomous and separate. It was deeply embedded in all powers of any sort lodged anywhere in the swarm of persons, bodies, institutions, and lesser 'states' that made up a territorial entity."[129] Perhaps Sixtus V, having realized the high visibility of the trial against members of the Bolognese nobility, might have advised the *legato* to pressure the *uditore* to give a verdict that scaled down the evidence regarding Paolo's psychological and physiological state and focused instead on the evidence of his escape—he was a murderer; he was noble; he escaped; he and his family and whoever helped him run away were negligent and needed to be punished. The hypothesis of a political involvement of various parties in the Barbieri trial needs to be kept in mind: papal politics, and not Paolo's insanity—or lack thereof—might have had very much to do with the final verdict.

CHAPTER 4

Witnessing and Chronicling

VERNACULAR ACCOUNTS OF THE MURDER

1588 Monday, October 24, the knight Paulo [*sic*] Barbieri of the Order of Santo Stefano of Florence and Pisa, son of the late Messere Antonio Maria Barbieri and of Madonna Hippolita [*sic*] Gessi Barbieri, and brother of Aurelio Barbieri, killed his wife, Madonna Isabella Caccianemici. She was the daughter of Messer Scipione Caccianemici, who threw himself in a well because he was melancholic, and of Madonna Angelica Bolognetti Caccianemici. [Isabella] was a young woman of fifteen, and most people say that she was five months pregnant. . . . She had seven wounds. It was a case worthy of great pity, that [the husband] had killed her for no reason, only because of [his] melancholic humor.[1]

Pirro Legnani probably wrote this entry in his "Diario, o sia cronaca delle cose accadute in Bologna (1555–1601)" shortly after the murder of Isabella. Legnani focuses on the family kinship of the murderer and the victim. He describes Isabella as the daughter of a melancholic man who committed suicide and as a fifteen-year-old girl who, according to the prevalent rumor (*dicono*), was five months pregnant when her husband stabbed her six times. That Paolo had killed Isabella for no reason, "only" because of his melancholic humor, calls for compassion for all involved, Legnani concludes. The reader cannot keep from wondering at Isabella's ill-fated life, marked by two men—her father and her husband—whose melancholy led one to take his own life and the other to inflict six fatal wounds on her body.

The hybrid nature of early modern chronicles reflects a manuscript culture expressing "the complex dynamics of interchange between written and oral culture."[2] "They say," Legnani writes, that Isabella was pregnant. This rumor circulated from the Barbieri household to the criminal court, and then to the streets of Bologna. While the rumor was ultimately unfounded, its circulation via chronicle demonstrates how information was disseminated through both oral and written vernacular narrations. Legnani uses this rumor to evoke at once an emotional response in his readership and the community's emotional reaction about Isabella's tragic fate—so young and carrying another life inside her!

Legnani's narration also calls attention to the notion of *fama*, which we introduced in the first chapter. It was common knowledge that Paolo was a knight of the Order of Santo Stefano and that he suffered from melancholic humors; it was common knowledge that Isabella was the scion of two important local families, and that her father committed suicide when she was a child. Legnani was neither a jurist nor a physician; he belonged to one of the most important senatorial families of Bologna and was a cleric at the cathedral of San Pietro.[3] His narrative constituted one of the vernacular "voices" that reported the Barbieri murder, along with several other chronicles and the depositions of witnesses and defendants at the trial. These narratives stand in contrast to the legal and medical Latin jargon of notaries, jurists, lawyers, and physicians, whose words and strategies we saw earlier. In court, witnesses and defendants adopted terms, filtered through the language of the notary and the judge, that reproduced the widespread knowledge of humoral theory but were also made of Italian words used in oral and written exchanges, like letters. Outside the court, chroniclers wrote reports of the event that revealed the authors' attitude toward city politics. Chronicles represented the response and commentary of different social groups and interests to the murder. Both in and out of court, the vernacular accounts of Paolo's insanity and murder presented several other rhetorical and narrative modes—pleading, condemnation, moral positioning, and obfuscation. Through these accounts, we can identify the interconnection between written and spoken language, through which the oral mode was "a network of transactions that shaped and were shaped by situated human relationships."[4] This connection also emphasized the perception and emotional state of the speakers at the time of the murder and its aftermath, which reverberated and left traces in the written records of court proceedings and chronicles;[5] and the positioning of the chroniclers who reported the murder in connection with the trial, the main actors of the event, and the community and social groups to which they belonged.

During the first few days of the trial, witnesses and defendants reported the words that Paolo pronounced once he left his dying wife covered in blood on the floor of their bedroom. They also expressed judgments on Paolo's state before and after the murder, which they often based on what they had heard from others. Sometimes those who reported Paolo's words were present when the *cavaliero* pronounced them, while others relied not only on what they had seen and heard, but also on what was the common opinion, or *fama*, of him when they described his condition.[6] When explaining Paolo's past behavior, the probable cause of the violent murder he perpetrated, and the way he interacted with them the day of the crime, witnesses and defendants used terms like *matto* and *pazzo* (synonyms, corresponding to the English "crazy" or "insane") or having "[melancholic] humors" (*humori*) or "furious frenzy" (*frenesia*). These words exemplified the city's common opinion. They were based on the judgment, accepted by the community, that people had of Paolo. While the first two terms belonged to everyday language, the last two had a medical undertone that testified to the circulation of specialized terms in the vernacular language in court, which was modeled by the arguments taking shape between witnesses and defendants on one hand and judge and notary on the other, and the power relations implied in these strategies.[7]

The defendants and several witnesses—friends, acquaintances, and servants of the Barbieri family—stated time after time that Paolo was a sort of a nutcase and that this was well known around Bologna. The servant Maddalena claimed that she heard from people living in the house—probably servants and family members—that Paolo had a "humore."[8] Ratta did not know the identity of the young man who entered his house brandishing the sword like a "matto" (crazy man), but Salani told him that "humors like this came to him [Paolo]" (*gli* [i.e., Paolo] *venivano così gl'humori*) from time to time.[9] Brocchi learned from Benini that Paolo "suffered a bit in the brain (*pateva un poco di cervello*), and probably a "humore" had fallen upon him "again" (*di nuovo*), hence his strange behavior. Aurelio claimed that this "humore" kept Paolo at home without saying a word for days on end, rejecting any social interaction.[10] Aurelio also described the effects that Paolo's "humore" had on him and on those around him: "Sir, he sat at the table and never talked, and he kept always his head down, and his behavior was torture."[11] Benini stated that Paolo had a "melancholic humor" that ascended to his head, using a description that shows traces of medical jargon ("dissi che questo doveva essere un humore che gli doveva essere montato").[12] He learned from Aurelio that Paolo had been suffering for quite some time from a threatening and violent "frenesia,"[13] although during one of Violano's interrogations Aurelio claimed that he thought that it would never reach this paroxysm of violence.[14] Benini also introduced the term *coglionarie* to describe Paolo's words and actions.[15] In this context, *coglionaria*, which was, and still is, a vulgar term normally used in the low register of speech, means "nonsense" or "foolishness."[16] Among the witnesses during the trial, only the *cursore* Ferrarini painted Paolo Barbieri as a cold-blooded murderer who killed his young wife and then escaped "pretending to have been the victim of an assault."[17]

THE CHRONICLERS' ACCOUNTS AND OPINIONS OF THE MURDER

During the trial two motives were ascribed to Paolo for murdering his wife: willful anger or insanity caused by melancholic humors. Anger would not keep Paolo from understanding what he had done and fleeing the scene to avoid being imprisoned and put to trial. On the other hand, melancholic humors may have caused a temporary loss of reason, so that Paolo did not realize the gravity of his actions. Several chroniclers chose only one motivation, while others accepted both explanations as equally valid, leaving the responsibility to determine the meaning to the reader.

The high social standing of the accused killer, his victim, and key defendants implicated in the trial ensured the story of the Barbieri murder a vast resonance in Bologna. Four citizens—Pirro Legnani, Valerio Rinieri, a member of the Bianchini family, and an anonymous member of the Lateran canons of the church of San Giovanni in Monte—reported the event in their manuscript chronicles shortly after it had occurred.[18] Antonio Francesco Ghiselli produced a highly detailed report almost a century later, combing information from earlier chronicles and the proceedings of the trial.[19] As in many other stories contained in his monumental work,[20] Ghiselli displays in the Barbieri story his great knowledge of local history and his ability to access disparate sources of information that were not always easily available. Ghiselli had a great interest in archival research, which he showed by diligently consulting documents in public, private, and religious archives.[21] His collage of various documents offers the most complete version of the crime and the trial, even though he somewhat exaggerates the ease with which the main defendants were freed on bail—an implicit criticism, perhaps, of papal justice, of which Ghiselli was a vocal critic.[22]

The chroniclers offered slightly different but equally plausible accounts of the murder and its aftermath. The disparity appears to rest on the perception and recollection that the chroniclers had of the event, and on their chronological proximity to it. Elaborating on Fentress and Wickham's notion of "social memory," the editors of *Chronicling History* maintain that chronicles "are construed to operate like oral traditions." By reading a chronicle, one can get a glimpse of the "material available to the authors, as well as the language, values, and cultural milieu of the intended readers of the texts" (xvii).[23] Chroniclers also showed a moral stance toward Paolo's actions, including his escape, which related to their attitude toward this violent crime and toward madness as its possible cause. Finally, the differences among the five reports of the Barbieri murder depend on the social and cultural groups to which the authors belonged and their links and allegiances to them. Many of the chronicles analyzed here can be described as chronological accounts centered on local events in Bologna, with forays into the national and international political situation, depending on the authors' and their families' level of involvement in the dealings of the city government. These texts can also be described as family chronicles, "which focus partly or wholly on events in the chronicler's own family, and which are written either as personal notes for the author's future reference, or to be read by other members of the same family. The boundary between family chronicles and diaries (which in their modern form also originated in the Renaissance) is fluid."[24]

In the sixteenth century the increasing emphasis on individuality promoted the genre of *diario*, in which authors inserted more personal information about themselves, their families, and their social networks, amidst local news and reports of cities and territories connected in one way or another to the politics and economy of Bologna.[25] In the two texts, by Rinieri and Legnani, that bear the title of *diario*, references to family members and evidence of their connections to powerful local families are numerous, especially in Legnani's manuscript, but they are also present in the *cronache* by Bianchini and the Lateran canon.[26] By the second half of the sixteenth century, the genres of *cronaca* and *diario* became intermingled, strengthening the link between familial ties and civic functions. Except for Ghiselli's *Memorie*, the chronicles examined in this chapter exemplified the merging of stylistic and thematic traits of the two genres. However, Bianchini, Rinieri, and the Lateran canon maintain some stylistic structures typical of earlier chronicles, such as giving a list of elected public officials at the beginning of each year, ending entries with the names of the ruling pope and the papal *legato*, or starting each entry with a religious reference, like the name of the saint of the day or the period of the Catholic liturgy when the event took place.

Also, the genre of chronicle changed along with the transformation of power dynamics in Bolognese society, especially in relation to the increasingly autocratic tendencies of papal authority. The chronicles analyzed here narrated primarily incidents occurred within the walls of the city. Foreign affairs of great importance were narrated from a local perspective, that is, emphasizing the way they impacted the local groups to which the authors of these texts belonged. Finally, while local chronicles written in earlier periods ranged over long periods of time, those by Legnani, Rinieri, the member of the Bianchini family, and the anonymous Lateran canon narrated less than a century of local and foreign events, and sometimes not even a decade.[27] Many of the episodes recounted occurred during the authors' lifetime: the member of the Bianchini family wrote his chronicle day by day, while Rinieri, the anonymous Lateran canon, and Legnani added and revised earlier entries at later times. Completed more than a century later, Ghiselli's *Memorie* embodied the aspirations of a group of intellectuals who, Janus-like, were living through the enormous political and cultural changes of the beginning of the eighteenth century but still looked up to the fading glories of an aristocratic class in decline.

None of the authors claimed that their texts constituted "history." When Legnani recounted the deaths of political and religious figures of international resonance, like those of Sixtus V in 1590, Alfonso II d' Este in 1597, and Philip II of Spain in 1598, he deferred the explanation of the political implications and consequences of these occurrences to the "Historie" and the "historiographi," thinking of himself as a chronicler.[28]

When chroniclers reported the Barbieri murder, they offered valuable information about their view of the event as members of different social and cultural communities. Even though these works were not printed, they "were not intended as private texts excluded from circulation,"[29] but were probably handed out in manuscript form among members of the authors' families and their social and cultural communities, which they portrayed in their writings.[30] Rinieri and Legnani, for instance, were active members of circles where information in the form of rumor and *fama*, news and historical accounts, was read and produced.[31] As Brian Richardson pointedly puts it, "Manuscript culture . . . needs to be studied in relation to the two other modes of circulation that were available in the sixteenth century: to the oldest of all, oral performance, and to the newcomer, the printed word."[32] The chroniclers who wrote about Paolo's murder of Isabella relied on the talk spreading in the urban community, including the *fama* of the main actors, their families, and their social groups, but also on information acquired through people involved in the trial and familiar with its proceedings—notaries, defense lawyers, and witnesses. In these chronicles, oral and manuscript modes complemented each other.[33] Fentress and Wickham emphasized that a past event becomes "social memory" once it is talked and written about: issues of truthfulness and reliability are not as important in the transmission of social memory as the way of its transmission and the meaning people give to it (ix–xi).[34] The analysis and interpretation of the five reports of the Barbieri murder assume that the authors' understanding and telling of the story depend on elements embedded in the authors' conception of their social and cultural groups, and in their connection to other social groups.

THE FIVE CHRONICLES OF THE MURDER: ORAL AND WRITTEN WORD, *FAMA* AND *RUMORE*

The chroniclers' reports of the Barbieri murder contain a similar core narration—the date of the killing, the young age of the woman killed, the name of the murderer, and his honorary title of *cavaliero*. These have the practical function of locating the event temporally, and of identifying the culprit. The victim's age and the honorary title of the murderer are given in slightly different versions. For instance, the younger the victim was reported to be, the more pitiful and moving her murder appeared. Paolo's honorific designation underlines the murderer's privileged social status and the fact that he and his family could afford to pay a vast amount of money to obtain this title.[35] One thing is clear: each author intended to emphasize from the beginning of his narrative that the protagonist of the story, the murderer, was someone important, whose social status and history of melancholy made his *fama* and whose story was worth being recorded in a chronicle. Several details vary from text to text, and identifying the cause of this variety may help us recognize a possible connection or even filiation among reports.

From what the chroniclers included in their reports, and what they left out, it is possible to draw some useful information regarding the authors' attitudes toward Paolo's murder and his insanity, and their perception of the repercussions of his act on the social and cultural groups to which the authors belonged. We will focus on specific topics that mark the hybrid nature of the genre of the chronicle in terms of oral/spoken and written mode and transmission, and the role of talk and *fama* in the construction of the main actors' identity and behavior. These topics are, first, the cause and circumstances of the murder; second, the identity of the victim and the killer, and third, the aftermath of the trial for Paolo's family and for the other defendants.

Marcantonio Bianchini is the name traditionally attributed to the author of a "Cronaca di Bologna," which covers the period from 1584 to 1638.[36] The person who wrote the chronicle claimed that he had started writing it on November 1, 1587,[37] and that he lived in the same house in Piazza Santo Stefano where the senatorial line of the Bianchini family resided. Bianchini's entry could be considered the closest we can get to a news report.[38] A careful reading of the entire chronicle shows that Bianchini is rather specific and generous with details about people and events, and in many of his entries he proposes two options as possible explanations for the event he narrates. The two explanations could represent the contrasting opinions that the community of Bologna held regarding a specific event, expressed and circulated as city talk and gossip.[39]

Bianchini adduces two causes for the murder of Isabella: "Some say it happened because of a fight, others because of the [melancholic] humor."[40] The presence of both explanations could reflect Bianchini's closeness to the event, which does not allow him to take a definite position, but only to report what he heard in spoken conversations around the city of Bologna. Rinieri, who wrote a hefty "Diario" in five volumes narrating more or less one hundred years of the history of Bologna (1520–1613),[41] states that Paolo "mercilessly" (*crudelmente*) killed his young wife because he was "oppresso da furore, et humore melancolico." It is important to observe that Rinieri's language reveals a tension between moral condemnation (Paolo killed Isabella *cruelly*) and lack of intent and therefore culpability (he was *melancholic* and overcome by *furor*),[42] which, in turn, suggests a conflict in the way the chronicler interpreted the crime and its causes. *Furore* and *humore melancolico* are the expressions with which several chroniclers describe Paolo's madness. As we saw earlier, *furore* was the classical legal term defining insanity, while "melancholic humor" was a medical expression. Members of groups outside of the legal and medical circles appropriated these terms, which circulated in the urban community.

As mentioned earlier, Rinieri was Paolo's brother-in-law; he married Diana Barbieri in 1577. She had seven children between 1578 and 1593.[43] Rinieri's family included judges and erudite scholars representative of the antiquarian and humanistic trend flourishing among sixteenth-century Bolognese chroniclers.[44] Valerio loved to write and kept records of everything, which is evident from the bulk of his "Diario" and from the innumerable handwritten records about disparate topics, from notable events that occurred in his family in a given year to daily expenses of his household. Rinieri was an erudite man who used a great array of documents to compose his text. In his work, he boasted of his connections to the most important families of Bologna by ties of patronage or social group.[45] He also reported news related to local notables and public officials, and to members of the university—students and professors.

Like Rinieri and Bianchini, Legnani attributes the senseless murder of Isabella and the wounding of the servant Maddalena to Paolo's "melancholic humor." The only author who appears to indicate that Paolo's insanity was intermittent is the anonymous Lateran canon, who characterizes Paolo as a man "violently moved by disorderly furor" (*rapito da disordinato furore*), who chased and stabbed his wife who tried to get between him and a servant with whom he was irate *(si sdegnò)* because either she did not obey the way he wanted or she did not understand his wishes. Paolo's "sdegno" becomes "disordinato furore": in this case *furore* appears to be used not as a legal term but as a semantic escalation of wrath and rage, which leads to uncontrolled fury. The connection between violent rage and furor is in line with the philosophical explanation present in classical literature, such as Cicero's *Tusculan Disputations*, and in vernacular texts, such as Petrarca's *Canzoniere*, where *ira* is considered a short-term *furore*.[46] The chronicler also writes that Paolo escaped from Bologna with his servant after he murdered Isabella because he understood the enormity of what he had done—to describe this moment the chronicler uses the phrase "when the husband realized this wicked and sinful act" (*avvedutosi il marito di questo misfatto*). When he reports that Aurelio sent clothes to his brother, the Lateran canon defines Paolo's murderous action as *errore*, which can mean fault but also offense and transgression. In Bianchini's report one of the explanations brought forward for the murder is that it was an episode of extreme domestic violence, caused by an external motive and by violent anger. Like the Lateran canon, Bianchini narrates that Paolo's fury could be caused by the servant Maddalena, who did not do as she was told; Isabella tried to intervene in the fight between servant and master, who ended up wounding Maddalena and killing his wife.

Bianchini lists Isabella and Maddalena as the victims of Paolo's criminal action but does not identify Isabella by her full name. Bianchini and the anonymous chronicler characterize the young woman only as the murderer's wife, and they might have chosen to do so because they wanted to keep the attention on Paolo and his family, leaving Isabella in the shadows as the "victim." Rinieri identifies Isabella as the daughter of Scipione Caccianemici and a young girl of fifteen, who was killed by her husband while sleeping in their matrimonial bed. Like the other chroniclers, Rinieri introduces Paolo by the name of his father and as a knight of the Order of Santo Stefano—as was customary in the early modern period—but does not recognize the murderer as a member of the family of his wife Diana, who was Paolo's sister.[47] Rinieri's reticence in stating his relationship with Paolo was probably due to his discomfort with the unpleasant matter of the murder, which brought unwanted publicity to his family. This short entry—the shortest of the group—could be interpreted as a way for Rinieri to distance himself from the crime, the murderer, and the victim.

Bianchini stated that Isabella was buried the following day in the church of San Domenico,[48] and that there were so many people inside the church that it could not contain them all, a sign of the incredible resonance that the event had in the city and of the strong emotional response from citizens of all social groups to the killing of the young woman.[49] As we saw at the beginning of this chapter, Legnani reports the hearsay that the young Isabella was five months pregnant, which the anonymous Lateran canon also conveys, not as a rumor, which turned out to be false, but as a fact ("And he killed her [his wife], who was five months pregnant").[50] The spoken rumor circulating in and out of the court about Isabella's pregnancy and indicated in Legnani's chronicle by the verb *dicono* becomes evidence in the Lateran canon's account.

The *strano* event, Rinieri concludes, should elicit pity—*compassione*—for both the victim and the perpetrator. *Strano* can be translated as both "unusual" and "extraordinary." This was, indeed, an extraordinary event for Rinieri, his wife, and his family, but he chooses to narrate the story not as a distraught relative but as a notable citizen, well informed of what was happening in Bologna and interested enough in this crime and in the high profile of the people involved to include it in his "Diario." Like Rinieri, Legnani seems to show compassion and sympathy for Paolo, and he defines the homicide as a pitiful case. In an additional note in the margin, which he probably wrote at a later stage, Legnani concludes the entry with the words "May God help him [Paolo]."[51] The anonymous chronicler also defines the murder as "worthy of great pity" (*degno di gran compassione*), but he also calls it an "eccesso," which gives a moralistic tone to the narration. In medieval and Renaissance Italy, *eccesso* meant not only a violent act characterized by excess, but also the trespassing of the boundaries of what was considered right, honest, and proper. Ultimately, it could also mean a sinful deed.[52]

The Lateran canon claims that the conditions surrounding the murder made Ratta and Aurelio Barbieri worthy of being helped: he writes that they left prison after three months, but only after having paid respectively three hundred and five hundred scudi, which corresponded to the amount of money recorded in the proceedings of the trial. Bianchini too seems to know the fines that Paolo's brother Aurelio, the Ratta family (li Ratta), and the notary (Benini) had to pay to the tribunal of the Torrone to be freed from prison, and that it was Paolo's servant Francesco who saved his master from being apprehended. Oral sources and updates from people who worked at the Torrone may have supplied the material with which Legnani wrote the entry about Isabella's murder. The hypothesis that Legnani had also contacts with people who worked at the Torrone or who were acquainted with the Barbieri trial seems supported by the fact that he knew the monetary penalties that were imposed on the four main defendants. Legnani was a representative of the local religious and social elite, and this privileged position allowed him to be in contact with people involved in the trial—the Ratta, the Barbieri, and the Rinieri.[53] We can speculate that the access to people informed of or involved in the trial allowed Bianchini, the Lateran canon, and Legnani to have more or less detailed information on the aftermath of the trial.[54]

The only chronicler who mentions Sixtus V's edict in relation to Aurelio Barbieri and Carlo Ratta is the anonymous Lateran canon. The chronicler's support of Sixtus V, whom several of the other chroniclers criticized harshly more or less openly in their texts,[55] could reflect a more general position of the religious collectivity to which he belonged toward the social elite of Bologna and its fractured relationship with papal authority. The devotion to Elena Duglioli (Bologna, 1472–1520), whose pious and saintly life was compared to that of Saint Cecilia, was tied to the Lateran canons of the church of San Giovanni in Monte.[56] During Duglioli's life this church became the focal point of aggregation for the local mercantile and professional middle class, which was favorable to the pope. Even though the church's importance as a focal point for the ascent and the establishment of the professional middle class in Bologna decreased during the sixteenth century, it is reasonable to suppose that the Order remained in favor of centralized papal power and against the control of the city by aristocratic oligarchies.[57]

At the beginning of Ghiselli's narration, entire sentences from Rinieri's chronicle are transcribed word by word. When he reports that Paolo and the servant Francesco went to Pisa after having escaped from Bologna, Ghiselli refers to the information found in the note that Legnani added at the margin of his entry. Ghiselli also had a chance to consult the proceedings of the trial. He quotes terms and phrases written by the notary Cambio during the depositions and interrogations of witnesses and defendants during the 1588 trial.[58] Ghiselli's narration is shaped not only by the composite collage of information gathered from earlier chronicles but also by the narration of the event given by people involved in the trial and filtered through the notary's transcription. Ghiselli underlines the high social standing of the families involved in the trial by stating that Giovanni Francesco Grato, whom he describes as one of the best lawyers of Bologna, was in Aurelio Barbieri's retinue—this information is not included in any of the other chronicles.

Ghiselli, a cleric and canon of the Basilica of San Petronio from 1685 to 1707, belonged to the petty local nobility. Born in 1634, he started composing his monumental work in ninety-two volumes, "Memorie antiche manoscritte di Bologna," at thirty-two. He died in 1730, the year after he completed the last volume. Composed more than a century after the trial and the other chronicles, Ghiselli's report of the murder emphasizes writing and reading as the predominant ways of communication and expression and exemplifies the layers of information and news, *rumori* and *fama*, that settled over time around the event until he organized it into a story. Ghiselli had a large amount of data available at his disposal to reconstruct events of local interest and of national and international standing, including the earlier chronicles reporting the murder of Isabella Caccianemici. Ghiselli claimed that he narrated the event from an objective, matter-of-fact point of view, which the biased nature of his sources, including the earlier chronicles discussed above that he collected to create his entries, calls into question.

In assessing Ghiselli's report of the murder, it is important to remember that he belonged to a group of intellectuals who did not have a clear social group of reference. Between the end of the seventeenth and the beginning of the eighteenth century the Bolognese nobility increasingly lost power vis-à-vis the centralizing aims of papal government, and those who were supposed to chronicle the life of the local nobility, like Ghiselli, were destined to report about a social and cultural community that was gradually declining. A new middle class, increasingly imbued with historiographical erudition and scientific progress, was replacing the local old nobility, but without a corresponding idealized self-image that was memorialized in chronicles and local histories. Ghiselli was famous for collecting and transcribing documents but never published any of his numerous works, including the "Memorie," because he disliked the printed page. For a writer who wished to adopt a journalistic mode in his chronicle, his attachment to the manuscript form exemplifies a deep contradiction in terms of spreading of information, mode of communication, and a strong allegiance to values "of honor, vengeance, and chivalric justice"[59] that characterize the ideology of the old local nobility, still rooted in oral performance and manuscript culture.

CONCLUSIONS

Witnesses and defendants during the trial used a mixture of vulgarized medical jargon and vernacular terms to describe what they saw and heard about Paolo's behavior and words. Their statements showed how humoral theory had seeped deep into the daily colloquial language of ordinary people, together with popular and vulgar terms belonged to a low linguistic register. These terms revealed the strategies that the speakers adopted to communicate with the notary and the judge to convey emotions of fear, disgust, and exasperation. Spoken and written dimensions interacted on the written page through the "rumor" and the "hearing" reported during the trial. As Elizabeth Cohen puts it, "the trial record itself, as a complex text, represents a highly structured, yet privileged site, where oral and written languages interact and shape each other."[60]

Outside the court, the murder of Isabella Caccianemici by Paolo Barbieri was a cause célèbre for several months. The sources from which the chroniclers drew their information were based on oral rumor and *fama*, manuscript chronicles, proceedings of the trial, and oral and written reports of members of the families involved in the trial. Fox and Woolf claim that "we are much better off conceiving of overlapping spheres of the oral and the literate, within which many of a culture's communicative activities occur in different ways depending upon a variety of factors such as time, location, purpose, and the identity and status of the communicators."[61]

The five chronicles discussed in this chapter offer narrations of the Barbieri murder and trial tinged by the authors' social and cultural communities. The bias of some chroniclers is evident in their attitude toward the victim and the perpetrator. The fact that Bianchini offered contrasting explanations of the cause of Isabella's murder exemplifies the divergent views produced at the spoken level, where talk circulated in and was shaped by social communities. The brevity of Rinieri's entry makes more sense if one reads his report of the murder within the conceptual frame offered by the notions of memory and social community. Rinieri seemed to vacillate between his role as a member of a family personally involved in this tragedy and as a representative of a social group that witnessed and commented on the behavior of one of its own. Legnani's identity, as expressed in his "Diario," is representative of what Pezzarossa calls the authority of biological and cultural endogamy of the production of civic memory in Bologna. Legnani's report of the murder seems to split its allegiances between the social group to which the author's family belonged and his religious role as the canon of one of the most important churches in Bologna. The anonymous Lateran canon had fully embraced the values and opinions of his community and interpreted the events he narrated through the lens of the post-Tridentine Church. He is also the only chronicler who articulated what the judge of the criminal trial and part of the urban community believed, that is, that Paolo Barbieri was aware of the gravity of his action, at least after he perpetrated the murder. Ghiselli's construction of an individual and social memory is composite and relies heavily on written records that expressed the values and opinion of several social and cultural groups, which he grafted together with no specific hierarchy. If it is true that Ghiselli showed his appreciation toward the new historiographical stance of L. A. Muratori, in the narration of Paolo Barbieri's murder he did not seem to discriminate among different sources.

These chronicles give precious information about the community in which they were produced, the "social memory" of their writers and readers, and the interaction between oral and written dimensions in a deeply hybrid culture and society as much as about the events they report. The readership of the chronicles included the authors' domestic, social, and cultural milieu, which was also in dialogue with the larger community where Isabella's murder and Paolo's flight resonated. In the end Isabella's gruesome murder and Paolo's rage or melancholic humors were representative of the way they were narrated, of what was occluded and what was emphasized, and of the "evidence" that could be extracted from these narrations. The story of a woman murdered by her crazy—or enraged—husband can show how early modern chroniclers perceived violent behavior and insanity and how they intertwined in their written accounts the talk of the town and the *fama* of the actors in this drama—the victim, the villain, and the supporting actors. In these stories the victim Isabella becomes prominent, while the killer Paolo is portrayed as someone who committed a heinous crime, whether led by violent rage or by melancholic humor and madness. Many chroniclers portray the event and the people involved in it as worthy of pity—Isabella was young, perhaps pregnant, and Paolo was insane—but some wonder if the murderer did it because he was enraged at not being obeyed the way he wanted, and if he was not insane after all. What should the modern reader conclude from these accounts? Was Paolo worthy of compassion, or should he be condemned in the harshest possible way, that is, by capital punishment? Either way, it was not only the murderer himself, but his entire family and their legacy, that would pay the price for his crime.

CHAPTER 5

The Aftermath

WHY IS PAOLO'S CASE EXCEPTIONAL?

When it comes to the fate of the insane in early modern Italy, medical and legal dimensions and public and private spheres should be considered together as forming a network that articulates and exemplifies contrasting interpretations of a person's madness. The exceptional nature of Paolo's story relies on the fact that we have all these interpretations, which develop a narrative of his criminal madness and its consequences on his family much more complete than in other cases of early modern insanity, which usually can be reconstructed only through trial proceedings or medical evaluations. Paolo's illness was real, and it had a destructive effect on his family. Whether because of honor, family duty, or genuine care, his brother Aurelio, his mother Ippolita, his sister Diana, and her husband Valerio Rinieri took care of Paolo until he died, on January 16, 1606, in Bologna. He outlived Aurelio and Ippolita, and he was buried in the same church where his wife Isabella, murdered almost twenty years earlier, was laid to rest.[1]

The events following Paolo's crime and escape lead us to several cities—Florence, Pisa, Lucca, Milan, and Rome—and to various private and public spaces—houses in Bologna and Rome, a hospital in Milan, courthouses in Bologna, Lucca, and Rome—where family and friends felt the consequences of Paolo's actions, which were recorded in both written disputes and legal documents. Ultimately, they developed into an entangled network of family quarrels over inheritance, dowries, and wills, all of which provide clues toward our understanding of the hostile atmosphere engendered by Paolo's madness and crime, the fallout of which lasted almost twenty years.

THE VERDICT

Paolo's flight convinced the *uditore* Alavolini that the murder of Isabella was the willful act of a sane person pretending to be mad to escape conviction. The judge's decision to reject the exceptions and articles regarding Paolo's madness proposed by Aurelio's defense lawyer, Giovanni Francesco Grato, was acceptable and reasonable under these circumstances. Only two categories of criminals were prevented from having a defense lawyer in early modern criminal courts: those who were caught *in flagrante delicto* and those who fled justice.[2] Paolo belonged to the second group, so any argument, even indirect, on his behalf was inadmissible in court. After having summoned to court Paolo and his servant Francesco on November 11 and 13, and seeing no sign of the two defendants, on November 15 Alavolini sentenced both to death by beheading and hanging, respectively. Since Paolo and Francesco were fugitives, neither capital punishment was executed. Alavolini also demanded that Paolo's property be confiscated, following the procedure for defendants *in absentia*.[3] On December 1, 1588, Alavolini allowed Ratta, Aurelio Barbieri, and Salani to move within the confines of the building of the Torrone. He imposed a stiff surety of one thousand golden scudi on Paolo's brother Aurelio and Ratta, the man into whose house Paolo ran after he killed Isabella, if they left the premises. He laid a much lower bond of five hundred golden scudi for the banker Salani and sentenced the notary of the Torrone Benini to exile—both men had the misfortune of being at Ratta's house the morning of the murder.[4]

Alavolini probably considered Aurelio Barbieri and Ratta the main culprits in Paolo's escape, while he judged Salani and Benini accessories. However, none of them was found innocent. Except for Benini, they were to be released on bail and had to find an affluent guarantor who would promise to pay the fine if they contravened the bond. Aurelio Barbieri, Ratta, and Salani had no trouble finding wealthy members of notable families—the Vidali, the Salimei, and the Bigosia.[5]

Also, on December 1, Benini's lawyer Salaroli submitted a petition (called in Italian *supplica* and in Latin *prex*) to the *vice-legato* Borghese, pointing to the "great harm" (*non modicum damnum*) that his client and family had suffered into since the beginning of the trial. After receiving Benini's petition, Borghese initially confirmed the penalty of exile and the fine of twelve golden scudi, but on December 19 he revoked the exile and the fee.[6] On December 9, Grato presented a petition vouching for Aurelio's freedom: Borghese was asked to "plenarie absolvere, et gratiose liberare" the defendant and restore him to his original "statum, gradumque famam et honores."[7] The *vice-legato* graciously granted Aurelio's freedom, but only after the Apostolic Office (Camera Apostolica) received five hundred golden scudi—a huge fine, which showed how wealthy Aurelio and his family were.[8] On December 11 and 15, Ratta and Salani followed suit with their petitions and had to pay, respectively, three hundred golden scudi and sixty golden scudi[9]—vast amounts of money, probably according with the two men's wealth.[10] However, in a sudden turn of events, on December 22 Borghese reversed Alavolini's judgment against Ratta and ordered that the hefty fee, already deposited, be given back.[11] Did Ratta's relationship with his powerful cousin Ludovico and his son, Monsignor Dionisio Ratta, the scion of the family with a bright ecclesiastical career, affect this reversal of justice? Dionisio Ratta might have expressed his displeasure with a sentence that would tarnish the *fama*, the good name, of his family, and the swift abolition of the verdict against Carlo Ratta with the restitution of the fee might support the hypothesis of political involvement in Alavolini's final decision.

Borghese overturned two of Alavolini's sentences—Benini's and Ratta's; still, the apostolic office received from Aurelio Barbieri and Ludovico Salani 560 golden scudi—a considerable amount of money, which ultimately went to benefit the papal treasury. The Barbieri family was wealthy and connected to influential figures in the local administration. However, it was not influential enough to have Aurelio ultimately pardoned and let go with just a slap on the wrist, as with Carlo Ratta. Aurelio had to pay a hefty fee to present his petition and to be freed. His punishment was not draconian—he was not tortured or kept for many months in jail—but it was severe enough that it could serve as an example. Rather than bringing to conclusion a nightmarish experience, the end of the trial was the beginning of Aurelio's financial woes. Alavolini's sentence against Paolo included the confiscation of all his properties, which meant that Aurelio's wealth too was confiscated— by testamentary disposition, the two brothers shared the Barbieri assets by an indissoluble bond.

PAOLO'S WANDERING AND THE HOSPITAL FOR MAD PEOPLE

The misfortunes of Paolo and Aurelio Barbieri and the Barbieri family continued for a long time after the trial: the devastating consequences of

Paolo's violent and murderous actions had profound repercussions on the economic, social, and private dimension of his family immediately after he killed his wife, and they continued until he died. From Bologna, Paolo wandered through Italy for a few years. It is not clear what he did or where he went between his escape from Bologna at the end of October 1588 and his arrival in Milan, probably at the beginning of the year 1590, where he was taken to the hospital of San Vincenzo in Prato. What we know is that Paolo went to Florence, Pisa, and Lucca, where he committed many *pazzie* (crazy things), for which he was put on trial.[12] However, it is unsure when Paolo was in the Tuscan city, what crazy actions warranted a trial, what the sentence was, and how long he remained there.[13]

In March of 1590, Grato appeared in front of the court reporting that for the merit he received by handing over to the justice in Rome a well-known murderer in October 1589, the sentence of Paolo's servant Francesco had been commuted to exile.[14]

The hospital of San Vincenzo in Prato hosted men and women who were considered mad (*furiosi*), from Milan and territories annexed to it, but also from outside the duchy.[15] In March 1590, thanks to a letter from the *legato* Peretti, the *vice-legato* Borghese granted permission to Paolo's brother Aurelio and his mother Ippolita to send seven golden scudi monthly for Paolo's care to the hospital without incurring punishment.[16] Since Milan belonged to the duchy of Milan, it did not have any obligation to return Paolo to Bologna, which was part of the Papal State, nor is there a trace of an agreement among the two states to extradite Paolo.[17] Paolo was probably there since the beginning of 1590; his name appeared for the first time during the patients' examination on May 16 of that year.[18] By the end of Paolo's stay, the fee was thirty-six scudi a month. Along with this, money was needed for clothes and shoes, while the hospital provided for food.

The extant documents of the Milanese hospital reporting its expenses and credits and the list of its patients help us reconstruct where Paolo lived, with whom, and under what conditions, between May 16, 1590, and April 8, 1598, when Paolo's brother-in-law Valerio Rinieri paid the hospital for Paolo's stay until that date and brought him back to Bologna.[19] What emerges is the way an Italian public health institution at the turn of the seventeenth century treated people deemed insane.[20] When the hospital of San Vincenzo in Prato admitted Paolo, it had existed for several centuries, and it had become part of the vast system aggregated around the Ospedale Maggiore, which Francesco Sforza, with the permission of Pope Pius II, had built on a piece of land located between the basilicas of

P A Z Z I A.

Di Cesare Ripa.

Carlo Marieri del.   Pazzia   Carlo Grandi inscp

FIG. 5 Cesare Ripa, "La pazzia," in *Iconologia* (first illustrated edition, 1603). Photo: The Picture Art Collection / Alamy Stock Photo.

Santo Stefano and San Nazaro in the second half of the fifteenth century. The hospital was completed at the end of the fifteenth century.[21]

The Sforza family aspired to provide the city with a hospital that, in architectural structure, function, and provision, offered a better life for patients suffering from different ailments. So the Ospedale Maggiore became the central entity to which the other nine hospitals, built over several centuries in the city, all responded, and from which they received financial support. A group of eighteen people constituted the chapter that supervised Milan's composite health structure: they made decisions in terms of money, treatment, organization, and staff for all the hospitals. No longer was the hospital a charitable institution open to anybody who was sick or in need.[22] The members of the chapter were elected from among the local nobility, were supporters of the duke's political power, and did not belong to the religious hierarchy of the church, nor were they lawyers or physicians. The chapter's composition exemplified the prince's desire to control the city's health system through the group of nobles who formed the chapter. Priests were still a daily presence in every hospital; their preaching arranged the life of the patients and those who took care of them. Even if physicians were not part of the decision-making made by the chapter, those who worked at the Ospedale Maggiore decided where each patient should be sent, according to his/her illness.[23] Every hospital accepted different categories of sick people, leaving the Ospedale Maggiore the care of patients with acute and short-term diseases that could be cured in a relatively brief amount of time. When, in 1508, Gian Giacomo Gilino, one of the eighteen members of the chapter, wrote a short document in Latin and Italian describing the functioning of the ten institutions, San Vincenzo in Prato had become the place where people suffering from various forms of insanity were sent.[24] However, as Gilino wrote, because the number of insane people was never very high, the hospital accepted two other categories of patients within its walls: older people and those suffering from ulcerations, with the exclusion of lepers.[25] In 1558, and later in 1642, more regulations were added to control the functioning of Milan's health system, but San Vincenzo in Prato remained the place where insane people from and outside the city were accepted and held.[26]

Between 1517 and 1640—years during which San Vincenzo in Prato recorded the "general visitations" (*visite*) of the members of the chapter to the hospital—the categories defining different types of insanity remained more or less the same. Some terms were of legal origin—*mentecapti, fatui*, and *furiosi*. Others, such as *matti, balzani, lochi, matochi*, and *bestie*, were of lay origin. Terms like *ispirtati* implied a religious dimension, while others, like *caschano dal letto, soffrono del mal caducho*, and *deboli di cervello*, seemed to refer to those patients who were affected by epilepsy and dementia. Starting in 1550, women—but not men—were recorded as suffering from melancholic humors (*patiscono humor melancholico*). Patients suffering from physical malformations due to congenital problems or accidents were described by the terms *stropiato, mutto*, and *orbo* in the book of examinations. No sign of treatment was recorded, except for the minimal care provided by a barber and a physician on staff. No medical opinion about the status of patients appeared in any of the hospital's extant documents; the interaction of the barber and the physician with the patients was irregular at best.[27] There were also *putti* and *putte*, abandoned children who might have suffered from some sort of disability. The hospital divided the patients according to gender and enlisted many of them to work in the hospital.[28] In general, patients were left free to move, and if confined to bed, it was because of other concurrent illnesses.[29]

Paolo belonged to the category generally called the *matti da catena*, which included patients who were perceived as violent toward themselves and others: they were chained to their beds or the wall because their behavior could not be restrained. Paolo was not the only patient who had committed violent crimes before he ended up, willingly or not, within the walls of this hospital. In the register of the annual examinations, some *matti/e da catena* were also defined as *condennati/e*, a term used to identify people who had been sentenced after a criminal trial. Like those who had epilepsy, the violently insane were placed in separate rooms with no more than four people sharing the same space. Many of the patients in these rooms, including Paolo, apparently paid the hospital a fee for board and lodging, which seemed proportionate to the patients' social and financial status. Paying patients were mostly from outside the city of Milan and its territory. In theory, patients who were not from Milan could not be accepted in any of the city's hospitals. In practice, these institutions received many "foreigners," probably because they needed the money to keep from drowning in debt.

San Vincenzo in Prato was like other hospitals for insane people in Italy. Its patients suffered from chronic illnesses and stayed in the hospital for a very long time, sometimes until the end of their days. The hospital's primary purpose was not to cure but to protect the public order from the disorderly conduct and violence of the insane people.[30] Some, like Paolo, left the hospital, but it is unclear if they had been cured of their illness and put back in the care of their relatives. Paolo's stay at the hospital of San Vincenzo in Prato constitutes an exemplary story of the fate that people suffering from insanity and their families had to endure. Liz Mellyn states that the release to the outside world of people like Paolo was due less to complete or partial healing than to the financial difficulty of continuing to pay for the hospital stay.[31] As will soon become evident, financial squabbles and legal feuds within the Barbieri family, and not his restored sanity, led to Paolo's release and return to Bologna.

PAOLO'S RETURN TO BOLOGNA: A FAMILY'S CALCULATED MOVE

On November 10, 1597, Bologna's *vice-legato*, Orazio Spinola, newly appointed by Pope Clement VII, received a petition in favor of Paolo Barbieri vouching for his return to Bologna. The document stated that Paolo had been "in a hospital for mad people" (*hospitali dementium*) in Milan since 1590, and that his murder of Isabella should be attributed to insanity,

not deceit—*furor*, not *dolus*.[32] It is noteworthy that Paolo's mother Ippolita and his brother-in-law Valerio Rinieri produced the petition asking
for Paolo's release a few months after Aurelio Barbieri had died in Rome,
between September 8 and 12, 1597, and after he had drawn a will in which
he bequeathed his estate, including Paolo's part, to the Roman religious
confraternity of the Santissima Annunziata.[33] We will see soon that Aurelio's decision created a chain of events through which it becomes evident
that Paolo's return to Bologna was not an act of maternal charity or compassion but a family strategy to regain control of what Aurelio had left to
the confraternity. Valerio Rinieri appeared to guarantee that if his mother-in-law did not take good care of her son, she would pay two hundred
golden scudi to the Apostolic Chamber. The *uditore* Giovan Battista Pellegrini reversed Paolo's conviction on December 17, 1597, and declared his
mother Ippolita his legal guardian, who was charged with taking care of
him in case he might be affected again by insanity.[34]

Pellegrini accepted the "truth" that Grato had tried in vain to argue and
that the then *uditore* Alavolini rejected as false almost ten years earlier,
namely, that Paolo had been raving mad when he killed Isabella. In April
of 1598, almost a decade after the homicide, Paolo left San Vincenzo in
Prato: accompanying him back to Bologna was neither his brother nor his
mother, who had died a few months before his release, but his brother-in-
law Valerio Rinieri.[35] After Ippolita died, his cousin Emilio Barbieri, who,
we may remember, was the only witness on behalf of Aurelio whom the
judge accepted during the 1588 trial, took over the role of Paolo's guardian
(*curator*) until at least 1602.[36] However, Valerio was very much involved in
Paolo's financial and medical welfare after the death of Aurelio and Ippolita. On September 6, 1598, Ludovico Lodi, one of the three physicians who
attested Paolo's insanity for Aurelio's defense during the 1588 trial, wrote
a letter narrating the improvement of Paolo's health under his medical
care since his return from Milan: walking, Lodi writes, would help Paolo's
condition significantly. The *vice-legato* Spinola allowed Paolo to walk the
streets of Bologna, as long as he was without weapons and accompanied.[37]
Pace Lodi's optimistic assessment of his state, Paolo was subject to fits of
violent behavior until he died: in the tediously detailed list of expenses
he incurred for Paolo's tending, his brother-in-law Valerio recorded the
purchasing of handcuffs, presumably to restrain Paolo, as he had been
by chains in San Vincenzo in Prato.[38] Besides impugning Judge Alavolini's verdict, Paolo's persistent insanity should make us reflect on the distance that hovered between his state of mind when the murder of Isabella

took place and the procedural events of the courtroom, between Paolo's madness as the experience of one individual and the normalization of this experience into prescriptive models adopted in courts of law and hospitals, unable to fully account for his behavior in medicolegal terms. Paolo's violent madness, the loss of reputation that not only he but his immediate family must have endured, and the financial and emotional sacrifices that his relatives experienced during his exile and when he was allowed to go back to Bologna have fallen through the cracks until now. What follows is an attempt to give voice to this unsung story and its actors.

FAMILY BATTLES AND THEIR STRATEGIES: INHERITANCE, WILLS, AND DOWRIES

Three major categories that frequently occur in the delineation of kinship in early modern Italian family households are essential in reconstructing Paolo's story after Isabella's murder: inheritance, wills, and dowries. Three episodes related to the aftermath of the trial against Paolo and his brother Aurelio and of Paolo's hospitalization in Milan exemplify these categories: the shared property between brothers, the value and attribution of a dowry—in particular, their restitution to the family that bestowed them initially—and the dispute of wills among surviving relatives after the death of a male family member without a male heir. This section of the chapter offers a glimpse into the complex network of emotional and social ties that existed among the members of the Barbieri family by interpreting Aurelio's testament and the ensuing legal dispute. We intend to interpret this network by reading between the lines of legal documents like testaments and their quarrels, and the legal opinions on these matters. These legal documents also raise questions concerning family and gender issues in Bologna at the turn of the sixteenth century. Finally, the story of the legal and financial woes of the Barbieri family exemplifies how the law was perceived as autonomous from its social context and, at the same time, "deeply bound up in the play of politics, class interest, and pressure of discrete groups, largely from among social elites."[39]

As recent studies demonstrate, medieval and early modern law and legal pursuits shaped and were shaped by emotions that communities as small as families and as big as neighborhoods and social groups considered appropriate and justified.[40] In this context Bourdieu's notion of *habitus* comes handy. Bourdieu states that "the structures characterizing a determinate class of conditions of existence produce the structures of

habitus, which in their turn are the basis of the perception and appreciation of all subsequent experiences. The *habitus*, a product of history, produces individual and collective practices—more history—in accordance
with the schemes generated by history."

He further explains that "being the product of a particular class of
objective regularities, the *habitus* tends to generate all the 'reasonable,'
'common-sense,' behaviors (and only these) which are possible within
the limits of these regularities, and which are likely to be positively sanc-
tioned because they are objectively adjusted to the logic characteristic of
a particular field, whose objective future they anticipate. . . . The *habitus*—
embodied history, internalized as a second nature and so forgotten as history—is the active presence of the whole past of which it is the product."[41]
Legal actions like contesting a will of a relative or claiming to be creditor
of someone with whom one used to be on amicable terms imply strong
emotions like hatred, vengeance, honor, and pride, which had their counterpart in humiliation and loss of one's good repute and honor, in other
words, of one's *fama*, in both social and legal terms.

Paolo's relatives and kin—his brother Aurelio; his mother Ippolita;
his sister Diana and her husband Valerio; his uncle Emilio Barbieri, who
became Paolo's legal guardian at the end of August 1598; his kin Francesco
Maria Bolognetti, the maternal uncle of the murdered Isabella and once a
partner in a business venture with the Barbieri patriarch, Antonio Maria,
and then with his sons Aurelio and Paolo in Bologna and Rome; and even
Grato, Aurelio's defense lawyer during the 1588 criminal trial, who was in
contact with his former client until shortly before the latter's death in September 1597—were all involved in this tangled web of emotions that found
expression in their choice of pursuing legal action against each other. The
vast number of legal documents following the 1588 trial chronicles the bit-
ter disputes for Paolo's property among his relatives and exemplifies the
vast and distressing effects of a person's insanity on his family and social
network; the documents also express deep conflicts that found a voice in
the legal actions that Paolo's kin and their representatives performed.

ONE INHERITANCE, TWO BROTHERS, AND A FAMILY IN TURMOIL

After two months of detention, Aurelio was released in December 1588.
He was in severe financial straits. Sometime between 1590 and 1597, he
moved to Rome to take care of various legal disputes, among them a trial
that involved a failed business venture with Francesco Maria Bolognetti.

In 1568 Bolognetti began a *banco* in Bologna with Antonio Maria Barbieri, Aurelio and Paolo's father, and Giulio and Pompeo Benci. After Antonio Maria Barbieri died in 1569, his sons became partners, first through a guardian and then in their own right once they reached adulthood.[42] In 1577 the Barbieri brothers renewed the *banco* with Bolognetti and Cesare Caravaggi and established another between Barbieri and Bolognetti in Rome.[43] The business started going south because of a dispute between Caravaggi and the other three partners and was dissolved in 1587, a year before Isabella was murdered. Aurelio accused Bolognetti of "erasing [and] falsifying the company's books" (*cancellare, falsificare i libri della compagnia*)[44] and of appropriating money that belonged to the Barbieri brothers. The dispute was brought before the criminal judge Alavolini in Bologna in July of 1589.[45] Bolognetti claimed that he did not want to have anything to do with the Barbieri family after Paolo murdered Isabella.[46] The trial came to an end on February 23, 1590: Bolognetti had to pay one thousand golden scudi to the apostolic office; however, most of the charges brought against him on behalf of Aurelio were dropped because they were unsubstantiated.[47] After the trial ended, Aurelio still expressed resentment and anger toward his former partner. In a petition to the pope, Aurelio, who at this point was already in Rome, stated that Bolognetti received excessive favors from the *vice-legato* Borghese, who was too lenient with him, and, in a letter written in 1597, Aurelio described Bolognetti as an "enemy" of the Barbieri family.[48] Bolognetti's desire to severe any contact with the Barbieri family and Aurelio's use of the term "enemy" reveal mutual animosity and resentment. Let us not forget that Bolognetti had placed a bounty of five hundred golden scudi on Paolo's head after he escaped capture, and that Aurelio might have decided to pursue Bolognetti legally because it was the most efficient way to express his hatred toward his former business partner and kin. He invested money and emotions in pursuing Bolognetti legally, intending to smear his name and reputation in Bologna.[49]

Aurelio's financial woes were made worse by the fact that many of the valuables he possessed were in the land and building properties that he shared with his brother Paolo, who was deemed incapable of making sound decisions. It appears that whatever their father, Antonio Maria Barbieri, left to his sons, Aurelio and Paolo, was bequeathed to them as indissoluble.[50] From a legal point of view, Paolo and Aurelio were considered a single entity, which constituted a huge problem, as Aurelio realized, when he needed to sell some of the property to pay outstanding debts. The issue of selling Paolo's property was a prickly one. Both Bologna's statutes and the

1585 bull of Sixtus V established that not only those who had been sentenced to death but also their families were supposed to be deprived of their assets. Managing a patrimony was essential for the well-being of the family, and "destructive conflicts . . . could erupt among brothers who had to share the same patrimony," fueled by anger and rivalry.[51] Paolo, though, was not directly involved in the conflict with his brother of managing and disposing of the patrimony; his mother Ippolita, his sister Diana and his brother-in law Valerio Rinieri represented Paolo's interests and the interests of the family and became Aurelio's antagonists. Therefore, the anger was transferred from brother to mother, sister, and brother-in-law.

Aurelio claimed that, given his mental status, Paolo was unable to determine his assets, including letting Aurelio sell the property that they shared. Aurelio needed money to pay the debts that he had incurred after and because of Paolo's murder and wanted to know how much money was left of the inheritance.[52] Ippolita and her representatives contended that Paolo could regain his sanity at any moment, and therefore could contest the decision made by her older brother to sell their shared property. In an exchange of letters between Aurelio and the lawyer Grato ranging from May 27 to August 13, 1597, Grato responds to Aurelio's request of finding a way to sell some of the properties he shared with his brother without going through his mother Ippolita, who Grato claims was swayed to reject Grato's help by her son-in-law Valerio Rinieiri. Ippolita certainly would not agree to the selling or would ask for part of the money on behalf of Paolo. Grato reminds Aurelio that since Paolo was still in the hospital in Milan, and not yet pardoned, the church had confiscated his share of the patrimony, following the 1585 edict of Pope Sixtus V against all violent criminals. A letter in the form of a *supplica* to the *vice-legato* Spinola in Bologna and the *legato* in Rome for the relinquishment (*cessione*) of the property that was confiscated upon payment of one or two hundred golden scudi could resolve the problem, without having Ippolita or any other relative involved in the division of the patrimony.

We do not have any of Aurelio's replies to Grato, but the lawyer's letters paint a rather bleak portrayal of Aurelio's family situation. According to Grato, Ippolita was turned against him by Valerio and his lawyer Fontana and refused to listen to Grato's repeated offers to help her manage the family patrimony. Rinieri and Fontana claimed that Grato had a debt of a few hundred lire with the business enterprise that the Barbieri family had with Bolognetti, while Grato states that the legal service he offered to Aurelio for the first two years since he moved to Rome should make things even. So he politely asks Aurelio to tell his brother-in-law and his lawyer to stop bothering him. Grato writes that he feels sorry for the way the Barbieri family members treated Aurelio, one of their own. Grato is also sad to learn that Aurelio's relatives sold some properties and did not help him pay debts and taxes that have bled him to the bone. Neither his family nor his friends moved a muscle to help him, while Grato, still loyal to him, would do everything in his power to be of assistance.[53] From the letters Grato sent to Aurelio, we also see Aurelio's frustration and resentment at the behavior of his mother and brother-in-law. Similar feelings of anger and vengeance appear in a story reported by the chronicler known as Marcantonio Bianchini: in 1602 a man left his property to charitable institutions and not to his daughters because he thought they were not his legitimate children.[54] This episode could be interpreted as the legal action of a father inflicting punishment on his daughters for reasons possibly driven by emotions: the wounded honor of a cuckolded husband, or the anger of a father spurned by his daughters. Litigants expressed their emotions, such as vengeance and hostility, through legal actions that lawyers shaped in the form of scripted documents. These documents—wills, civil suits against former business partners, the retraction or denial of credit given to a relative, former friend, or associate—were composed for economic reasons and to achieve economic and financial goals. Still, they might be the result of strong emotions expressed in documents, like the letters that Aurelio Barbieri and Grato exchanged in 1597.

Three other documents appear to shed partial light on what happened next. One is a copy of a letter that Aurelio wrote, in which Grato's advice seems to have been put to use.[55] The second is a copy of a rebuttal written by the lawyer Fontana, who represented the interests of Paolo Barbieri through the initiative of his mother Ippolita and her daughter Diana Barbieri-Rinieri. Fontana argued that the confiscation of the patrimony of criminals who escaped justice was never enforced, unless for cases of lese-majesty, and that Aurelio did not have the right to ask the *legato* for Paolo's part of the patrimony because it never was in the church's possession after all.[56] The third document is a letter to the *vice-legato* of Bologna Orazio Spinola written by Marcello Vestri Barbiani, secretary to Pope Clement VIII (1592–1605), on his behalf. The pontiff stated that Aurelio should be permitted to sell some of the property he shared with his brother Paolo but only to pay for outstanding debts and expenses accumulated over the years because of Paolo's *eccesso*: the fines for the trial, the establishment of a dowry for a younger sister, and the expenses for the prosecution and those incurred in legal disputes and the never-ending lawsuit against Bolognetti. Having received the papal brief, the *vice-legato* Spinola permitted Aurelio to sell a land whose property he shared with his brother, called "la possession del Palazzo."[57]

Victory must have been sweet but was undoubtedly short-lived: while trying to find a buyer for the possession, Aurelio died in Rome between September 8 and 12 of 1597.[58] Aurelio must have been exhausted and distraught by the financial problems directly and indirectly caused by Paolo's murder of Isabella. As we saw from Grato's letters, Aurelio felt, and was, estranged from his mother Ippolita, his sister Diana, and his brother-in-law Valerio Rinieri. On September 7, 1597, a few days before he died, Aurelio created a will, stating that he did not want to die without one, and wishing to avoid that a cause for disputes arose among his relatives ("nolens intestatus decedere ne inter suos post eius mortem aliquod scandulum [*sic*] litis super eius bonis oriatur").[59] Unmarried and childless, he devolved what he considered his own real and personal patrimony to the powerful Roman religious confraternity of Santissima Annunziata. The confraternity, which was funded in 1460 and had had its headquarters at the church of Santa Maria sopra Minerva since the second half of the fifteenth century, received a vast amount of donations, which were used to provide young Roman women of marriageable age, the so-called *zitelle*, with dowries. It was not uncommon to leave one's inheritance to religious institutions: in his testament, Giambattista Rinieri, son of Valerio Rinieri and Diana Barbieri, bequeathed his property to the Order of the Eremitani of Saint Augustin.[60]

Aurelio might have written other testaments before, but he rendered them void with his last will. Did the previous versions differ from the last? Had he bequeathed in them properties to his family? In his last testament, Aurelio left five hundred scudi to his mother, stipulated the restitution of her dowry, and established a monthly payment of seven scudi for Paolo's care at the hospital in Milan. He also bequeathed a considerable amount of money—seven hundred scudi—to a woman named Lucia De Brodis, who lived in the same building in Rome where Aurelio had his rooms: Aurelio hoped that with this money she could marry within a year of his death. Perhaps this suggests that Aurelio and Lucia had an intimate relationship; it is not clear. In his will Aurelio also named Cecilia Guerrieri and Giovan Antonio de Gottardis, Lucia's niece and nephew, to whom he left respectively fifty and forty scudi.[61] If he had died without a will, his patrimony would probably have gone to his sister Diana, the oldest of the remaining children of Ippolita Gessi and Antonio Maria Barbieri, since there was no other male heir in the Barbieri household and Paolo was not deemed capable of managing a patrimony because of his *pazzia*. Kuehn reports a similar story that happened in fifteenth-century Florence: "Giovanni di Nuto died without male heirs. He had designated an unrelated man as his heir. To three agnatically related women . . . he left only dowries. Had Giovanni di Nuto died intestate, these three women would have split the property." Therefore, the three women in Giovanni's family contested his testament.[62] Ippolita, too, composed a testament before she died on February 14, 1598, and Diana appeared to have inherited from his mother according to Ippolita's last will.[63] The legal documents analyzed so far, and Grato's letters to Aurelio, seem to reveal deep fractures among the family members of the Barbieri household.

Much has been written on the history of emotions.[64] Contrary to the conventional view, according to which legal courts and justice should be impervious to emotions, the analysis in this chapter follows in the footsteps of the works of Smail, Terry Maroney, Kimberly-Joy Knight, Laura Kounine, Martha Nussbaum, and Merridee L. Bailey, among others, who view the legal system and emotions as linked rather than mutually exclusive.[65] The increased interest in the history of emotions, which has produced a vast amount of publications and created a cluster of interrelated fields across disciplines, periods, and geographical areas,[66] has generated a growing scholarship focused on investigating the link between the legal system and emotions. Let us also remember that producing emotions in the courtroom was a goal of the Greek and Latin rhetoricians, who worked at the service of the law—Aristotle and Cicero come to mind.[67] Sylvia Junko Yanagisako states that "law is only one of the complex and sometimes contradictory forces of kinship that shape the reformulation and renegotiation of the sentiments, interests, and strategies of family members."[68] Terry Maroney has defined the study of emotions and law as an interdisciplinary movement or field.[69] Maroney proposes six categories for studying the relevance of emotions in the legal system and legal documents. She observes that, in general, the six approaches that she suggests are seldom applied individually, but rather in combination. Maroney argues that "any exploration of law and emotion should strive to identify which emotion(s) it takes as its focus; distinguish implicated emotion-driven phenomena; explore relevant and competing theories of the emotions; limit itself to a particular type of legal doctrine; expose underlying theories of law; and make clear which legal actors are implicated."[70] The last category in Maroney's list, the "legal actor's approach," investigates and interprets how specific emotions shape or are meant to shape the people who are involved in legal actions with specific official roles. Smail's work on criminal and civil court cases in thirteenth- and fourteenth-century Marseille offers a valuable historical contextualization of Maroney's approaches. He argues that the increased number of legal disputes in medieval Marseille does not reflect a repression or smoothing of emotions. Rather, it reflects their full display and expression through the legal script of civil and criminal cases, contested wills, and debt litigation, through which personal and family feelings of love and trust on one hand and hatred, vengeance, and humiliation on the other were performed, as people looked for emotional satisfaction for the wrong they perceived had been done to them. As indicated earlier, in the debt litigation between Aurelio and Francesco Maria Bolognetti, Aurelio invested a vast amount not only of money, but also of emotions. For the feelings of trust and friendship at the basis of the business that the two families had established decades before, he substituted the desire to humiliate his former business partner and kin.

A CONTESTED WILL

Anger, fear, and vengeance can be connected to Aurelio's will, its resulting legal documents, and its dispute with his family members after his death. From the letters exchanged between Aurelio and Grato, we see how hurt Aurelio felt when he did not receive the financial help he thought he deserved from his family members while he lived in Rome. Aurelio was there mainly because of the trial that ensued with the end of the Barbieri brothers' business venture with Bolognetti. The former partner was accused of embezzling money that belonged to the Barbieri family. After Aurelio's death, the confraternity of SS. Annunziata received the Barbieri property. Diana believed it belonged to her and her mad brother Paolo. Through her husband, Valerio Rinieri, and a network of legal actions performed in Bologna and Rome, she contested the property's bequeathal to the confraternity. Now that her older brother was dead and her younger brother was in a hospital for mad people in Milan, she thought of herself as the legitimate successor in line for the inheritance and feared that none of it would come to her. In the end, Diana got her wish. As the last living member of the Barbieri family, she received a sizable amount of money. Paolo was not capable of living and operating on his own. Diana and her husband had him released from the hospital not because he was healed but because his supposed improvement was essential for recovering the family property. This cluster of emotions dovetails with the legal determination about the distribution of property and goods in cases of contested inheritance. The actors of these legal actions were the judge, the defendant(s), and the parties involved in the contested will, while the emotions that the actors expressed and that were entangled in the legal actions were anger and fear. These legal actors functioned according to social codes of behavior specific to the early modern period. They also embodied changes related to the rules instituted by the "emotional communities" to which they belonged.

Did Aurelio have the right to leave property and money to a religious confraternity instead of to members of his family? The family in Bologna did not think so. Through her husband Valerio, Diana contested Aurelio's will, and a legal dispute followed. According to Diana and Valerio, Paolo, who had been out of the hospital since April of 1598, had the right to request his part of the inheritance. It seems that Paolo never fully recovered, however, so this claim was probably a pretext to bring back to the Barbieri/Rinieri family what Aurelio had bequeathed unjustly—according to Diana and Valerio—to the Roman religious confraternity of the Santissima Annunziata. Diana came to an agreement with the confraternity. A legal document written in 1600 states that an evaluation was requested by both parties for a piece of land in Castagnoli, outside of Bologna, worth one thousand nine hundred golden scudi. In the end, the confraternity surrendered the inheritance (*cessio bonorum*) that Aurelio left to them on May 5, 1600, and gave the one thousand nine hundred scudi to Diana. Although the devolution of his patrimony to a religious society might have satisfied some spiritual debt that Aurelio had with the confraternity while living for long periods in Rome, Diana's reaction, like the reaction of the three unnamed women left out by the testament of the Florentine Giovanni di Nuto, reveals brewing conflicts within the household. Female members of the family felt slighted by the main male heir, who, childless and/or unmarried, or with no legitimate or natural children formally recognized while he was alive, chose to leave by testamentary disposition what they considered property of their household, which they tried to keep intact, or at least not excessively fragmented. Fear was an emotion linked to inheritance: early modern families strove to keep their property whole and feared its fragmentation due to marriages, deaths, and debts.

In the dispute that erupted around the patrimony shared by the two brothers, the female figures—their mother Ippolita, their older sister Diana, and even the murdered young wife Isabella—appeared through the legal actions and decisions of the men of their respective families. "Women's interests were not easily separable from men's," writes Kuehn. "The protection of female rights meant that property was available for a woman's children and use by her husband or brother."[71] Ippolita's dowry was listed in the joint patrimony of Aurelio and Paolo, which they inherited from their father when he died in 1569, to which they added Isabella's dowry when she married Paolo in 1585; when the two women died, the Gessi and Caccianemici families reclaimed both dowries, as was common in early modern Italy.

CONCLUSIONS

In this chapter, we examined the dismal financial and economic consequences of a violent crime committed by a man deemed insane not only for his family but also for his kin and business associates. We also examined how the limited agency exercised by women in their original households and the household into which they were assimilated by marriage expressed itself in reinforcing the patrimony of their family of origin when they died and the inheritance of their new household when they were still alive. The restitution of Isabella's and Ippolita's dowries exemplifies the first instance, while Diana's contestation of her brother Aurelio's will and her remuneration represent the second. We also used complex legal documents—testaments, dispositions, briefs—as expressions of fractured interactions among sons and mothers, brothers, and brothers and sisters, which were exacerbated by the aggravating circumstance of the insanity attributed to one of the actors of this family drama.

Shame, pity, fear, and anger are traceable in the wording of the legal documents we analyzed and evident in the legal decisions that family members made in conflict to each other. The legal doctrine of intermittent insanity and the legal determination regarding the distribution of property and goods in cases of contested inheritance revealed emotions couched in private and official letters, and the legal actors—the judge, the defendant(s), and the parties involved in the contested will—expressed the same emotions in the legal actions that they performed. Both sets of documents are linked to social codes of behavior specific to the early modern period. They also express changes related to the codes instituted by the emotional communities to which the legal actors belonged. In a society increasingly less inclined to feel pity for the poor, the maimed, and the

insane, shame in relation to slighted honor grows in emotional importance. The dramatic changes that occurred in the Barbieri family between
the end of the sixteenth and the beginning of the seventeenth century are
expressed through conflicts that found a voice in the legal actions that its
family members and their representatives performed.

A few decades after Paolo Barbieri died, on January 16, 1606, this branch
of the Barbieri family was extinguished.[72] With no male heirs to speak of,
and with a vast amount of debt accumulated during Aurelio's life in order
to face the expenses of the trial for Paolo's murder of Isabella Caccianemici, the patrimony seemed to have been eroded by creditors, including the heirs of the families of Isabella and Ippolita and the household of
Diana's husband, Valerio Rinieri. The house on Piazza Calderini had been
sold; the main actors of this sensational story of insanity, violence, exile,
and estrangement were long dead. However, the fight between the local
aristocracy and the pope and his officials over whether the latter could
confiscate the lands and properties of those citizens who escaped justice
and were condemned to death continued long after Paolo, his family, and
his friends and enemies had ceased to exist.[73] The harsh sentence against
Paolo and his family was not unique. However, if we look at the real reason why Paolo committed the crime, his manifest insanity, and the strategies that the surviving members of his family used to regain the family's
wealth in his name, we cannot help but think that the opinion held by the
fourteenth-century jurist Baldo degli Ubaldi, that insane people could not
be considered guilty for crimes they had committed and therefore could
not be punished because they "[are] punished enough by [their] insanity,"
was devastatingly accurate.

Conclusion

The story of Paolo Barbieri is more than just the tale of an unfortunate crime—it is an example of the exercise of central authority over the demands and privileges of the local elite. It is a manifestation of the tension existing between legal and medical representatives facing the daunting task of categorizing such a slippery and vague notion as madness. It is an illustration of how the news of a tragic murder involving noble and notable people traveled throughout the city in the form of rumor, affecting the public opinion of individuals and families alike, and was reported in the chronicles of citizens of Bologna living in this period. It is a model of how social, cultural, and emotional communities filtered their perception of insanity, violence, and justice in written accounts. It is an instance of how oral and written modalities interacted in a manuscript culture and society like the Bolognese urban community at the turn of the seventeenth century. It is, in the end, the account of families devastated by illness, exile, and death, of hatred and animosity within a family and among kin and business partners, all of which found expression through legal action.

Unlike other early modern insanity narratives, the story follows Paolo's melancholic furor from its warning signs to its tragic outcomes. It travels from the open squares to domestic spaces, from the courtroom to the hospital for the insane, connecting cities in various Italian early modern states—the Papal State, the grand duchy of Tuscany, the republic of Lucca, and the duchy of Milan. Paolo Barbieri, his insanity, the murder he committed, and the fate of exile, hospital internment, and house confinement that marked his life from the moment he left Bologna until he died unfolded between the end of the sixteenth and the beginning of the seventeenth century. During this period, criminal justice in the Papal State was the stage on which the pope's central authority and his representatives, the *legato* and *vice-legato* and the *uditore* and *sotto-uditore* in Bologna, on the one hand, and the local aristocracy on the other, performed a wrestling match in which the former came out the winner in the end, but only after a long fight that lasted at least until the end of the seventeenth century, as pointed out by Colin Rose in his study on violence and homicide in early modern northern Italy.[1] The 1588 trial for the murder of Isabella Caccianemici appears to exemplify this fight fully: the murderer and his presumed accomplices were noble or notable, their actions needed to be punished through their *bona*—their money and their properties—mainly because the primary defendant and his accomplice escaped and capital punishment could not be performed on their bodies. The punishment implied that Paolo was sane, even though the rumor circulating in the city was that for years before the murder the young man manifested bizarre and threatening behavior, the signs of which both jurists and physicians recognized as those of a mad person. The verdict trumped legal and medical expert opinions and showed the discrepancy between theory and practice in the legal arena in terms of proof and evidence. Papal justice clearly expressed its intent to control the trial's proceedings, first by establishing that Paolo was a criminal fugitive, not a man out of his mind, then by enforcing Pope Sixtus V's bull regarding the confiscation of fugitives' property and that of their relatives. The threat of confiscation was not new, since earlier pontiffs had issued bulls with similar content. However, it appears that after Paolo's escape and conviction in absentia, his property was in fact confiscated, creating devastating effects on his family's financial situation, and resentment, ill will, and even hatred among its members.

The good or bad opinion in which a person or a family was held, their *fama*, both in and of the courtroom, played an important role in characterizing this story's main characters. Rumors contributed to creating their legal *fama* in the courtroom and affected the perception of the case, its actors, and its aftermath in the reports made by local chroniclers.

Paolo spent almost eight years in a hospital for mad people in Milan, away from his family, kept in shackles in a room he had to share with other people like him, raving mad and violent toward themselves and others. The irony is that his family requested the papal representatives in Bologna to release him not because they believed his condition had improved, but because they needed to show that he was sane enough to claim the part of his inheritance that his brother Aurelio had given away as if it had been all his. First papal justice, and then his family members, exploited Paolo's actions as a pretext to advance their interests.

Paolo was stripped of his title of knight of the Order of Santo Stefano, even if people kept calling him *cavaliero* until he died. When Paolo passed away at the beginning of the year 1606 at forty-two, the big house in Piazza Calderini, the theater of the gruesome murder of the young Isabella Caccianemici, had been sold to pay the family's debts. His mother and brother were dead, and so was Francesco Maria Bolognetti, the man who had placed a bounty on Paolo's head and required an autopsy on his niece's body. Only his sister Diana and her husband Valerio Rinieri, the fastidious chronicler of family assets and local events alike, were still alive. Valerio reported the expenses that he had to incur for Paolo's funeral ceremony and his burial, and nothing more.

Many things have changed since the Barbieri affair in terms of the assessment and management of civil and criminal justice, the medical interpretation of madness, and the organization and treatment of insane people. However, in the end, at the cost of sounding essentialist and ignoring the myriad circumstances that make the story of insanity in the early modern era different from the present day, some elements have not changed. Insanity still has nefarious effects on the people who suffer from it and their families, who must carry the brunt of caring emotionally and financially for someone whose actions they do not understand and may even condemn. The story that this book narrates is not like any other story of early modern insanity. In this book, madness is reconstructed in the context of Bologna's political life at the turn of the seventeenth century and the development of its particular medical and legal frameworks. In this story, madness is not an abstract concept, but is embodied in the lives of the murderer, the victim, and their relatives, branding them for life.

INTRODUCTION

1. Anonymous, "Cronaca di Bologna 1588–1595." The chronicle was written by a Lateran canon of the church of San Giovanni in Monte in Bologna who was active in the second half of the sixteenth century.

2. See Gardi, *Stato in provincia*, 213–15.

3. Smail, *Consumption of Justice*.

4. Foucault, *Histoire de la folie*.

5. Midelfort, *History of Madness*; Gowland, *Worlds of Renaissance Melancholy*.

6. T. Cohen, *Love and Death in Renaissance Italy*; Robisheau, Cohen, and Sijártó, *Journal of Medieval and Early Modern Studies*; Magnusson and Sijártó, *What Is Microhistory?*

7. The scholarship on Bolognese chronicles is vast and has developed exponentially since the early 1990s. See at least Pezzarossa, "Prima verifica"; Pezzarossa, "'Cose che non debbono assolutamente vedere la luce'"; Quaquarelli, *Per singulare memoria*; Antonelli and Pedrini, "Parte I: Il codice BUB 1994"; Bastia and Bolognani, *Memoria e la città*.

8. Dale, Lewin, and Osheim, *Chronicling History*; Dunphy, *Encyclopedia of the Medieval Chronicle*, s.v. "Chronicles (Terminology)."

9. E. Cohen, "Moving Words."

10. Kuehn, *Heirs, Kin, and Creditors*; Smail, *Consumption of Justice*.

11. Rosenwein, "Worrying About Emotions," 842–43; Rosenwein, "Problems and Methods," 11; Bourdieu, *Logic of Practice*, 54–56.

CHAPTER 1

1. Anonymous, "Cronaca di Bologna 1588–1595," xx.

2. See figure 1 for the location of the Barbieri house.

3. ASB, *Torrone* 2133, 12r–13r, 14v.

4. Ibid., 13r, 14v, 16v.

5. Ibid., 15r.

6. Ibid., 17r.

7. Ibid., 8r.

8. Ibid., 29r. During the first day of the trial, Giovanni Fantoni, Barbieri's coachman, a new hire who did not live at the Barbieri house, stated that he heard a rumor from the women of the Barbieri house that Isabella was pregnant.

9. Ibid., 15r.

10. Ibid., 13v.

11. Ibid., 17v (Cornelia's deposition). Aurelio's servant Andrea Ghirardi confirmed what Maddalena and Cornelia stated about Aurelio's words and actions. See ibid., 10r.

12. Antonio Maria Barbieri died on August 29, 1568. *Miscellanea di memorie storiche bolognesi*, BAB, B 1283, folder 19/3, 497r. Paolo Barbieri was born on March 22, 1563. AAB, *Registri battesimali della Cattedrale*, 23, 59. Giuseppe Guidicini calls the Barbieri family "noble and ancient," while Salaroli lists members of the family who were elected to the offices of ambassador and *gonfaloniere* of justice, and who were part of the General Council (called also, at different times, the Council of Five Hundred or Six Hundred) and of the Council of the "Anziani" of Bologna. The house where the Barbieri family lived and where Isabella was murdered was located in Piazza Calderini, and the church of San Domenico hosted the burial of many of its members. The Barbieri family ceased to exist by the first half of the seventeenth century, and its properties passed to the Malvezzi family. See Guidicini, *Cose notabili della città di Bologna*, 1:160–61; Salaroli, "Famiglie della città di Bologna," BAB, B 802, 97; Galeati, "Palazzi e case nobili della Città di Bologna," BAB, B 93, 87–88.

13. Carrati, "Li matrimoni contratti a Bologna," BAB, B 900, 49. Isabella belonged to the Caccianemici family, who were also called Braiguerra or Odaldi, from the name of their ancestor Odaldo. According to the eighteenth-century scholar Carlo Salaroli, among the ancestors of the Caccianemici family there was also a pope, Lucius II, who lived in the twelfth century. Isabella was buried in the church of San Domenico, where other members of the Caccianemici Braiguerra family were laid to rest. For further information on the connection between Pope Lucius II and the Caccianemici family, see Salaroli, "Famiglie della città di Bologna," 228–29; Guidicini, *Cose notabili della città di Bologna*, 4:247, 5:143; Guidicini, "Alberi genealogici," BAB, cc. 27, 33; Giuliano Milani, "Lucio II," *Enciclopedia dei papi*, vol. 2.

14. Several contemporary chronicles report Scipione Caccianemici's suicide; see, for instance, Alamanno Bianchetti, "Annali di Bologna dall'edificazione della città fino al 1599," BAB, Malvezzi 61, 3:166r.

15. See Casini, *Cavalieri degli Stati Italiani*, 7–14. By establishing the Order, Cosimo I aimed at having a fleet able to fight the ships of the Ottoman Empire and pirates and increase the activities of Tuscan ships with Genoa, Sicily, and Marseilles. Casini, *Cavalieri degli Stati Italiani*, 7–9; Trivellato, *Familiarity of Strangers*, 108.

16. For the idea of objects as metonymies of early modern lay culture, see T. Cohen, *Love and Death in Renaissance Italy*, 226.

17. ASPI, *Fondo dell'Ordine di S. Stefano*, "Provanze di nobiltà," filza n. 41 inserto 47, 610, 12v–13r; Guarnieri, *Ordine di Santo Stefano*, 1:114; Casini, *Cavalieri degli Stati Italiani*, 12–13.

18. ASPI, *Fondo dell'Ordine di S. Stefano*, "Provanze di nobiltà," filza n. 41 inserto 47, 617–18, 20v–21r. The children of Antonio Maria Barbieri and Ippolita Gessi were cousins of the senator Girolamo Guastavillani, brother of the cardinal Filippo Guastavillani. See "Memoriale di casa di Valerio Rinieri," ASB, *Demaniale San Giacomo*, 95/1701, 6v.

19. ASPI, *Fondo dell'Ordine di Santo Stefano*, "Suppliche e informazioni," 1095, 617r.

20. The military knights embraced the vows of charity—help others in need; chastity—be faithful to their spouses; and obedience—follow the orders of their superiors. Guarnieri, *Ordine di Santo Stefano*, 114; Casini, *Cavalieri degli Stati italiani*, 12–14.

21. Giorgio Vasari built the palazzo for the Order between 1562 and 1564. Guarnieri, *Ordine di Santo Stefano*, 115.

22. For the date of Paolo's admission to the Order, see ASPI, *Fondo dell'Ordine di S. Stefano*, "Provanze di nobiltà," filza n. 41 inserto 47, 0589.

23. ASPI, *Fondo dell'Ordine di S. Stefano*, "Processi criminali / cause criminali," 3065, 656–57.

24. Ibid., 657.

25. ASB, *Demaniale San Giacomo*, 96/1702. Enea narrated his misadventures with Paolo in Pisa in 1584 and in Bologna in 1587 in a letter dated November 16, 1588, at the invitation of Giovanni Francesco Grato, Aurelio Barbieri's defense lawyer, during the trial for the murder of Isabella.

26. Count Ulisse Bentivogli Manzoli belonged to one the most important families of Bologna, the Bentivogli, which had ruled the city during the fifteenth century. Ulisse's mother, Isotta Manzoli, had married Alessandro Bentivogli, hence the double name of this branch of the family. See Gardi, *Stato in provincia*, 215. In 1576 Ulisse married Pellegrina Cappello, daughter of Bianca Cappello, who in 1579 became the second wife of the grand duke of Tuscany, Francesco I. Cicogni, *Delle inscrizioni veneziane*, 2:211.

27. ASB, *Demaniale San Giacomo*, 96/1702. Ulisse Bentivogli wrote a letter on November 17, 1588, also at the invitation of Grato. Neither the letter written by Enea Rasi nor that written by Ulisse Bentivogli was admitted in court.

28. ASB, *Demaniale San Giacomo*, 96/1702.

29. Marescalchi, *Cronaca 1561–1573*, 19.

30. ASB, *Torrone* 2461, 278r.

31. The story of Mazzetti's murderous action and subsequent punishment, both performed in public spaces of Bologna, can be reconstructed by weaving together the account given in the catalogue of capital punishments carried out in Bologna between 1030 and 1653, which from 1540 were extracted from the book of the Conforteria of the Company of Santa Maria della Morte, and the accounts in several contemporary chronicles. See ASB, *Catalogo di tutte le giustizie in Bologna*. Mazzetti was apprehended and then sentenced to death by hanging on April 10, 1593. Bianchetti, "Annali di Bologna," BAB, Malvezzi 62, 322; Bianchini, "Cronaca di Bologna," BUB 296, 1:28v; Galliani, "Cose notabili ed importanti, 1589–1600," ASB, Demaniale, Malvezzi-Campeggi, iv, 47/707, 62r.

32. For information about the University of Bologna, its professors, students, and governance, see Salterini, *Archivio dei Riformatori dello Studio*; Brizzi et al., *Università a Bologna*, vol. 2; Capitani, *Università di Bologna*; *Philosophiae ac medicinae scholarium Bononiensis Gymnasii Statuta.*

33. Gowland, "Problem of Early Modern Melancholy," 83–84.

34. On hypochondriac melancholy, see Calabritto, "Medicina practica, consilia."

35. The judge asked the same question to Aurelio and the female servants: why did Paolo kill Isabella? They all responded that they could not think of anything else but his "humors" and "insanity." When the judge asked the servant Angelica if there had been any "conflict" (*differentia*) between Paolo and Isabella, she said there was none, and that Paolo "loved" (*voleva bene*) his wife. ASB, *Torrone* 2133, 36r, 63r, 67v, 69v.

36. E. Cohen, "Moving Words," 70.

37. Mellyn, *Mad Tuscans and Their Families*, 128–60.

38. Legnani Ferri, "Diario," BUB 896, 2:71r.

> Monday night . . . Sir Paolo Turchi, son of Sir Floriano and massaro of the
> Monte di Pietà of San Pietro, jumped at night into a well, naked, because of
> a melancholic humor, leaving behind three children and his wife Madonna
> Eugenia Valentini, and the previous year his brother, Sir Girolamo, wounded
> himself in order to end his life, but he recovered, however, he does not leave
> his house out of shame, may God guard everyone from such misfortune. In
> fact, Paolo was a reputable man, he shocked everyone; they buried him at
> night with four priests in San Giovanni in Monte.

39. The Monte of San Pietro was established in 1531 and was located in spaces made
available by the cathedral of San Pietro. See Carboni, *Credito disciplinato*, 35. See also
Delbianco, *Sedi storiche del Monte di pietà di Bologna*, 25–28.

40. In his "Diario" Valerio Rinieri (1547–1613), a contemporary of Legnani and an
important character in the Barbieri saga—he was Paolo's brother-in-law—added that,
even if Turchi committed suicide, the archbishop of Bologna allowed his body to be
buried in the church of San Giovanni in Monte, probably because of his social status.
Rinieri, "Diario 1520–1613," BUB 2137, 2:60v.

41. "Within traditional societies . . . the fluidity of the boundary between law, mor-
als, and custom is very high. In these societies, the quarrels between the members of
a community do not only offend the law, but the fundamental rules of everyday life.
Therefore, conflicts, even private ones, have a supra-individual character." Niccoli, *Perdonare*, 63–64 (my translation).

42. Barbagli, *Congedarsi dal mondo*, 106; Strocchia, "Women on the Edge," 55–57;
Healy, "Suicide in Early Modern and Modern Europe," 908.

43. Cesarina Casanova examines the case of Lucia Marzocchi in *Crimini nascosti*,
98–100. Massimo Giansante wrote a very interesting article on this trial ("Caso di Lucia
da Varignana," 303–21), on which I base my discussion and to which I refer for the text
of the trial. The proceedings can be found in ASB, *Torrone* 6987, file 12.

44. This is what Lucia herself said to the judge the first time she was questioned:
"Because the evening of past Carnival, if I was not mistaken, somebody burned my withe,
that is, a band of twisted twigs that I had made to herd the sheep during the winter, I
got so angry for the vexation I felt that my cattle would suffer that I started thinking of
killing myself; and because I did not want that my granddaughters stay and suffer after
my death, this morning I resolved to kill them, which I did." Giansante, "Caso di Lucia
da Varignana," 307 (my translation).

45. Ibid., 312–15.

46. Ibid., 319.

47. When the judge of the Torrone asked her to explain again the motives behind the
killing, Lucia replied, palpably annoyed, that she had already explained herself immediately after she committed the murder and did not feel like elaborating. Ibid., 311.

48. Even though she had already killed herself in her cell, Lucia was hanged publicly,
"de ordine auditoris . . . ad exemplum aliorum": the judge decided that the death penalty had to be performed anyway. Ibid., 312. Modern readers may find the infliction of

further punishment on a corpse unduly harsh. However, in this period both ecclesiastical and civil institutions still considered suicide an act more egregious than murder; also, killing oneself after committing a crime was interpreted as a clear sign of guilt, and executions postmortem of the corpses of criminals were not unusual. Minois, *History of Suicide*, 36, 61. In early modern France and England families of suicides were at risk of losing the victim's property. Minois, *History of Suicide*, 135; Strocchia, "Women on the Edge," 55. For an overview of recent publications on early modern suicide in Europe, see Healy, "Suicide in Early Modern and Modern Europe," 903–12. The story of Lucia Marzocchi is also narrated as an example of early modern suicide in Barbagli, *Congedarsi dal mondo*, 45–46.

49. Sbriccoli, "Giustizia negoziata, giustizia egemonica," 345–64; Sbriccoli, "Giustizia criminale," loc. 3200–583 of 4611, Kindle.

50. The Torrone presided over the proceedings of criminal trials in Bologna from at least 1525 to 1796. On the constitution and functioning of the Torrone in the sixteenth and seventeenth centuries, see Verardi Ventura, "Ordinamento bolognese"; Di Zio, "Tribunale criminale di Bologna"; Pastore, *Crimine e giustizia in tempo di peste*, 73–76; Casanova, *Crimini nascosti*, 27–36; Angelozzi and Casanova, *Giustizia criminale*; Rose, "Violence and the Centralization of Criminal Justice."

51. Rubin Blanshei and Cucini, "Criminal Justice and Conflict Resolution," 356.

52. Dall'Aglio and Rospocher, introduction to Dall'Aglio, Richardson, and Rospocher, *Voices and Texts*, 2.

53. Ibid., 5; E. Cohen, "Moving Words," 72.

54. Burke, "Oral and Manuscript Cultures," 23.

55. De Caprio and Senatore, "Orality, Literacy, and Historiography," 131–32.

56. Niccoli, "Voci, scritture, stampe," 224.

57. Richardson, *Manuscript Culture*, xi.

58. Fox and Woolf, *Spoken Word*, 8.

59. Niccoli, "Voci, scritture, stampe," 224.

60. Kuehn, "Fama as a Legal Status," in Fenster and Smail, *Fama*, 28.

61. See Bettoni, "Fama, Shame Punishment."

62. Fenster and Smail, introduction to *Fama*, 3.

63. ASB, *Torrone* 2204, 25r. See Bettoni, "Fama, Shame Punishment" and, by the same author, "Voci malevole." See also the collection of essays in Fenster and Smail, *Fama*.

64. See Strange and Cribb, introduction to Strange, Cribb, and Fort, *Honour, Violence and Emotions*, 13.

65. See ibid., 9–13. Honor and shame are significantly absent in the stories of women's suicide and murder. Apparently, women were led to acts of violence against themselves and others by loneliness, domestic abuse, and social and economic impoverishment. Lucia, the only woman here who committed murder, explained her actions as caused by material factors, even if only expected and not yet at hand.

66. ASB, *Torrone* 2133, 5v.

67. Bourdieu, *Logic of Practice*, 56.

68. See Strange and Cribb, introduction to Strange, Cribb, and Fort, *Honour, Violence and Emotions*, 9–10.

69. Rosenwein, "Problems and Methods," 11.

70. Boari, *Qui venit contra iura*; De Renzi, "Medical Expertise"; De Renzi, "Natura in tribunale"; Maclean, "Evidence, Logic, the Rule"; Maclean, *Interpretation and Meaning*; Maclean, *Logic, Signs and Nature in the Renaissance*; Crawford, "Legalizing Medicine."

71. Maclean, "Evidence, Logic, the Rule," 228–30; De Renzi, "Medical Expertise," 318–21; Burke, "Images as Evidence," 276; Ginzburg, "Clues," 96–125.

72. Davis, *Return of Martin Guerre.*

73. Snyder, *Dissimulation and the Culture of Secrecy.* Among the modern scholars who studied the notion of dissimulation in the early modern period, see Villari, "Elogio della dissimulazione"; Zagorin, *Ways of Lying*; Zarri, *Finzione e santità*; Eliav-Feldon, *Renaissance Impostors*; Gordian, "Culture of Dis/simulation."

74. Pastore, "Maladies vraies et maladies simulées."

75. For the figure of Selvatico, see also ibid., 20, and Michael Gordian, "Culture of Dis/simulation," 152–58.

76. "Fit persaepe, ut delirare nonnulli, desipereque simulent, quos ex praecedentibus caussis, ex habitu simulantis, & ex privatione notarum delirii, ac melancholiae levi negocio deprehenduntur." Giambattista Codronchi, *De vitiis vocis, libri duo*, 157. I thank Ian Maclean for bringing Codronchi's text to my attention for the first time. For information about Codronchi's life and work, see Giovanni Battista Codronchi, *Methodus testificandi*, 125–31.

77. "Nullus morbus fere est, qui facilius & frequentius simulari soleat, quam insania, nullus item, qui difficilius possit deprehendi." Zacchia, *Quaestiones medico-legales*, *liber* 3, *titulus* 2, *quaestio* 5 ("De Simulata Insania"), 160. Zacchia (1584–1659) published the *Quaestiones* in installments from 1621 until 1635. For information on Zacchia's life, family, and work, see De Renzi, "Per una biografia di Paolo Zacchia," and Duffin, "Questioning Medicine," 150–55.

78. The information of Bolognetti's bounty on Paolo's head is included in a letter that Aurelio himself presumably wrote years after the murder to the *vice-legato* to be granted permission to sell property that he shared with his brother Paolo. ASB, *Demaniale S. Giacomo*, 97/1703, 50r.

CHAPTER 2

1. Francesco Ciabattini had the misfortune of bearing the letter from Firenzuola, where he made a stop with a group of French horsemen who were traveling from Rome to Bologna, and he was held in jail as soon as he arrived at the city. ASB, *Torrone* 2133, 90r. Battistino, the owner of the inn where Paolo and his servant Francesco were staying, asked Ciabattini to bring a letter to Bologna. The text of the letter was put on record and transcribed in the proceedings of the trial on November 28, 1588. Ibid., 160v–61r, together with the original document.

2. During the trial several witnesses described Francesco as a *tosazzo* (bad boy)—see, for instance, ibid., 10v. Nowhere in the proceedings can one find the reason for this pejorative attribute.

3. "Vi prego havere compassione della fortuna del Cavaliero et ancora vi aviso che chi viene o messo o lettere non lo rabuffi, per non lo cavare piu del senno di quel che è." Ibid., 161r.

4. See chapter 1.

5. The doctors' letter is in ASB, *Demaniale*, 96/1702, 3–7.

6. "Far dispiacere ad altri, et nocergli nela vita notabilmente." Ibid., 4.

7. Ibid., 3.

8. "Then the autumn arrived, [the period] during which the above-mentioned humors become more painful and provoke the individual to commit horrendous and wild acts." Ibid., 6.

9. Ibid., 15. The letter's handwriting corresponds to Grato's in other signed documents.

10. Ibid., 6.

11. Ibid., 7.

12. De Renzi, "Natura in tribunale."

13. In 1588 Mercuriale received a yearly salary of five thousand four hundred lire, a very large sum compared to what Gasparo Tagliacozzi and Ludovico Lodi were paid in the same period, respectively six hundred and four hundred lire. For information about Mercuriale's life in Bologna, see Paoletti, *Girolamo Mercuriale e il suo tempo*; Simili, "Gerolamo Mercuriale lettore e medico di Bologna"; Simili, "Gerolamo Mercuriale nell'ombra e nella luce," 170–80; Simili, *Gerolamo Mercuriale lettore e medico a Bologna. Nota II*; Simili, "Gerolamo Mercuriale lettore e medico a Bologna. Nota III"; Seneca, "Fallito tentativo di Girolamo Mercuriale."

14. Simili, "Gerolamo Mercuriale lettore e medico di Bologna," 163; Seneca, "Fallito tentativo di Girolamo Mercuriale," 162. Mercuriale had a very long résumé that warranted this prestigious position at the University of Bologna. It included works as varied as *De arte gymnastica* (1569), an erudite multivolume work on the history of gymnastics; *De morbis muliebribus* (1582), a gynecological treatise; and *De decoratione* (1585), a work on cosmesis, that is, on ways to improve one's physical appearance. In the treatise *De arte gymnastica* Mercuriale showed a great interest in antiquarianism, which may have secured him his first appointment as a professor of medicine at the University of Padua in 1570. For an analysis of Mercuriale's deep interest in antiquarianism and its influence in his medical works, see Siraisi, "History, Antiquarianism, and Medicine," and Agasse, "Bibliothèque d'un Medecin Humaniste," particularly 215–53, which reproduce the list that Mercuriale composed of the books in his library.

15. For an exhaustive analysis of Tagliacozzi's life and work, see Gnudi and Webster, *Life and Times of Gaspare Tagliacozzi*.

16. In *De curtorum chirurgia per incisionem* (1597), Tagliacozzi first described his procedure in a letter to Mercuriale in 1586. Gnudi and Webster, *Life and Times of Gaspare Tagliacozzi*, 135–42. For an analysis of the relationship between Tagliacozzi and Vincenzo Gonzaga, see Finucci, *Prince's Body*. For a discussion of the figure of Tagliacozzi and a contextualization of his treatise on rhinoplastic surgery, see Savoia, *Cosmesi e chirurgia*.

17. In 1577 Lodi started his university career by teaching logic, then between 1578 and 1599 he taught courses in the theory of medicine, which consisted of "philosophy of medicine and principles of physiology and pathology," and of its practice, namely, "the study of specifics of diagnosis and treatment." Siraisi, *Medieval and Early Renaissance Medicine*, 73. In 1619, the year he died, he was invited to teach *lecturae supraordinariae*

of practice of medicine, which were paid much better than the other courses. For further information on Lodi's life, see Mazzetti, *Repertorio dei professori*, 183–84; for the topics he taught and the years he taught them, see Dallari, *Rotuli dei lettori legisti ed artisti*, vol. 2; for an explanation of the different types of *lecturae—extraordinaria, ordinaria* and *supraordinaria*—see also Dallari, *Rotuli dei lettori legisti ed artisti*, vol. 2, vii.

18. ASB, *Demaniale San Giacomo*, 96/1702, 7.

19. Angelo Michele Sacco taught surgery at the University of Bologna, and Tagliacozzi and Aranzio were his more famous colleagues. See Dallari, *Rotuli dei lettori legisti ed artisti*.

20. "Sir, those young women in the house said that the *cavaliero*'s wife was pregnant." ASB, *Torrone* 2133, 29r.

21. ASB, *Demaniale San Giacomo*, 90/1696, 91/1697, 96/1702, 97/1703; ASR, *Archivi dei 30 Notari Capitolini Officio* 37 (1592).

22. According to Sacco, Bolognetti told him that Alavolini gave permission to perform the autopsy on Isabella's body: "Francesco Maria [Bolognetti] answered me ... we have permission from the judge." ASB, *Torrone* 2133, 137v. For information on Orazio Alavolini and his role in the criminal system of early modern Bologna, see chapter 3.

23. Sacco's deposition was treated as if it were part of the inquisitorial phase of the trial (*pro Curiae informatione*), even if Alavolini began the defensive phase of the trial a few days before, on October 29. For a description of the structure of an early modern trial, see chapter 3. At the beginning of the fourteenth century, legal documents started referring to dissections in relation to processes of canonization. In the Bolognese juridical system, recourse to the dissection of a victim appeared to be the exception rather than the practice. See Chandelier and Nicoud, "Entre droit et médecine," 242, 264–65.

24. ASB, *Torrone* 2133, 137v–138r. Katharine Park observed that "because the umbilical cord and placenta had not yet formed, it wasn't yet receiving nourishment from the mother, which means that it wasn't yet alive, since the most basic form of animation is that provided by the nutritive soul. Anything that isn't exercising some kind of nutritive function therefore can't be alive" (Katharine Park, email conversation, September 2005).

25. Chandelier and Nicoud, "Entre droit et médecine," 274 and 292.

26. In medieval and early modern continental Europe, only a few physicians could be called as medical experts in legal proceedings, and their duties, emoluments, and qualifications were regulated by statute. Crawford, "Legalizing Medicine," 93. In 1252 Bologna developed what appears to be the first set of provisions meant to regulate medical investigation in cases of offences against people. Ortalli, "Perizia medica a Bologna"; Simili, "Beginning of Forensic Medicine in Bologna," 91–95; Chandelier and Nicoud, "Entre droit et medicine," 238–39.

27. From the thirteenth century onward, Spanish and Italian surgeons and physicians were called as expert witnesses, sometimes working in collaboration, in cases of suspicious wounds or suspicious and violent death: Chandelier and Nicoud, "Entre droit et médecine," 236, 259, 270, 273. For the sixteenth and seventeenth century, see Paolo Zacchia's *consilium* 15 in *Quaestiones medico-legales*, 9:688–91 as discussed by De Renzi, "Medical Expertise," 320–21; Wear, "Medicine in Early Modern Europe," 237;

Park, *Doctors and Medicine*, 96; Ruggiero, "Cooperation of Physicians and the State," 15; De Renzi, "Witnesses of the Body," 220; Maclean, *Logic, Signs and Nature*, 86; Pastore, *Medico in tribunale*, 102; Pastore, *Veleno*, 161–89.

28. Savoia, *Cosmesi e chirurgia*, 40–45.

29. "Ipsis ergo peritis semper magis erit credendum; quam aliis testibus: . . . hoc unum tamen est verum, cuilibet docto in arte sua esse credendum." Vincenzo Carrari, *De medico* (Ravenna, 1581), 187. De Renzi, "Natura in tribunale," 805, 819 and note 24; Ascheri, "'Consilium sapientis' perizia medica e 'res iudicata,'" 541.

30. See Chandelier and Nicoud, "Entre droit et medicine," 242, 244–45; Boari, *Qui venit contra iura*, 71.

31. De Renzi, "Natura in tribunale," 803–6; De Renzi, "Witnesses of the Body," 224–25; Pastore, *Veleno*, 86–87. Pastore also underlines the contradiction existing among medical opinions in cases of suspected poisoning, which reflected contrasting interests—that is, of the defense and the prosecution. Pastore, *Veleno*, 111, 125.

32. De Renzi, "Witnesses of the Body," 223–25. In fact, in some cases a productive collaboration occurred between the medical investigation and report and the judicial procedure. See Pastore, *Veleno*, 156.

33. Colombero, "Il medico e il giudice," 365.

34. Ibid., 365; Boari, *Qui venit contra iura*, 60, 70.

35. Siraisi, *Medicine and the Italian Universities*, 226; Siraisi, *Avicenna in Renaissance Italy*; Maclean, *Interpretation and Meaning*, 15; Boari, *Qui venita contra iura*, 38; Bylebyl, "School of Padua"; Wear, "Galen in the Renaissance."

36. For an exploration of the subjective dimension of madness in the early modern period, see Hodgkin, *Madness in Seventeenth-Century Autobiography*.

37. ASB, *Demaniale San Giacomo*, 96/1702, 6.

38. "It remains that he could have been overtaken by diabolical and wild images and thoughts, which the vapors of the above-mentioned humors usually bring with them, and which did not allow him to recognize that the person whom he was wounding with his sword was his wife. Then, when somehow, he realized that he had killed her in such a state of furor, he reasonably chose to escape. Alternatively, these imaginations could have shown to him that his wife was worth being killed and therefore he could have reached such excess through a fit of madness. When he came to his senses, he himself realized what he had done without any reason, and therefore he escaped." ASB, *Demaniale San Giacomo*, 96/1702, 6–7.

39. Mantica, *De coniecturis*; Mascardi, *Conclusiones probationum*; Menochio, *De praesumptionibus*. Francesco Mantica (Vanzone 1534–Rome 1614) taught at the University of Padua. Pope Sixtus V appointed him "uditore di Rota," and Pope Clement VIII made him cardinal. For information about Mantica's life and work, see Feci, "Mantica, Francesco Maria." For information about Mascardi's life (1540/45–1585) and activity, see Sinisi, "Mascardi, Giuseppe." Mascardi published the first two volumes of his treatise in 1584, while his brother Alderamo Mascardi edited and added the third volume in 1588. During his long life (1532–1607) Menochio taught with success at the Universities of Pavia, Mondovì, and Padua. For information about Menochio's life and professional activities, see Valsecchi, "Menochio, Giacomo." See also Burke, "Images as Evidence," and Boari, *Qui venit contra iura*, 37–70.

40. "Et certe quilibet praesumitur sanae mentis esse, & ei, qui dicit, testatorem fuisse furious, vel mentecaptum, onus probandi incumbit." Mantica, *De coniecturis*, book 2, 19r; "An si qui semel fuerit furiosus, semper praesumatur furiosus," Mascardi, *Conclusiones, conclusio* 825 and in particular paragraphs 13, 17, 18.

41. Zacchia, *Quaestiones medico-legales, quaestio* 23, *liber* 2, *titulus* 1.

42. Boari, *Qui venit contra iura*, 162 (my translation).

43. "La différence de registre, entre ce qui est attendu de la justice, savoir l'établissement de la vérité des faits, et ce que les médecins sont en mesure d'affirmer, en fonction de leur savoir et de ce que les signes corporels leur permettent de déduire. Et c'est bien en cela que réside la difficulté de devoir accorder ces deux registres, celui de la vérité et celui au mieux d'une certaine vraisemblance ou plausibilité." Chandelier and Nicoud, "Entre droit et médecine," 269. "Justice demands uniformity, and jurists are therefore bound to reduce as far as they can variation between cases." Maclean, "Evidence, Logic, the Rule," 241. For the *consilium* as expression of shared knowledge between law and medicine, see Pastore, *Veleno*, 90.

44. For a discussion of the *dilucida intervalla* of the *furiosus* in the tradition of criminal law, see Boari, *Qui venit contra iura*, 30, 130–40.

45. Mercuriale, *Medicina practica* (1602), book 1, 27. Mercuriale's *Medicina practica* was based on the physician's lectures at the University of Padua (1569–1587).

46. Ibid., 53 and 61.

47. Mercuriale, *Responsorum et consultationum medicinalium in duo volumina digesta* (1589), book 2, *consultatio* 9 and 101; book 3, *consultatio* 86. Mercuriale wrote his medical consultations between 1563 and 1603, and they were printed in four volumes between 1587 and 1604. For a bibliography of Mercuriale's printed works, including the various editions of his *consilia*, see Cerasoli and Garavini, "Bibliografia delle opere a stampa di Girolamo Mercuriale"; for a description of the organization of Mercuriale's *consilia* in successive editions, see also Siraisi, "Psychology," 338n33.

48. Mercuriale, *Consultationes et responsa medicinalia* (1620), book 3, *consultatio* 86.

49. For a definition of "epistemic genre," see Pomata, "Observation Rising."

50. Taddeo Alderotti wrote one of the earliest substantial collections of medical *consilia*. Siraisi, *Taddeo Alderotti and His Pupils*, 271; Agrimi and Crisciani, *Consilia médicaux*, 62; Lockwood, *Ugo Benzi*, 44.

51. Rossi, *Consilium Sapientis Iudiciale*; Ascheri, "'Consilium sapientis' perizia medica e 'res iudicata'"; Ascheri, "'Consilia' come acta processuali," 310–11; De Renzi, "Witnesses of the Body," 224.

52. For a definition and an exhaustive analysis of the genre of the medical *consilium*, see Agrimi and Crisciani, "Individuale nella medicina"; Lockwood, *Ugo Benzi*, 47; Agrimi and Crisciani, *Consilia médicaux*, 19; Crisciani, "'Consilia,' responsi, consulti."

53. Agrimi and Crisciani, *Consilia médicaux*, 67.

54. Ibid., 77, 97; Agrimi and Crisciani, *Edocere medicos*.

55. Among the patients for whom Mercuriale wrote his *consilia* were aristocrats, wealthy merchants, lawyers, and young rich scholars coming from abroad, who could be cured at home.

56. Chandelier and Nicoud, "Entre droit et médecine," 248–73.

57. Ibid., 283–93.

58. See De Renzi, "Medical Expertise," and Duffin, "Questioning Medicine."

59. Mercuriale, *Responsorum et consultationum medicinalium* (1589), vol. 2, *consultatio* 65.

60. Mercuriale, *Consultationes et responsa medicinalia* (1620), *consultatio* 47.

61. For the use of erudite quotations in medical *consilia*, see Agrimi and Crisciani, *Consilia médicaux*, 55 and 98; Siraisi, "Anatomizing the Past," 6; Calabritto, "Examples, References and Quotations."

62. For *consilia* in which the doctor discusses the patient's fate and eventual death, see Cristoforo Guarinoni's *Consilia medicinalia* (Venice, 1610), as discussed in Calabritto, "Curing Melancholia," 643–47.

63. Chandelier and Nicoud, "Entre droit et médecine," 282.

64. Mercuriale, *Consultationes et responsa medicinalia* (1620), *consultatio* 47.

65. When talking about Paolo's behavior, the three physicians referred to the "six nonnatural things" (*sex res non naturales*)—air and weather, food and drink, motion and rest, sleep and wakefulness, evacuation and repletion, and passions of the mind, which included worries and excessive intellectual exertion. The Galenic tradition considered these elements as belonging to the realm of nature, but external to the body. Garcia-Ballester, "On the Origin of the 'Six Non-natural Things,'" 105.

66. Carrari, *De medico*, 5–6, 183. I thank Vivian Nutton for bringing to my attention this text. Carrari, a priest who studied law, addressed his treatise to judges who received advice from physicians "ut lites diriment." For information about Carrari's life, see Ascari, "Carrari, Vincenzo,"; Boari, *Qui venit contra iura*, 68.

67. Mascardi, *Conclusiones, conclusio* 826, † 23, 226.

68. "In hac classe succedunt Melancholici Hypochondriaci, qui cum [paraphreniticis] in hoc conveniunt, quod eorum delirium non ex proprio cerebri vitio, sed ex Hypochondriorum morbo, & intemperie excitatur. . . . Hypochondriaci autem habent quidem accessiones, & exacerbationes, non tamen quotidianas, tertianas, aut quartanas, sed potius menstruas, aut annuas, & longiores multo sunt; recrudescit enim morbus in his certis quibusdam temporibus, ut Vere, sive Autumno, cum in aliis mente satis constent." Zacchia, *Quaestiones medico-legales*, book 1, I, *quaestio* 21.

69. ASB, *Demaniale San Giacomo*, 96/1702, 6–7.

70. Mascardi, *Conclusiones probationum* (1584), 225. The list is part of *conclusio* 526 ("Ex quibus probetur furor"), where Mascardi discusses the most important issues in common law related to proving a defendant's insanity. In his list Mascardi also enumerated signs of insanity that related to people's standing and perceived behavior in their social group and community.

71. "Furor cum nil aliud sit, qum a quaedam mentis aegritudo, animique morbus, proinde latens intus, sub nostrum sensum cadere non possit; necessarium est, ut nisi per actus et signa, quae extrinsecus proveniant, aliter probari non possit." Ibid.

72. Giambattista Da Monte (1489–1551) stated in his *consilia* that the narration of the accidental was easy to know and report, but that the difficulty consisted in probing the hidden causes. "Haec sunt accidentia ab eo recitata, quae omnia sunt facilia cognitu: sed in causis indagandis est summa difficultas, nec possum mihi satis facere," *consilium* 23; "Haec [symptomata] ad suas causas reducenda sunt, ut inveniatur curatio," *consilium* 234; "Quia non curamus symptomata, sed ea solum consideramus in hoc

finem, ut veniamus in cognitionem morbi, quo cognito & invento omittimus omni illa signa & accidentia: nam nullum symptoma trahit curam ad se, nisi sub ratione morbi: venio igitur ad affectum & morbum, hoc est, melancholiam hypocondriacam," *consilium* 236; "Oportet nos indagare causam, ut deveniamus ad curam," *consilium* 242. Da Monte, *Consultationes medicae* (1583).

73. "Proof theory, like medical theory, was a body of principles and rules that prescribed how the evidence of particular cases should be collected and interpreted, and what actions should be taken (by judge or physician) in different circumstances." Crawford, "Legalizing Medicine," 98. See also De Renzi, "Medical Expertise," 318.

74. For a definition and description of the genre of the *observatio*, see Gianna Pomata, "Sharing Cases."

75. Ibid., 204–6.

76. See Maclean, "Evidence, Logic, the Rule," 229–30.

77. Boari, *Qui venit contra iura*, 39–40, 69–73, 159, 162. For a thorough examination of the development of the interpretive skills in sixteenth-century law, see Maclean, *Interpretation and Meaning*.

78. "The former [the inartificial proofs] of these include brute signs ('signa nuda') of all kinds: circumstantial evidence, rumours, the depositions of witnesses, the *ipsissima verba* of documents and altercations, the results of torture and interrogation; the latter (the 'artificial proofs') are what the art of the advocate can make of them for the benefit of his client." Maclean, "Evidence, Logic, the Rule," 242.

79. In mid-sixteenth-century Bologna a controversy appeared between prosecutors/judges and lawyers. "The former were controlled by the provincial 'rettore,' who is appointed by the pope, while the latter were subject to the jurisdiction of the Senate.... [T]he ways of exercising justice become an instrument of political struggle between local authorities and central power." Ago, "Giustizia personalizzata," 407 (my translation). See also Evangelisti, "Gli 'operari delle liti'"; Brambilla, "Genealogia del sapere."

CHAPTER 3

1. For records on Leone Benini, see Gardi, *Stato in provincia*, 421. It appears that Benini was active at the Torrone between 1578 and 1590 in the capacity of "substitute" for the notaries who were elected by the Monte di Pietà, which the senatorial oligarchy of the city controlled. See Gardi, *Stato in provincia*, 114, and Angelozzi and Casanova, *Giustizia criminale*, 49–50.

2. ASB, *Torrone* 2133, 6r.

3. Ibid., 18r, 21r–v.

4. Ibid., 5v. Benini's and Ratta's depositions confirm each other (6v). Ibid., 18r (Benini's deposition).

5. Ibid., 21v–22r. See also ibid., 77v, where Benini gives the same information during his second interrogation. When the judge Violano asked Aurelio whether he ever wrote a letter of this kind to his brother Paolo, Aurelio denied it. Ibid., 60r–60v.

6. "Tremava tutto, con quella spada nuda in mano come fa un matto." Ibid., 7v.

7. Ibid., 20v–21r. (Benini); ibid., 17v–19v (Salani).

8. Ibid., 5v, 6v, 18v, 21r, 22r.

9. Ibid., 22v, words reported by Benini in third person singular.

10. Ibid., 18r–v.

11. Ibid., 6r.

12. For a brief description of the building called the *Torrone* and its use as a prison, see Terpstra, "Confraternal Prison Charity and Political Consolidation," 218–20. The pope elected the *legato* every three years and could confirm him in his position for more terms. Underneath the *legato* were three judges, all foreigners, who administered justice: the *uditore generale* for civil trials, the *uditore del Torrone* for penal trials, and the *uditore di camera* for trials related to public finance and economy. See Verardi Ventura, "Ordinamento bolognese," 386–425.

13. The *cursore*, which literally means "runner," was a city official charged with bringing summonses to defendants. See Angelozzi and Casanova, *Giustizia criminale*, 55.

14. The *bargello* corresponded to a police captain, and he chose the *sbirri* who worked for him. Angelozzi and Casanova, *Giustizia criminale*, 52. For the relationship between *auditore, sotto-auditore*, and *legato* (or *vice-legato*, in the absence of the *legato*), see Gardi, *Stato in provincia*, 206; Verardi Ventura, "Ordinamento bolognese," 373; Rose, "Violence and the Centralization of Criminal Justice," 105–6; Angelozzi and Casanova, *Giustizia criminale*, 43–48.

15. ASB, *Torrone* 2133, 85v–94r.

16. When Domenico de Cortesi was questioned, he confirmed what Lazaro had already said. The only discordant detail concerned the piece of cloth dropping out of the young man's cloak: Domenico first said it was white and then "bloody." Ibid., 91r–94r (deposition of Domenico dei Corteli/Cortesi).

17. "We heard by I don't know who that a woman of the Barbieri family had been hit, and then we said between us 'bloody me, maybe the one we saw with that bloody cloth might have been him, who must have done this evil." Ibid., 88v.

18. On October 31 Violano questioned Carlo Ratta about the version of the events given by Lazaro dei Bernabo and Domenico de Cortesi. It does not seem that Violano thought that Paolo was one of the men described by Lazaro and Domenico, but he wanted to check if they could have been servants who brought clothes to or took away the sword from Paolo, who was already at Carlo Ratta's house. Ratta rejected their report: whether or not the two men described by Lazaro and Domenico entered his house, he did not know.

19. ASB, *Torrone* 2133, 19v, 25r.

20. Ibid., 8r ff.

21. See Gardi, *Stato in provincia*, 213–15.

22. See Angelozzi and Casanova, *Giustizia criminale*, 392 and 652. For a discussion of the tribunal of the Torrone in the early modern period as the official tool to manage violence in early modern Bologna, see Rose, *Renaissance of Violence*, 80–157.

23. Angelozzi and Casanova, *Giustizia criminale*, 477 and 553.

24. ASB, *Torrone* 2133, 29v–30r.

25. Treatment of insanity in civil trials was already present in Justinian's *Institutes*, issued in 535 CE, which included large extracts from the *Digesta*, the most important text of Roman jurisprudence. The *Digesta* was already a few centuries old when the commission established by Emperor Justinian sat to organize Roman law. In the

Institutes one can already find allusions to the notion of intermittent insanity in connection with the composition of wills. The will of an insane person made during a lucid interval or "before the onset of madness" was considered legally valid. The *Institutes* stated that those who were considered "insane and wasteful" (*furiosi . . . et prodigi*) "are put under the supervision of their agnates [relatives by male line] by the Twelve Tables" and could not make a will or perform any transaction "as [they] cannot even understand" and "[do] not know what [they are] doing." See *Institutes*, I, 23, 3; III, 19, 8 II, 12, 1. For a description of the *Institutes*, see Birks and McLeod, introduction to Justinian, *Justinian's Institutes*, 8–13; for the importance of the *Digesta* and its "rediscovery" by Italian medieval jurists, see Alessi Palazzolo, *Processo penale*, 23–39.

26. Santarelli, *Esperienza giuridica basso-medievale*, 59–67. See also Gardi, *Stato in provincia*, 215; Vallerani, "Criminal Court Procedure," 28; Boari, *Qui venit contra iura*, 57, 87–88, 112.

27. Degli Ubaldi, *Consilia sive responsa* (1575), vol. 3, *consilium* 347 ("Homicidium commissum per furiosum an puniatur"); and Boari, *Qui venit contra iura*, 96. See also Menochio, *Consilia*, vol. 1, *consilium* 82, † 211, 172v ("Praeterea † furiosus satis ipso suo furore punitur")

28. See *Justinian's Institutes*, I, xxiii.3, "De curatoribus," and Boari, *Qui venit contra iura*, 22–25.

29. Menochio, *Consilia*, vol. 1, *consilium* 82, † 204, 172r; Boari, *Qui venit contra iura*, 86.

30. For a discussion of these terms, see Boari, *Qui venit contra iura*, 42–43; Mantica, *De coniecturis ultimarum voluntatum*, 19r–20r; Mascardi, *Conclusiones probationum omnium*, 210–28; Menochio, *De praesumptionibus*, bk. 6:297v–300r.

31. *Dizionario giuridico romano*.

32. Ibid.

33. Ibid.; Boari, *Qui venit contra iura*, 43; Angelozzi and Casanova, *Giustizia criminale*, 473–76.

34. Boari, *Qui venit contra iura*, 43–50; Burke, "Images as Evidence," 276.

35. Menochio and Mascardi wrote that a person could be presumed insane if his relatives and neighbors claimed so. Menochio, *De praesumptionibus*, bk. 6, *praesumptio* 45, † 44–45, 299r; "Furoris probandi aliud est argumentum, ut cum a patre sic furiosus existimatur . . . vel ab affinibus, & consaguineis ita habaeatur, vel ab alijs, & denique comiter sic iudicaretur." Mascardi, *Conclusiones probationum omnium*, conclusio 826, † 5, 225. For the notion of social and legal *fama*, see Bettoni, "Fama, Shame Punishment"; Bettoni, "Voci malevole"; Fenster and Smail, introduction to *Fama*; Kuehn, "Fama"; Angelozzi and Casanova, *Giustizia criminale*, 503–12.

36. Menochio, *De praesumptionibus*, bk. 6, *praesumptio* 45, † 46, 299r.

37. Mascardi, *Conclusiones probationum omnium*, conclusio DCCCXXVI, nn. 10, 14, 17, 19, 20, 30; Mantica, *De coniecturis* 20r–v, paragraphs 10, 11, 13, 15.

38. "Sextum est signum & coniectura . . . quis ad rem non respondet, ut si una de re interrogatur, de altera respondeat. . . . Furoris, et dementiae signum est, quando quis loquitur verba inordinate, fatua, et talia, quae ab homine sanae mentis proferri non solent." Menochio, *De praesumptionibus*, bk. 6, *praesumptio* 45, †† 36, 39, 297v. "Furor colligitur cum quis ad rem ipsam, de qua agitur, non respondet"; "30. qui enim fatue

loquitur fatuus praesumitur." Mascardi, *Conclusiones probationum omnium, conclusio* 826, † 20, 224 and † 30, 225.

39. "Ita pariter si probatur te exivisse domum districto e cruento gladio, & cruenta veste; et in domo repertum esse cadaver: solumque te fuisse mortui inimico, urgens inde oritur coniectura et praesumptio, ducta a ratione humana, & coniecturis ita apparentibus confirmata, ut dicendum sit, te illum occidisse." Menochio, *Consilia*, bk. 6, *consilium* 82, † 85, 169v.

40. "Illud vero notandum est, furoris probationem difficilem esse." Mantica, *De coniecturis*, vol. 2, † 16, 20r. "Furiosum quem esse cum difficiliter possit probari, quo pacto sit intelligendum furiosum ex coniecturis et praesumptionibus probari." Mascardi, *Conclusiones probationum omnium, conclusio* 824, *argumentum* 220. "Sciendum est, † stultitiam, dementiam, insaniam & furorem difficile esse probationis, quippe quae sunt de his, quae latent in hominis animo & passim cognita non sunt, nisi diu cum eo quis sit & versetur, & ob id Baldus in l. 2 ss de testa. scribit, mentis sanitatem esse quid invisibile, & proprie non percipitur visu vel auditu, sed magis iudicio rationis. & ideo (ut dixi) difficilis probationis est." Menochio, *Consilia*, bk. 1, *consilium* 82, † 211, 172v.

41. "Iudex in iudicando aliquem furiosum plenam adhibere debet causae cognitionem, cum multi tales se fingant." Menochio, *De praesumptionibus*, 297v, pr. 45, 23.

42. "5. Sed hinc prius non discedam, quam te admoneam, furiosum in † dubio neminem praesumi, cum quilibet sanae mentis esse praesumatur. . . . 6. Cuius rei ratio illa reddi potest, quia haec praesumptio sanae mentis, propria ipsius naturae praesumptio est, ut scilicet sensus & ratio naturalis in quolibet homine praesumitur. . . . 8. hinc propterea est, ut qui furiosum † aliquem esse dixerit, id ei onus probandi incumbat." Mascardi, *Conclusiones probationum omnium, conclusio* 824, 221. "Natura ipsa parit homines sanae mentis: & ideo † qui asserit aliquem esse insanum repugnat ipsi naturae; atque ita ei adversatur praesumptio, quae a natura ipsa descendit." Menochio, *De praesumptionibus*, bk. 6, *praesumptio* 45, † 22, 298v. "2 . . . & ei, qui dicit, testatorem fuisse furiosus, vel mentecaptum, onus probandi incumbit." Mantica, *De coniecturis*, 19r.

43. Mascardi, *Conclusiones, conclusio* 825, † 10, 223; Menochio, *De praesumptionibus*, bk. 6, *praesumptio* 46, †† 63–65, 300r; Boari, *Qui venit contra iura*, 112.

44. Boari, *Qui venit contra iura*, 121, 130–40.

45. Menochio, *De praesumptionibus*, 297, pr. 45, 23.

46. Menochio, *Consilia*, vol. 1, *consilium* 94, †† 35–36, 211v.

47. For Sixtus V's papal bull, see Zanardi, *Bononia manifesta*, 234. For an analysis and interpretation of the bull and the reaction of the senatorial aristocracy to it, see Angelozzi and Casanova, *Giustizia criminale*, 218–21; Gardi, *Stato in provincia*, 72.

48. Angelozzi and Casanova, *Giustizia criminale*, 218.

49. For the history and functioning of Bologna's "governo misto," see De Benedictis, *Repubblica per contratto*, and Gardi, *Stato in provincia*, for the years of Sixtus V's papacy. For a view of the relationship between Bologna's senatorial nobility and the Roman *curia*, see Reinhardt, "Quanto è differente Bologna?," 107–46.

50. Gardi, *Stato in provincia*, 174. Alavolini was Bologna's *uditore* from 1587 to 1591, while Violano left his post as *sotto-uditore* at the end of June of the year 1589 and came back to Bologna in the same capacity between the end of 1592 and the first few months of 1593. I thank Andrea Gardi for his generosity in sharing with me his data archive

detailing Violano's and Alavolini's careers in the ranks of the justice system in the Papal State.

51. Angelozzi and Casanova, *Giustizia criminale*, 220.

52. ASB, *Torrone* 2133, depositions of Benini, Ratta, Brocchi, Salani. Battista Tacconi, Carlo Ratta's servant, testified that when Paolo got into his master's house, they thought he was crazy (37v), and the servant Maddalena stated that everybody in the Barbieri house said that her master "had a humor" (*haveva un humore*) (67v).

53. "Io credo sia stata una pazzia io [*sic*], perche so che non haveva ragione nessuna di far questo et era un humore cosi che stava qualche volta cosi, tre e quattro di in casa che non parlava." Ibid., 36r.

54. "Che sempre haveva l'humore e non si sapeva che cosa havesse." Ibid., 40v–41r.

55. Ibid., 31r–31v. "And in that instant, I heard above my room making noises as if people were running . . . the servant of my brother's wife, called Madalena, arrived at the door of my room and knocked I said who is it, she said it's me, run, that the cavaliero has wounded us all. Fearing that he would come down for me, I double locked the door of my room, even if it was already locked, and I got dressed. Then I opened the door of my room and went out and saw that that servant was wounded on one hand, and cried and screamed hoime my hand, hoime my hand."

56. Ibid., 34r.

57. Ibid., 32r–33v.

58. When Violano questioned Benini for the first time as a witness, he wanted to know if the notary had suggested that Aurelio send clothes to his brother. Benini denied it, even though at Ratta's house several people reported that he said so. Ibid., 25v.

59. ASB, *Torrone* 2133, 33r; 35v; 43.

60. "C'è di peggio ha ferito sua moglie et credo la sia morta." Ibid., 80v–81r.

61. "Signore, ho io mo a patir per questo io." Ibid., 35v.

62. "Signore no[n] io ero fora di me et non sapevo che cosa mi facesse, et tanto mi era andar la quanto a venir qua mi et non di meno se Vostra Signoria si contenta io dico che il mio Procuratore rispondera a questo interrogatorio et a questo processo." Ibid., 47v.

63. Ibid., 54v.

64. Ibid., 84r–84v.

65. "Signore mi butto nelle vostre braccia se ho mancato in cosa nessuna et errato è stato ignorantemente et ve ne dimando perdono eccomi qua fate quello che voi volete et cosi è la verità." Ibid., 76v–77r.

66. Ibid., 6r.

67. For the life and career of Dionisio Ratta and a brief story of the Ratta family, see Casanova, "Ratta, Dionisio."

68. ASB, *Torrone* 2133, 6r–7v.

69. Ibid., 48r.

70. Ibid., 39r–39v (Grato's request), 39v–40r (Fontana's request).

71. "Signore io non lo dissi mo alla corte ne a nessuno che era li che il cavaliero fosse stato in casa mia et che s'era partito verso porta di stra Castioni perché non mi venne fantasia." Ibid., 53v.

72. "Perché in quelli fatti cosi che l'homo non crede havere a render di conto non

pone piu mente che tanto, et casa mia sempre sta aperta et ci vene sempre della gente che io non sto a dimandare chi sia et chi non sia." Ibid., 97r.

73. Ibid., 22v–23r and 23v–24r. When questioned again on October 27, this time as a codefendant, and asked about the words exchanged between Paolo Barbieri and the men present in Carlo Ratta's house the morning of the murder, Benini stated that "the knight kept saying nonsense and screamed 'leave me my sword, I am a knight, my honor is at stake if I am without arms, I am dead, I am wounded, they will kill me, they are following me' . . . then he hugged everybody and begged us not to leave him." Ibid., 78v.

74. Ibid., 24v. At the time of Sixtus V, there were eight notaries and one head notary; each notary could choose up to three assistant notaries. Gardi, *Stato in provincia*, 159. See also Rose, "Violence and the Centralization of Criminal Justice," 106–7.

75. "No[n] mi andò alla fantasia." ASB, *Torrone* 2133, 26v.

76. Ibid., 25v–26r.

77. Ibid., 18r–19v.

78. "Questa è la verità et in summa fu andato prima a quell' altra casa dei Ratta che vi ho detto perché intesi fosse quella perché . . . c'è una Madonna sul muro." Ibid., 101r, 103r.

79. Ibid., 94v.

80. Ibid., 94r–95r. Benini's lawyer Salaroli is not mentioned, but he must have received a copy as well if on November 2 he produced questions and exceptions for the defensive phase of the trial. For the explanation of the expression *alla larga*, see Angelozzi and Casanova, *Giustizia criminale*, 499.

81. For the structure of the early modern criminal trial, see ibid., 449–683.

82. ASB, *Torrone* 2133, 104v. The *exceptiones cum articulis* presented by Buratto, Salaroli, Fontana, and Grato are placed at the end of the volume containing the proceedings of the trial, on single sheets, probably handwritten by each of the four lawyers. It is worth mentioning that, according to the proceedings of the trial, on October 25 Grato was the defense lawyer of Ludovico Salani; however, a few days later, on October 29, Buratto became Salani's lawyer until the end of the trial. Ibid., 58v (Grato); 95r–95v (Buratti). This was perhaps Salani's attempt to distance himself from Aurelio and Paolo Barbieri.

83. Ibid., unnumbered loose sheets of paper included in the volume; they refer to 104r of the volume, where Salani's lawyer, Buratto, is said to have presented his expectations and questions for the witnesses *pro parte*. The numbered sheets of the volume *Torrone* 2133 stop at 182r. Loose sheets of paper were included in the volume, and they have numbers on their top left margin that refer to numbered pages in the bounded volume.

84. Ibid., unnumbered loose sheets of paper.

85. Ibid., 141v.

86. "Vir[um] prob[um], obedient[em] et bonae conditionis, opinionis et famae." Ibid., unnumbered loose sheets of papers.

87. Kuehn, "Fama."

88. On the "arte" of the *strazzaroli* in Bologna, see Gardi, *Stato in provincia*, 134.

89. Violano questioned the witnesses called by Buratto on November 3, 4, and 15. ASB, *Torrone* 2133, 106v–14v; 130v–32v; 134v–36v; 146r–48r; 148v–52r.

90. "Homo da bene veridico, et degno di fede et homo di bonissima vita et fama conditione et oppenione." Ibid., 130v.

91. Ibid., 132r–v.

92. Ibid., 146r (Fantuzzi); 148v (Leonori).

93. Ibid., 148r (Fantuzzi's deposition); ibid., 151r (Leonori's deposition).

94. Ibid., 146v.

95. Ibid., 149r, 149v.

96. See Burdick, *Principles of Roman Law*, 415. In juridical terms, *negligentia* is one of the forms of criminal guilt. See D'Angelo and del Giudice, "Colpa."

97. "Lui è stato sempre obediente alli ordini de superiori anzi so che dalli signori auditori che ci son stati qui pro tempore è stato tenuto e ben voluto et si son serviti di lui senza riserva et lui gl'ha obediti et serviti fedelmente con ogni deligentia." ASB, *Torrone* 2133, 116r. Curzio Rumuli was questioned both for Salani and Benini.

98. "Since he would have been excessively negligent in wasting so much time before reporting the news of the event and the aftermath to the court" (Poi che saria stata troppo grande negligentia in perder tanto tempo prima che se ne havesse dato notizia alla corte del fatto e caso seguito). Ibid., 121v.

99. "'Fu temporeggiato non poco che prima che si mettesse assieme li sbirri si dovette esser temporeggiato un quarto d'hora incirca poi tutti di compagnia il Capitano de condusse in stra Castiglione in casa di Monsignor Ratta." Ibid., 124v.

100. Ibid., unnumbered loose sheets of paper.

101. Members of the Seccadinari and Volta families figured among the representatives of the Senate of Bologna, and the Accursi family counted among its ancestors the famous thirteenth-century jurist Accursio.

102. "Gentil homo di buona virtù timorata consientia et di bona fama e conditione" and "solito a vivere cristianamente." ASB, *Torrone* 2133, 126r (Seccadinari's deposition), 143r (Volta's deposition). In his deposition Accursi uses wording very similar to that of Seccadinari (128r).

103. ASB, *Demaniale San Giacomo*, 96/1702.

104. Diana Barbieri, Paolo and Aurelio's sister, married Valerio Rinieri in 1577. ASB, *Demaniale San Giacomo*, 95/1701. Later, a descendant of the Rinieri family bequeathed some of the family property to the Augustinian friars of the church of San Giacomo Maggiore, along with all the documents pertaining to those properties. A folder included in this collection of documents contains two sets of defenses for Aurelio Barbieri, written by the same hand, which I recognize as that of Grato. Ibid., 96/1702.

105. Daston, "Marvelous Facts and Miraculous Evidence," 243.

106. ASB, *Torrone* 1233, 138r–139v.

107. ASB, *Demaniale San Giacomo*, 96/1702, 26.

108. Ibid., 26–27.

109. Ibid., 22–23.

110. Menochio, *De praesumptionibus*, bk. 6, *praesumptio* 59, 299v.

111. Menochio, *De praesumptionibus, praesumptio* 45, 298v; Mascardi, *Conclusiones probationum omnium, conclusio* 826, † 23, 224.

112. ASB, *Demaniale San Giacomo*, 96/1702.

113. ASB, *Torrone* 2133, 143r/v; 133r.

114. Ibid., 145v.

115. ASB, *Demaniale San Giacomo*, 96/1702.

Id potius fecit pro honore familiae ipsius Domini Aurelij de Barberijs in Civitate Bononiae nobilis etiam reputatae, et ne ire, et stare idem Paulus nudus, et solum cum interula visus fuisset, et ne cogeretur pudibunda, et cetera membra eius uti nuda ostendere, et demonstrare, et etiam officium pietatis quia ipsi Domino Aurelio dictum fuit, quod uti nudus, et ob frigiditatem temporis tremebat potiusquam quod idem Dominus Aurelius pan(n)os . . . mitti iussisset domino Paulo, ut ei auxilium vel opem prestare, stante maxime quod audiverat eum nudum in capiteque, et in pedibus et dorso excepta sola interula, et cum ense enudato per stratas cur(r)ere tamquam furiosum, et insanum factum.

116. At the end of his life Aurelio seemed to have thrown his "officium pietatis" out of the window when he decided to leave nothing to his sister Diana and bequeathed all his goods to a religious confraternity in Rome. For the narration and discussion of the aftermaths of Paolo's murder on his family, see chapter 5.

117. ASB, *Demaniale San Giacomo*, 96/1702.

118. ASB, *Torrone* 2133, unnumbered loose sheets of paper.

119. Ibid., unnumbered loose sheets of paper.

120. Early modern men and women wore hats and headdresses for protection and decorum at the same time. For an interpretation of hats and headdresses in the context of the early modern network of market economy, urban communities, and court fashion, see Welch, "Art on the Edge."

121. ASB, *Torrone* 2133, unnumbered loose sheets of paper. Their depositions are not recorded.

122. ASPI, *Suppliche e informazioni* 1095 doc. 212, 617r; ASPI, *Fondo dell'Ordine di S. Stefano, Provanze di nobiltà* (Paolo Barbieri) filza n. 41 inserto 47, 0626. ASB, *Torrone* 2133, 133r–134r; 155r–60r (Emilio Barbieri's deposition). Emilio was the only witness called by the defense who was questioned at home.

123. ASB, *Torrone* 2133, 155r.

124. Ibid., 156v–57v.

125. "Et per tale quale tengo io detto Signor Aurelio credo sia tenuto et reputato da tutti gli altri, et in questo non credo habbi bisogno di prova che si sa a Bologna chi è il Signor Aurelio." Ibid., 158r.

126. "Giovene honesta virtuosa quieta et di bonissima conversatione." Ibid., 158v.

127. "Per pietà et per honore della fameglia sua." Ibid., 159v.

128. Ibid., 144v. For Fontana's use of Paolo's insanity in his defense of Carlo Ratta, see ibid., unnumbered loose sheets of paper.

129. Fosi, *Papal Justice*, 2.

CHAPTER 4

1. Legnani, "Diario," 2:69r–v.

1588 Adi 24 d'Ottobre in lunedì, il Cavaliere Paulo Barbieri dell'ordine di Santo Stefano di Fiorenza et Pisa, figliolo fu di Messere Antonio Maria Barbieri, et di Madonna Hippolita Gessi Barbieri, sua madre che vive, fratello di Messer Orelio Barbieri, ammazzò sua moglie Madonna Isabella Caccianemici fu figliola di Messere Scipione Caccianemici che per humore malenconico si gittò in uno pozzo, et figliola di Madonna Angelica Bolognetti Caccianemici, giovinetta di XV anni, et dicono de più era gravida di 5 mesi . . . havea da 7 ferite, caso degno de grande compassione, haverla (?) ammazzata senza causa, solo per humor malenconico.

2. De Caprio and Senatore, "Orality, Literacy, and Historiography," 131.

3. For information on the Legnani family and on Pirro Legnani, see Guidicini, *Alberi genealogici delle famigli nobili bolognesi*, ASB, vol. 3, s.v. "Legnani"; Fantuzzi, *Notizie*, 5:49; Quaquarelli, *Memoria Urbis: I*, 133. Before becoming a priest, Legnani had been elected to several prestigious city offices. In March 1588 Cardinal Antonio Carafa encouraged Legnani to become a cleric. To achieve this position, Legnani rushed through the three orders of "letterato, esorcista e studioso" by dispensation. In his "Diario, o sia cronaca delle cose accadute in Bologna (1555–1601)," Legnani wrote that he officiated his first Mass on March 28, 1595, in a small chapel restored by a relative of his, Veronica Savii Legnani, widow of Antonio Legnani. Veronica was unable to leave her house and therefore had an oratory built inside her residence. Legnani, "Diario," 1:163v. Legnani left the position of canon of the cathedral of San Pietro in 1618 and died in 1622.

4. E. Cohen, "Moving Words," 69.

5. For the presence of emotions in legal depositions, see Smail, *Consumption of Justice*, 14–16, 92, 93–94.

6. See chapter 3.

7. E. Cohen, "Back Talk," 101–2.

8. ASB, *Torrone* 2133, 67v.

9. Ibid., 6v.

10. Ibid., 36r.

11. "Lui Signore stava a tavola e non parlava mai lui[,] e stava con la testa bassa sempre mai che era una morte il fatto suo." Ibid., 40v.

12. Ibid., 21v/22r.

13. Ibid., 21v.

14. Ibid., 33r.

15. "Il C.ro diceva delle coglionarie et gridava lassateme la mia spada son cavaliero si tratta del honor mio a star senz'arme io son morto io son ferito mi amazzaranno mi seguitano"; "Mi arrivaranno a dosso e mi amazzaranno e in somma dava nelle coglionarie." Ibid., 78r/v. The notary used the same term again when he qualified what Salani said of Paolo's nonsense: "Arivo li il Salame [sic] et cominciò a far allegrezza e con le mane e con la cera raccontando le coglionarie che diceva la il cavaliero." Ibid., 80v.

16. For the meaning of *coglionerìa*, see *Dizionario degli Accademici della Crusca* (1691).

17. "Fingendo d'essere stato assaltato da gente et esser stato offeso." ASB, *Torrone* 2133, 122v. Ferrarini submitted his *denuntia* (accusation) against Paolo the day of the murder, after he visited the Barbieri house with the *sotto-uditore* Violano and the notary Cambio. However, Ferrarini's accusation was put on record on November 3. Ibid., 122r–v.

18. Rinieri, "Diario," 2:55v; Bianchini, "Cronaca di Bologna," BUB 296, 1:13r;

anonymous, "Cronaca di Bologna 1588–1595," 3. The church of San Giovanni in Monte had been an important center for the Order in Emilia Romagna since the twelfth century and produced a significant number of *predicatori* (preachers) who were sent to other churches in Bologna because of their rhetorical skills and religious preparation. At the end of the sixteenth century, a good number of the canons were from Bologna, including the abbot, further reinforcing the already strong link that the institution had with the fabric of the city. For information about the church of San Giovanni in Monte, see Raule, "Chiesa di San Giovanni in Monte," and Fanti and Degli Espositi, *Chiesa di San Giovanni in Monte*. For a detailed history of the Order of the Regular Lateran Canons, see Egger, "Canonici regolari," in *Dizionario degli Istituti di perfezione*, ed. Pelliccia and Rocca.

19. Antonio Francesco Ghiselli, "Memorie antiche manuscritte di Bologna raccolte, et accresciute sino a' tempi presenti," BUB 770, vol. 18, 600–603.

20. Ghiselli's work, in ninety-two volumes, ranges from the origins of Bologna to 1729.

21. An example of Ghiselli's archival research is the multivolume *Scritture varie concernenti la città di Bologna*. For a detailed account of Ghiselli's life, see Ciuccarelli, "Antonio Francesco Ghiselli."

22. "Finally, after Aurelio, Carlo, Lodovico, and Leone stayed a few days in jail [*alla larga*], as I said [earlier], all submitted petitions, paid money for them, and they too were freed" (*Finalmente dimorato Aurelio, Carlo, Lodovico, e Leone alcuni giorni come ho detto alla larga, tutti supplicarono, e pagarono per le suppliche denari, e furono anch'essi liberati*). Ghiselli, *Memorie*, vol. 18, 603.

23. Fentress and Wickham, *Social Memory*; Dale, Lewin, and Osheim, *Chronicling History*.

24. Dunphy, *Encyclopedia of the Medieval Chronicle*, s.v. "Family Chronicles."

25. The Lateran canon reported events that happened in the city of Bologna, like the killing of a young boy who worked for a goldsmith in the city and the arrival in Bologna of a bearded young woman, and in the rest of Europe, like the murder of the king of France, Henry III, whom he condemned, along with his followers, as heretics: he hoped that the king of Spain, instrument of the "triumphant" post-Tridentine Church, would exterminate them all. See Pezzarossa, "Prima verifica," 3:133–34.

26. The chronicler boasted that he was the cousin of Camillo Sighicelli (or Sighiulli), who worked as a secretary of cardinals Filippo Guastavillani (1541–1587) and Enrico Caetani (1550–1599), two very important figures during Sixtus V's papacy. For the information about the relationship between the anonymous chronicler and Camillo Sighicelli, see anonymous, *Cronaca*, 16. For the identity of Camillo Sighicelli and his diary of the trip to France at the retinue of Cardinal Caetani, see Manfroni, "Legazione del Cardinale Caetani in Francia."

27. Bianchini, "Cronaca di Bologna"; Rinieri, "Diario 1520–1613"; Legnani, "Diario"; Anonymous, "Cronaca di Bologna 1588–1595."

28. Legnani, "Diario," 2:94v, 185v, 195r. Ercole Mamelini wrote a note in the chronicle of his father Andrea about the difference between *cronaca* and *historia*, which is that the former gives narrations of events as they happened, while the latter is biased and subject to external influences. Andrea Mamelini, "Liber Memorialium," BA, B 1156,

11r. For a discussion of the corpus of chronicles written by different generations of the Mamelini family, see Montanari, *Cronaca e storia bolognese*, 5–70, and in particular 5.

29. De Caprio and Senatore, "Orality, Literacy, and Historiography," 130.

30. See Richardson, *Manuscript Culture*, xx.

31. For information on the cultural and social circles in which Rinieri and Legnani operated, see Antonelli and Pedrini, "Criteri editoriali," xxxi–xxxvi; Pezzarossa, "Alcune osservazioni," 511.

32. Richardson, *Manuscript Culture*, xi.

33. Niccoli, "Manoscritti, oralità, stampe popolari," 178.

34. Halbwachs, *On Collective Memory*; Fentress and Wickham, *Social Memory*.

35. See chapter 1 for the laborious and expensive process through which candidates and their families had to go in order to be considered eligible to become knights of the Order of Santo Stefano.

36. Bianchini, "Cronaca di Bologna," 5 vols.

37. "Il primo Novembre 1587 comintiai a scrivere questo libro." Ibid., 1:149r. A careful reading of the entire chronicle presents the reader with a few interesting elements that confirm what Quaquarelli has argued, namely, that, although not the count Marcantonio Bianchini, the author of this chronicle was a member of this noble senatorial family. Quaquarelli, *Memoria Urbis: I*, 59–61.

38. Quaquarelli argues that Bianchini wrote his chronicle day after day. See Quaquarelli, *Memoria Urbis: I*, s.v. "Bianchini, Marcantonio."

39. The expressions *si dice/disse*, *si diceva*, and *dicono* are frequent in the chronicle. See, for instance, Bianchini, "Cronaca di Bologna," 1:45v, 87v, 96v/97r, 141v, 213r/v, 242r, 282r/283r, 291r/292r, 311r; 2:33r, 225r; 4:121r.

40. "Chi dice esser avvenuto per lite, altri per humore." Ibid., 13r.

41. Rinieri, "Diario 1520–1613," BUB 2137, 5 vols.

42. "Overwhelmed by madness [*furore*] and melancholic humor." Rinieri, "Diario 1520–1613," 55v.

43. Among the many documents he compiled during his lifetime, Rinieri wrote a short account of the Barbieri family in which he reported Paolo's killing of Isabella, his blood relation with Rinieri's wife Diana, and his death in 1606. Rinieri, "Raccolta delle famiglie di Bologna et loro fatti et parentadi," BUB 2136B, 1:281r–286r, and in particular 282v, 286v; 2:188–211, and in particular 207v–8r.

44. Valerio's father Giovambattista was one of the main *procuratori* of Bologna, and his mother Pantasilea belonged to the powerful family of the Moneti alias Scanabecchi. Valerio's uncle Giacomo Rinieri combined his profession of antiquarian with a great passion for ancient times and a penchant for writing chronicles. See Antonelli e Pedrini, "Parte I: Il codice BUB 1994," 26, 235. Because of his family's social standing in Bologna, Rinieri held various positions in the local government—he was elected one of the *tribuni della plebe*, and one of the *anziani*. See Antonelli e Pedrini, "Criteri editoriali," xii.

45. For the affectionate words Rinieri uses in reference to the death of Cardinal Filippo Guastavillani, which occurred on August 17, 1587, in Rome and that of the prothonotary apostolic Valenti on November 1588, see Rinieri, "Diario 1520–1613," 2:18v, 57r.

46. Cicero, *Tusculan Disputations*, book 4, chap. 23; Petrarca, *Rerum vulgarium fragmenta*, 232; *Vocabolario degli Accademici della Crusca* (1612).

47. Rinieri did identify Paolo as his brother-in-law elsewhere in his chronicle—for instance, when Paolo attended the funerals of Giovanni Paolo Castellani, prior of the church of Santo Stefano in Bologna. Rinieri, "Diario 1520–1613," 2:26r/v.

48. About twenty years later her murderer was buried in the same church. ASB, *Demaniale San Giacomo*, 91/1697.

49. "They buried her the following morning in the church of San Domenico, and there were so many people that there was no space on the sides [of the church]." Bianchini, "Cronaca," 13r.

50. Anonymous, "Cronaca di Bologna 1588–1595," 3.

51. Making additions in the margins at a later stage is a characteristic of Legnani's way of writing his chronicle.

52. For the definition of the term *eccesso*, see *Grande Dizionario della lingua Italiana*.

53. Legnani also reported that Paolo had found refuge in the house of Carlo Ratta, who did not know that Paolo had killed his wife and thought that his behavior was caused by "melancholic humor." Besides being further proof of Legnani's acquaintance with the proceedings of the trial, this information could also be evidence of the author's close relationship with the Ratta family, since it corresponded with what Ratta said during his first deposition. Legnani seems also to imply that Ratta was somehow obliged to accept Paolo's presence in his home because somebody else brought him in.

54. The anonymous chronicler seemed to be abreast of what happened during the trial and of the argument that the judge used to sentence Ratta and Aurelio Barbieri to pecuniary fees, so that they could be punished "if not with their lives, at least with a great sum of money."

55. After the pope's death, Rinieri stated that everybody hated him, and Legnani and Bianchini wrote that he was too greedy and haughty. Rinieri, "Diario 1520–1613," 2:94r–v; Legnani, "Diario," 2:94v; Bianchini, "Cronaca," 1:5r.

56. For the life of Elena Duglioli and her connection with the church of San Giovanni in Monte, see Romanello, "Elena Duglioli," and Zarri, "Altra Cecilia."

57. For the oligarchy established by the Bentivogli family throughout most of the fifteenth century, see Gardi, *Stato in provincia*, 97–105.

58. One example is when Ghiselli reports that Salani and Benini suggested that Aurelio Barbieri send Paolo some clothes to Carlo Ratta's house, and Aurelio responded that "something worse has happened, as he [Paolo] killed his wife." Another example is when Ghiselli recounts the grave mistake that the *bargello* made when he searched the house of the wrong Ratta on Strada Castiglioni while looking for Paolo and the servant Francesco. A third example is when Ghiselli narrates that Paolo asked Carlo Ratta for some water, allegedly to wash his hands, so that he could escape with his servant without being noticed or stopped by anyone. Ghiselli relates this information with no reference to the biased nature of the depositions from which he obtained them.

59. Casanova and Angelozzi, *Nobiltà disciplinata*, 18.

60. E. Cohen, "She Said, He Said," 405–6.

61. Fox and Woolf, introduction to *Spoken Word*, 5.

CHAPTER 5

1. ASB, *Demaniale San Giacomo*, 91/1697.

2. Smail, *Consumption of Justice*, 188.

3. ASB, *Torrone* 2133, 151v–52r. See Sacco, *Statuta civilia, et criminalia*, 472, for the rules regulating the seizure of a murderer's property (rubrica 51, "De poena homicidae et mandantis fieri homicidium et eius, cuius dolo commissum fuerit homicidium"). On the same topic, see also *Reformatio offici Turroni*, 27v/28r ("Quando de paena capitali ageretur, vel pecuniaria & corporali simul") and Verardi Ventura, "Ordinamento bolognese," 375–78. Francesco's last name appears nowhere during the trial; however, when Paolo was in the hospital of San Vincenzo in Prato in Milan, and after he returned to Bologna in 1598, he was accompanied by a male servant by the name of Francesco Di Menghioli (or Di Mengoli), who received periodic payments for his service. See ASB, *Demaniale San Giacomo*, 91/1697 ("Spese fatte in diverse cause, et liti delli Barbieri proprij"), 16. For the inquisitorial procedure against defendants, see Angelozzi and Casanova, *Giustizia*, 479–92.

4. ASB, *Torrone* 2133, 161r–165v.

5. Ibid., 161v, 164r–v.

6. Ibid., 161v–162r, 171v.

7. Ibid., 166v. During Sixtus V's papacy there was "a large recourse to the 'supplica,' with which defendants request pardon (maybe upon payment of a pecuniary 'settlement') for their crimes: the *legato*, as the pope's alter ego of and holder of his sovereign authority, grants the dismissal of criminal actions in 1007 cases (199 per year)" (my translation). Gardi, *Stato in provincial*, 204.

8. ASB, *Torrone* 2133, 167r. Two thousand one hundred twenty-five lire were also paid to submit this petition to the apostolic office. Ibid., 167v.

9. Ibid., 168v, 171r. Ratta had to pay 1275 lire and Salani 255 to submit their petitions to the apostolic office.

10. "The uditore of the Torrone questions the legato . . . before issuing the sentences for the most serious causes . . . [he] signs the release warrants" (my translation). Gardi, *Stato in provincia*, 206.

11. ASB, *Torrone* 2133, 171v.

12. ASB, *Demaniale San Giacomo*, 97/1703, 50r–v. This statement is part of a letter written by Aurelio Barbieri, which the office of the *vicelegato* of Bologna put on record on July 24, 1597.

13. No trial or sentence against Paolo Barbieri is recorded in Lucca's criminal proceedings between the end of 1588 and the beginning of 1590. They report, though, the aggressive behavior and injurious words of a Florentine knight by the name of Bartolo (or Jacopo Bartoli) in the public squares of Lucca between September and December 1589. While the two times he hit people in the face did not warrant any form of penalty, after he proclaimed that all citizens of Lucca were traitors and assassins, the judge banned Bartolo from the city and the state of Lucca, never to return. Could this knight have been Paolo in disguise? His actions and words are reminiscent of Paolo's behavior, but until more evidence is unveiled, this remains a conjecture. ASLU, *Potestà di Lucca, Inquisizioni*, 650, 108r–v; 651, 60r, 163r; *Sentenze e Bandi*, 302, 926v–927r; 303, 13r–v.

14. ASB, *Torrone* 2133, 172r–176v.

15. For information on the hospital of San Vincenzo in Prato, see chapter 33 of the untitled treatise written by Gian Giacomo Gilino and published in 1508. The original version of the treatise, in Latin, and the text in Italian are reproduced in Cosmacini, *Carità e la cura*, 87–160 and 162–83.

16. ASB, *Legato*, Expeditiones 104, 281r–v. A copy of the letter is also in ASB, *Demaniale San Giacomo*, 94–1700b.

17. In the seventeenth century other hospitals in Bologna, Florence, and Rome required relatives to pay a monthly fee for the admission of insane people. See Roscioni, *Governo della follia*, 112–13.

18. AOM, *Origine e dotazione, Aggregazioni, San Vincenzo Ospedale*, 86 (Amministrazione: visite, 1517–1640).

19. AOM, *Libro Mastro Entrate* (1594–98), fol. 415, s.v. "Hospitale de Santo Vincenzo."

20. In her book *Governo della follia*, Lisa Roscioni discusses other Italian hospitals that admitted people considered insane by their relatives and community between the second half of the fifteenth century and the nineteenth century. She examines in detail the Hospital of Santa Maria della Pieta' in Rome, which was founded in 1548.

21. The first mention of the church of San Vincenzo in Prato occurred in 822. The hospital, which was built next to the church, was probably established in the twelfth century. See De Peri e Panzeri, "Origine dell'assistenza ai folli," 21, 24; Cantù and Venosta, *Milano Diamante*, 342.

22. Roscioni, *Governo della follia*, 45.

23. De Peri and Panzeri, "Origine dell'assistenza ai folli," 21–23.

24. Gilino was born in the mid-fifteenth century in the castle of Caravaggio, where his father Tomaso, who was prefect of the duke of Milan at that time, was commander of the fortress. Gilino was chancellor, secretary, and ducal councilor of both Gian Galeazzo and Ludovico Sforza. For further information on Gilino's life, see Spinelli, introduction to *La relazione ai deputati*, 30–34. See also Roscioni, *Governo della follia*, 22.

25. Cosmacini, *Carità e la cura*, 176.

Capitolo XXXIII. . . . Se de cervello manchino, sive sono furiosi, hanno la receptione sua separata nel hospitale de Sancto Vincentio, qual numero, perché sole per la più parte del tempo essere picolo, se li agiongeno infirmi de altre due qualitate, cioè o de vechieza o de qualche ulcerazione, fora de lazarosi.

Chapter XXXIII. . . . If they are brainless, or if they are furious, they have their separate reception in the hospital of San Vincenzo; because the number [of its patients] is in general small, two other qualified categories are added, the elderly and people suffering from some forms of ulceration, except for those caused by leper. (my translation)

26. Canetta, *Cronologia del'Ospedale Maggiore*, 100; De Peri and Panzeri, "Origine dell'assistenza ai folli," 25.

27. AOM, *Origine e dotazione, Aggregazioni, San Vincenzo Ospedale*, 86 (Amministrazione: visite, 1517–1640).

28. A rigid separation according to gender could be also found in the Hospital of

Santa Maria della Pietà. In general, patients in the hospitals for insane people were more or less forced to work. Roscioni, *Governo della follia*, 246.

29. De Peri and Panzeri, "Origine dell'assistenza ai folli," 30–31. AOM, *Origine e dotazione, Aggregazioni, San Vincenzo Ospedale*, 86 (Amministrazione: visite, 1517–1640).

30. Roscioni, *Governo della follia*, 34–37. By the end of the sixteenth and the beginning of the seventeenth century some institutions like the Hospital of Santa Maria della Pietà and Santa Dorotea in Florence seemed interested in organizing and coordinating therapies for their patients. Roscioni, *Governo della follia*, 221–22.

31. Mellyn, *Mad Tuscans and Their Families*, 58–93.

32. ASB, *Legato*, Suppliche, 55 (1597–99), 48r. The petition is also transcribed in the proceedings of the trial. ASB, *Torrone* 2133, 179v.

33. For the date of Aurelio's death, see ASR, *Archivi dei 30 Notari Capitolini*, Officio 6, 1597 (Notaio Girolamo Tranquilli) 286r, where Aurelio draws up his will on September 7, 1597, and *Collegio dei Notari Capitolini*, vol. 748 (1596–97; Notaio Vincenzo Foschi) 694r, where are listed the objects found in the rooms where Aurelio died.

34. ASB, *Torrone* 2133, 181r–v.

35. Ippolita died on February 14, 1598. For the date of Ippolita's death, see ASB, *Demaniale San Giacomo*, 91–1697 ("Quinterno delle heredità della signora Hippolita Barbieri"). In this document, written by Valerio Rinieri, are listed the expenses in which he incurred for his mother-in-law's funeral, and the items found in her house at the time of her death.

36. ASB, *Demaniale San Giacomo*, 91/1697, 90/1696.

37. Both Lodi's letter and Spinola's permission are in ibid., 94–1700 ("Scritture, processi, e carte diverse relative all'eredità Rinieri").

38. ASB, *Demaniale San Giacomo*, 91/1697 and AOM, *Origine e dotazione, Aggregazioni, San Vincenzo Ospedale*, 86 (Amministrazione, visite, 1517–1640). For the treatment of the violently insane, see De Peri and Panzeri, "Origine dell'assistenza ai folli," 33 and n. 86.

39. Kuehn, *Heirs, Kin, and Creditors*, 17.

40. Smail, *Consumption of Justice*; Rosenwein, "Worrying About Emotions"; Rosenwein, "Problems and Methods"; Lemmings, "Law," 192–95; Wiener, Bornstein, and Voss, "Emotion and the Law."

41. Bourdieu, *Logic of Practice*, 54–56.

42. Rinieri, "Raccolta delle famiglie di Bologna et loro fatti et parentadi," vol. 1, BU 2138.

43. ASB, *Demaniale San Giacomo*, 90/1696.

44. Ibid., 94/1700.

45. Ibid., 91/1697.

46. Ibid., 91/1697.

47. Ibid., 94/1700.

48. Ibid., 96/1702, 97/1703.

49. "Centralized courts of law in late medieval Europe would not have developed so rapidly without the monetary and emotional investment of ordinary users of law. . . . I would insist only that the pursuit of grudges, rather than a reasoned preference for

rationality or a desire to achieve an outcome, was a chief motive for the investment." Smail, *Consumption of Justice*, 17.

50. The *pater familias* Antonio Maria Barbieri died in 1569, when his two sons were still very young. In the preface to his book *Heirs, Kin, and Creditors* Kuehn writes that tackling the topic of inheritance is too complicated because of its vastness and intricacies (xi). Luckily for us, our goal is not as sophisticated and vast as that which Kuehn and other excellent scholars in the field have set up in their articles, essays, and books. On the topic of inheritance, see also Tamassia, *Famiglia italiana*; Besta, *Successioni nella storia del diritto italiano*; Goody, Thirsk, and Thompson, *Family and Inheritance*; Klapisch-Zuber, *Women, Family, and Ritual*.

51. Kuehn, *Heirs, Kin, and Creditors*, 89.

52. ASB, *Demaniale San Giacomo*, 97/1703.

53. Ibid., 96/1702, "Lettere del Signor Giovan Francesco Grato scritte al Signor Aurelio Barbieri in Roma." Grato wrote three letters to Aurelio in Rome on May 27, July 2, and August 8, 1597.

54. "April 17, 1602. A man bequeaths his properties to charity and not to his two daughters because he says they are not his. The day before, he had been mortally wounded with a harquebus and stab wounds to the face; makes a will and dies with great contrition." Bianchini, "Cronaca," 85v–86r.

55. ASB, *Demaniale San Giacomo*, 97/1703.

56. Ibid., "Scritture delli Signori Aureglio et Cavaliere Paollo Barbieri."

57. Ibid. A copy of the pope's letter, dated April 10, 1597, appears also in ibid., 94/1700 with the heading "Breve de Nostro Signore Clemente ottavo in favor del signor Aurelio Barbieri," and in ASR, *Archivio 30 Notari capitolini* Officio 6 1597 12r–18r.

58. ASR, *Fondo Arcinconfraternita SS. Annunziata*, "Officio della curia del cardinale vicario in Roma Officio 33," 622r.

59. ASR, *Archivio del Collegio dei Notai Capitolini*, vol. 748 (1596–97), 705r.

60. ASB, *Demaniale San Giacomo*, 90/1696. The transfer of the inheritance of Giovan Battista Ranieri, son of Valerio, to the priors and friars of Santo Giacomo di Bologna of the order of Sant' Agostino was finalized on January 5, 1633.

61. ASR, *Archivio del Collegio dei Notari Capitolini*, vol. 748 (1596–97), 705v–6v.

62. Kuehn, *Law, Family, and Women*, 249.

63. ASB, *Demaniale San Giacomo*, 95/1701. See Tamassia, *Famiglia italiana*, 289; Kirshner, *Marriage, Dowry, and Citizenship*, 88–92.

64. The humoral theory and the thought systems of Freud and Darwin exemplify the hydraulic model. In the second half of the twentieth century, the cognitive and social constructionist outlooks completely replaced the hydraulic model of emotions. The work of Martha Nussbaum, the Stearnses, and Antonio Damasio is an example of the cognitive model, where emotions are recognized as having a cognitive element and are the result of a process of appraisal and judgment of what is beneficial for an individual and/or a community. The work of Barbara Rosenwein and William Reddy exemplifies the social constructionist model, in which societies and social groups shape, encourage, or discourage certain emotions. The interpretation in this chapter inclines toward the social constructionist model of the study of emotions. However, a combination of

the cognitive and constructionist model can benefit the field and the analysis of a legal situation or document.

65. Smail, *Consumption of Justice*; Bailey and Knight, "Writing Histories of Law and Emotion"; Maroney, "Law and Emotion"; Nussbaum, *From Disgust to Humanity*. Kounine is the editor of an issue of the *Journal of Social History* entirely devoted to the intersection of emotion, reason, and body in the courtroom (*Journal of Social History* 51, no. 2 [2017]).

66. Relying on a social constructionist model of emotions, Susan Matt describes the effect that society had on one particular emotion, namely, envy, between the end of the nineteenth and the beginning the twentieth century, and how this emotion appeared to be intertwined with a radical change in American economy and its attitude toward consumerism. Matt, *Keeping up with the Joneses*.

67. Bailey and Knight, "Writing Histories of Law and Emotion," 122; Remer, "Rhetoric, Emotional Manipulation, and Political Morality."

68. Yanagisako, *Producing Culture and Capital*, 83.

69. Maroney, "Law and Emotion," 119n1.

70. Ibid., 119.

71. Kuehn, *Law, Family, and Women*, 255–56.

72. ASB, *Demaniale San Giacomo*, 95/1701, "Origine della famiglia de Rinieri di Bologna et lor disendenti." Girolamo Barbieri, the only male survivor of the family, died in 1626. He was the first cousin of Paolo and Aurelio Barbieri and became too a knight of the Order of Santo Stefano. See Rinieri, "Raccolta di scritture delle famiglie di Bologna et loro dignità e origine, et degli huomini illustri che di quelle sono," BUB 2138, 5 vols.

73. In 1624 Domenico and Cristoforo Barbetti were condemned to death in absentia, accused of having committed crimes and collaborated with bandits. Their sentence and the confiscation of their goods were the culmination of a bloody feud between the Barbetti and Tanari families. The consequences of the sentence reverberated for years, at least until 1635. See Angelozzi and Casanova, *Giustizia criminale*, 244–53; ASB, *Assunteria del Torrone* 9 ("Miscellanea di varii casi di Confiscationi, Multe, et altri pregiudicij intentati dalla Corte criminale contro le prerogative della Città et i rimedij procurati dal Pubblico per esimersi da detti pregiudicij Tomo Primo"), 57r–120r.

CONCLUSION

1. Rose, *Renaissance of Violence*.

BIBLIOGRAPHY

PRIMARY SOURCES

Anonymous. "Cronaca di Bologna 1588–1595." BAB, *Fondo Gozzadini* 287.

Bianchetti, Alamanno. "Annali di Bologna dall'edificazione della città fino al 1599." 5 vols. BAB, *Fondo Malvezzi*, 59–63.

Bianchini, Marcantonio. "Cronaca di Bologna 1584–1638." 5 vols. BUB 296.

Carrari, Vincenzo. *De medico et illius erga aegros officio Opusculum varia, et non spernenda eruditione refertum: omnibus, praecipue in foro versantibus utile, Et pernecessarium.* Ravenna, 1581.

Carrati, Antonio Maria. "Li matrimoni contratti a Bologna. Tomo I: Fedelmente estratti da loro originali parrocchiali libri dal Conte Antonio Maria Carrati." BAB, Fondo speciale manoscritti B, 900.

Catalogo di tutte le giustizie in Bologna dall'anno 1030 sino al 1539 estratto da varie croniche e manuscritte e stampate, come si vede dalle note in margine. Dall'anno poi 1540 sino al tempo presente dalli libri della Conforteria. ASB, Sala Studio.

Cicero, Marcus Tullius. *Cicero on Emotions: Tusculan Disputations 3 and 4.* Translated by Margaret Graver. Chicago: University of Chicago Press, 2002.

Codronchi, Giovanni Battista. *De vitiis vocis, libri duo. . . . Cui accedit Consilium de raucedine, ac Methodus testificandi, in quibusvis casis medicis oblatis, postquam formulae quaedam testationum proponantur.* Frankfurt, 1597.

———. *Il methodus testificandi.* Edited and translated by Clemente Puccini, M. Bini, Giovanni Chieregatti, and Chiara Sabattani. Bologna: Forni, 1987.

Da Monte, Giambattista. *Consultationes medicae.* Basel: Henrichum Petrum et Petrum Pernam, 1583.

Galeati, Domenico Maria. "Palazzi e case nobili della Città di Bologna da chi possedute anticamente ed in oggi per quanto si è potuto sapere, e ricavare da instrumenti da Istorie e da altre notizie e dello stato presente della Città sino all'anno 1771." BAB, Fondo speciale manoscritti B, 93.

Galliani, Francesco Maria. "Cose notabili ed importanti, 1589–1600." ASB, *Demaniale, Malvezzi-Campeggi,* iv, 47/707.

Ghiselli, Antonio Francesco. "Memorie antiche manuscritte di Bologna raccolte, et accresciute sino a' tempi presenti." Vol. 18. BUB 770.

Guidicini, Giuseppe. "Alberi genealogici delle famiglie nobili bolognesi." ASB, vol. 3, s.v. "Legnani."

———. *Cose notabili della città di Bologna ossia storia cronologica de' suoi stabili sacri, pubblici e privati.* 5 vols. Bologna, 1868–73.

Justinian. *Justinian's Institutes*. Translated by Peter Birks and Grant McLeod. London: Duckworth, 1987.

Legnani Ferri, Pirro. "Diario, o sia cronaca delle cose accadute in Bologna (1555–1601)." 2 vols. BUB 896.

Mamelini, Andrea. "Liber Memorialium." BAB, *Fondo speciale manoscritti B*, 1156.

Mantica, Francesco. *De coniecturis ultimarum voluntatum libri duodecim*. Venice, 1580.

Marescalchi, Giovan Battista. *Cronaca 1561–1573*. Edited by Ilaria Francica. Bologna: Costa Edizioni, 2002.

Mascardi, Giuseppe. *Conclusiones probationum omnium quae in utroque foro quotidie versatur*. 3 vols. Venice, 1584.

Menochio, Giacomo. *Consultationes et responsa medicinalia quattuor tomis comprehensa*. Venice: Iacobo Franciscis, 1620.

———. *De praesumptionibus, coniecturis, signis et indicis, commentaria*. 2 vols. Venice, 1587–90.

Mercuriale, Girolamo. *Medicina practica*. Frankfurt am Main: Johann Theobald Schönwetter, 1602.

———. *Responsorum et consultationum medicinalium in duo volumina digesta*. Venice: Giolito, 1589.

"Miscellanea di memorie storiche bolognesi." BAB, *Fondo speciale manoscritti* B, 1283.

"Miscellanea di varii casi di Confiscationi, Multe, et altri pregiudicij intentati dalla Corte criminale contro le prerogative della Città et i rimedij procurati dal Pubblico per esimersi da detti pregiudicij Tomo Primo." ASB, *Assunteria del Torrone* 9.

Petrarca, Francesco. *Rerum vulgarium fragmenta*. Edited by Giuseppe Savoca. Florence: Olschki, 2008.

Philosophiae ac medicinae scholarium Bononiensis Gymnasii Statuta sub feliciss. Auspiciis Illustrissimi, ac Reverendiss. Card. Justiniani Bonon. De Latere Legati instaurata MDCIX. Bologna, 1612.

Rinieri, Valerio. "Diario 1520–1613." 2 vols. BUB 2137.

———. "Raccolta delle famiglie di Bologna et loro fatti et parentadi." Vol. 1. BUB 2136B.

———. "Raccolta di scritture delle famiglie di Bologna et loro dignità et origine, et degli huomini illustri che di quelle sono stati." 5 vols. BUB 2138.

Salaroli, Carlo. "Famiglie della città di Bologna, loro origine, Arme, Case, e Sepolture. Loro Dignità, e de magistrate esercitati, Nobili, Antiche, e Moderne. Sino all'anno 1740. Forma il secondo libro della Nobiltà di Bologna." BAB, Fondo speciale manoscritti B, 802.

Tagliacozzi, Gaspare. *De curtorum chirurgia per incisionem*. Venice, 1597.

Ubaldi, Baldo degli. *Consilia sive responsa*. 5 vols. Venice, 1575.

Zacchia, Paolo. *Quaestiones medico-legales*. 5th ed. Avignon, 1657.

SECONDARY SOURCES

Accademia della Crusca, ed. *Lessicografia della Crusca in rete*. http://www.lessicografia.it/index.jsp.

Agasse, Jean-Michel. "La Bibliothèque d'un Medecin Humaniste: L'Index Librorum de Girolamo Mercuriale." *Les Cahiers de l'humanisme* 3/4 (2002–3): 202–53.

Ago, Renata. "Una giustizia personalizzata. I tribunali civili di Roma nel XVII secolo." *Quaderni Storici* 34, no. 2 (1999): 389–412.

Agrimi, Jole, and Chiara Crisciani. *Les consilia médicaux.* Translated by Caroline Viola. Turnhout, Belgium: Brepols, 1994.

———. *Edocere medicos: Medicina scolastica nei secoli XIII–XV.* Naples: Guerini e Associati, 1988.

———. "L'individuale nella medicina tra Medio Evo e Umanesimo: I 'consilia.'" In *Umanesimo e medicina: Il problema dell'individuale,* edited by Roberto Cardini and Mariangela Regolosi, 1–32. Rome: Bulzoni, 1996.

Alessi Palazzolo, Giorgia. *Il processo penale. Profilo storico.* Bari: Laterza, 2001.

Angelozzi, Giancarlo, and Cesarina Casanova. *La giustizia criminale in una città di antico regime: Il tribunale del Torrone di Bologna (sec. XVI–XVII).* Bologna: CLUEB, 2008.

———. *La nobiltà disciplinata: Violenza nobiliare, procedure di giustizia e scienza cavalleresca a Bologna nel XVII secolo.* Bologna: CLUEB, 2003.

Antonelli, Armando, and Riccardo Pedrini. "Criteri editoriali." In *Cronaca di Giacomo Rinieri 1535–1549,* edited by Armando Antonelli and Riccardo Pedrini, xv–li. Bologna: Costa Edizioni, 1998.

———. "Parte I: Il codice BUB 1994." In Giovanni, *Cronaca di Bologna 1443–1452,* edited by Armando Antonelli and Riccardo Pedrini, 25–92. Bologna: Costa Edizioni, 2000.

Ascari, Tiziano. "Carrari. Vincenzo." In *Dizionario Biografico degli Italiani,* vol. 20.

Ascheri, Mario. "I 'consilia' come acta processuali." In *La diplomatica dei documenti giudiziari (dai placiti agli acta—secc. xii–xv). Atti del X Congresso internazionale della Commission Internationale de Diplomatique, Bologna 12–15 Settembre 2001,* edited by Giovanna Nicolaj, 309–28. Vatican City: Scuola Vaticana Paleografia, 2004.

———. "'Consilium sapientis' perizia medica e 'res iudicata': Diritto dei 'dottori' e istituzioni comunali." In *Proceedings of the Fifth International Congress of Medieval Law, Salamanca 21–25 September 1970,* edited by Stephen Kuttner and Kenneth Pennington, 533–79. Vatican City: Biblioteca Apostolica Vaticana, 1980.

Bailey, Merridee L., and Kimberly-Joy Knight. "Writing Histories of Law and Emotion." *Journal of Legal History* 38, no. 2 (2017): 117–29.

Barbagli, Marzio. *Congedarsi dal mondo: Il suicidio in Occidente e Oriente.* Bologna: Il Mulino, 2009.

Bastia, Claudia, and Maria Bolognani, eds. *La memoria e la città: Scritture storiche tra Medioevo ed età moderna.* Bologna: Il Nove, 1995.

Battaglia, Salvatore, ed. *Grande Dizionario della lingua Italiana.* 21 vols. Turin: UTET, 1967–2002.

Besta, Enrico. *Le successioni nella storia del diritto italiano.* Padua: CEDAM, 1935.

Bettoni, Antonella. "Fama, Shame Punishment and Metamorphoses in Criminal Justice (Fourteenth–Seventeenth Centuries)." *Forum historiae iuris* 24 (2010) https://forhistiur.net/2010-03-bettoni.

———. "Voci malevole: Fama, notizia del crimine e azione del giudice nel processo criminale (secc. XVI–XVII)." *Quaderni Storici* 41, no. 1 (2006): 13–38.

Birks, Peter, and Grant McLeod. Introduction to Justinian, *Justinian's Institutes*, 8–13.

Blanshei, Sarah Rubin, and Sara Cucini. "Criminal Justice and Conflict Resolution." In *A Companion to Medieval and Renaissance Bologna*, edited by Sara Rubin Blanshei, 335–60. Leiden: Brill, 2018.

Boari, Marco. *Qui venit contra iura: Il furiosus nella criminalistica dei secoli XV e XVI*. Milan: Giuffrè Edizioni, 1983.

Bourdieu, Pierre. *The Logic of Practice*. Translated by Richard Nice. Stanford: Stanford University Press, 1990.

Brambilla, Elena. "Genealogia del sapere: Per una storia delle professioni giuridiche nell'Italia padana secoli xiv–xvi." *Schifanoia* 8 (1989): 123–50.

Brizzi, Gian Paolo, Lino Marini, Paolo Pombeni, and Enrica Baiada, eds. *L'università a Bologna: Maestri, studenti e luoghi dal XVI al XX secolo*. 2 vols. Bologna: Cassa di Risparmio di Bologna, 1988.

Burdick, William L. *The Principles of Roman Law and Their Relation to Modern Law*. Clark, NJ: Lawbook Exchange, 2004.

Burke, Peter. "Images as Evidence in Seventeenth-Century Europe." *Journal of the History of Ideas* 64, no. 2 (2003): 273–96.

———. "Oral and Manuscript Cultures in Early Modern Italy." In Innocenti, Richardson, and Sbordoni, *Interactions Between Orality and Writing*, 21–30.

Bylebyl, Jerome. "The School of Padua: Humanistic Medicine in the Sixteenth Century." In *Health, Medicine and Morality in the Sixteenth Century*, edited by Charles Webster, 335–70. Cambridge: Cambridge University Press, 1979.

Calabritto, Monica. "Curing Melancholia in Sixteenth-Century Medical Consilia, Between Theory and Practice." *Medicina nei secoli* 24, no. 3 (2012): 627–64.

———. "Examples, References, and Quotations in Sixteenth-Century Medical Texts." In *Citation, Intertextuality, and Memory in the Fourteenth and Fifteenth Centuries*, edited by Yolanda Plumley, Giuliano Di Bacco and Stefano Jossa, 58–73. Exeter: University of Exeter Press, 2011.

———. "Medicina practica, Consilia and the Illnesses of the Head in Girolamo Mercuriale and Giulio Cesare Claudini: Similarities and Differences of the Sexes." *Medicina e storia* 12 (October 2006): 63–83.

Canetta, Pietro. *Cronologia del'Ospedale Maggiore*. Milan, 1884.

Cantù, Ignazio, and Felice Venosta. *Milano Diamante*. Milan, 1877.

Capitani, Ovidio. *L'Università di Bologna: Personaggi, momenti e luoghi dalle origini al XVI secolo*. Cinisello Balsamo: Silvana Edizioni, 1987.

Carboni, Mauro. *Il credito disciplinato: Il Monte di Pietà di Bologna in età barocca*. Bologna: Il Mulino, 2014.

Casanova, Cesarina. *Crimini nascosti: La sanzione penale dei reati "senza vittima" e nelle relazioni private (Bologna XVII secolo)*. Bologna: CLUEB, 2007.

———. "Ratta, Dionisio." In *Dizionario Biografico degli Italiani*, vol. 86.

Casini, Bruno. *I cavalieri degli Stati Italiani membri del Sacro Militare Ordine di Santo Stefano Papa e Martire*. Vol. 1. Pisa: ETS, 1998.

Cerasoli, Giancarlo, and Brunella Garavini. "La bibliografia delle opere a stampa di Girolamo Mercuriale." *Medicina & Storia* 6 (2006): 85–119.

Chandelier, Joël, and Marilyn Nicoud. "Entre droit et médecine: Les origines de la médecine légale en Italie (XIIIe–XIVe siècles)." In *Frontières du savoir*, edited by Joël Chandelier and Aurélien Robert, 233–93. Rome: École française de Rome, 2015.

Cicogna, Emanuele Antonio. *Delle inscrizioni veneziane raccolte ed illustrate da Emmanuele Antonio Cigogna cittadino Veneto*. Vol. 2. Venice, 1827.

Ciuccarelli, Cecilia. "Ghiselli, Antonio Francesco." In *Dizionario Biografico degli Italiani*, vol. 54.

Cohen, Elizabeth. "Back Talk: Two Prostitutes' Voices from Rome, c. 1600." *Early Modern Women Journal* 2 (2007): 95–126.

———. "Moving Words: Everyday Oralities and Social Dynamics in Roman Trials Circa 1600." In Dall'Aglio, Richardson, and Rospocher, *Voices and Texts*, 69–83.

———. "She Said, He Said: Situated Oralities in Judicial Records from Early Modern Europe." *Journal of Early Modern History* 16 (2012): 403–30.

Cohen, Thomas. *Love and Death in Renaissance Italy*. Chicago: University of Chicago Press, 2004.

Colombero, Carlo. "Il medico e il giudice." *Materiali per una storia della cultura giuridica* 16 (1986): 363–81.

Cosmacini, Giorgio, ed. *La carità e la cura: L'Ospedale Maggiore di Milano nell'età moderna*. Milan: Pizzi, 1992.

Crawford, Catherine. "Legalizing Medicine: Early Modern Legal Systems and the Growth of Medico-Legal Knowledge." In *Legal Medicine in History*, edited by Michael Clark and Catherine Crawford, 89–117. Cambridge: Cambridge University Press, 1984.

Crisciani, Chiara. "'Consilia,' responsi, consulti: I pareri del medico tra insegnamento e professione." In *Consilium: Teorie e pratiche del consigliare nella cultura medievale*, edited by Carla Casagrande, Chiara Crisciani, and Silvana Vecchio, 259–79. Florence: Sismel-Edizioni del Galluzzo, 2004.

Dale, Sharon, Alison Williams Lewin, and Duane J. Osheim, eds. *Chronicling History: Chroniclers and Historians in Medieval and Renaissance Italy*. University Park: Penn State University Press, 2007.

Dall'Aglio, Stefano, Brian Richardson, and Massimo Rospocher, eds. *Voices and Texts in Early Modern Italian Society*. London: Routledge, 2017.

Dall'Aglio, Stefano, and Massimo Rospocher. Introduction to Dall'Aglio, Richardson, and Rospocher, *Voices and Texts*, 1–19.

Dallari, Umberto. *I rotuli dei lettori legisti e artisti dello Studio Bolognese dal 1348 al 1799*, vol. 2. Bologna, 1889.

D'Amelio, Mariano, and Arturo del Giudice. "Colpa." In *Enciclopedia Italiana*. Rome: Istituto dell'Enciclopedia Italiana, 1931. https://www.treccani.it/enciclopedia/colpa_%28Enciclopedia-Italiana%29.

Davis, Natalie Zemon. *The Return of Martin Guerre*. Cambridge, MA: Harvard University Press, 1984.

De Benedictis, Angela. *Repubblica per contratto: Bologna; Una città europea nello Stato della Chiesa*. Bologna: Il Mulino, 1995.

De Caprio, Chiara, and Francesco Senatore. "Orality, Literacy, and Historiography in Neapolitan Vernacular Urban Chronicles of the Fifteenth and Sixteenth

Centuries." In Innocenti, Richardson, and Sbordoni, *Interactions Between Orality and Writing*, 129–43.

Delbianco, Maria. *Le sedi storiche del Monte di pietà di Bologna*. Florence: Olschki, 1999.

De Peri, Francesco, and Laura Panzeri. "L'origine dell'assistenza ai folli in provincia di Milano: l'ospedale di San Vincenzo in Prato." In *Tempo e catene: Manicomio, psichiatria e classi subalterne; Il caso milanese*, edited by Alberto De Bernardi, Francesco de Peri, and Laura Panzeri, 15–54. Milan: Franco Angeli, 1980.

De Renzi, Silvia. "Medical Expertise, Bodies, and the Law in Early Modern Courts." *Isis* 98, no. 2 (2007): 315–22.

———. "La natura in tribunale: Conoscenze e pratiche medico-legali a Roma nel XVII secolo." *Quaderni storici* 36, no. 3 (2001): 799–822.

———. "Per una biografia di Paolo Zacchia: Nuovi documenti e ipotesi di ricerca." In *Paolo Zacchia, 1584–1659: Alle origini della medicina legale*, edited by Alessandro Pastore and Giovanni Rossi, 50–73. Milan: Franco Angeli, 2008.

———. "Witnesses of the Body: Medico-legal Cases in Seventeenth-Century Rome." *Studies in History and Philosophy of Science* 33, no. 2 (2002): 219–42.

Di Zio, Tiziana. "Il tribunale criminale di Bologna nel secolo XVI." *Archivi per la storia* 4 (1991): 125–35.

Dizionario Biografico degli Italian. Rome: Istituto dell'Enciclopedia Italiana, 1977. https://www.treccani.it/enciclopedia/vincenzo-carrari_(Dizionario-Biografico).

Dizionario degli Istituti di perfezione. Edited by Guerrino Pelliccia and Giancarlo Rocca. Rome: Edizioni Paoline, 1975.

Dizionario giuridico romano. 3rd ed. Naples: Edizioni Giuridiche Simone, 2000.

Duffin, Jacalin. "Questioning Medicine in Seventeenth-Century Rome: The Consultations of Paolo Zacchia." *Archives and Artifacts / Archives et artefacts de la pratique médicale* 28, no. 1 (2011): 149–70.

Dunphy, Graeme. *Encyclopedia of the Medieval Chronicle*. Leiden: Brill, 2016.

Egger, Carlo. "I canonici regolari di Sant'agostino." In *Dizionario degli Istituti di perfezione*. Edited by Guerrino Pelliccia and Giancarlo Rocca. Rome: Edizioni Paoline, 1975.

Eliav-Feldon, Miriam. *Renaissance Impostors and Proofs of Identity*. London: Palgrave Macmillan, 2012.

Evangelisti, Claudia. "Gli 'operari delle liti': Funzioni e status sociale dei procuratori legali a Bologna nella prima età moderna." In *Parlare, scrivere, vivere nell'Italia di fine Cinquecento: Quattro saggi*, 89–103. Rome: Carocci, 2018.

Fanti, Mario, and Carlo Degli Espositi. *La chiesa di San Giovanni in Monte in Bologna: Guida a vedere e a comprendere*. Bologna: Pubblicazione a cura della Parrocchia di S. Giovanni in Monte, 1994.

Fantuzzi, Giovanni. *Notizie degli scrittori bolognesi raccolte da Giovanni Fantuzzi*. 9 vols. Bologna, 1781–94.

Feci, Simona. "Mantica, Francesco Maria." In *Dizionario Biografico degli Italiani*, vol. 69.

Fenster, Thelma, and Daniel Lord Smail, eds. *Fama: The Politics of Talk and Reputation in Medieval Europe*. Ithaca: Cornell University Press, 2003.

Fentress, James, and Chris Wickham, *Social Memory*. Oxford: Blackwell, 1994.

Finucci, Valeria. *The Prince's Body. Vincenzo Gonzaga and Renaissance Medicine.* Cambridge, MA: Harvard University Press, 2015.

Fosi, Irene. *Papal Justice: Subjects and Courts in the Papal State, 1500–1700.* Translated by Thomas Cohen. Washington, DC: Catholic University of America Press, 2011.

Foucault, Michel. *Histoire de la folie à l'âge classique.* Paris: Plon, 1961.

Fox, Adam, and Daniel Woolf, eds. *The Spoken Word: Oral Culture in Britain, 1500–1850.* Manchester: Manchester University Press, 2003. http://library.oapen.org/handle/20.500.12657/34996.

Garcia-Ballester, Luis. "On the Origin of the 'Six Non-natural Things' in Galen." *Sudhoffs Archiv. Beihefte* 32 (1993): 105–15.

Gardi, Andrea. *Lo stato in provincia: L'amministrazione della legazione di Bologna durante il regno di Sisto V (1585–1590).* Bologna: Istituto per la Storia di Bologna, 1994.

Giansante, Massimo. "Il caso di Lucia da Varignana: Psicopatologia della vita quotidiana in un processo per infanticidio del 1672." *Atti e Memorie Nuova Serie* 44 (1993): 303–21.

Ginzburg, Carlo. "Clues: Roots for an Evidential Paradigm." In Ginzburg, *Clues, Myths, and the Historical Method*, translated by John and Anne Tedeschi, 96–125. Baltimore: Johns Hopkins University Press, 1989.

Gnudi, Martha Teach, and Jerome Pierce Webster. *The Life and Times of Gaspare Tagliacozzi Surgeon of Bologna, 1545–1599: With a Documented Study of the Scientific and Cultural Life of Bologna in the Sixteenth Century.* New York: Harbert Reichner, 1950.

Goody, Jack R., Joan Thirsk, and Edward Palmer Thompson, eds. *Family and Inheritance: Rural Society in Western Europe, 1200–1800.* Cambridge: Cambridge University Press, 1976.

Gordian, Michael. "The Culture of Dis/simulation in Sixteenth- and Seventeenth-Century Europe." PhD diss., University of London, 2014. https://core.ac.uk/download/pdf/33337697.pdf.

Gowland, Angus. "The Problem of Early Modern Melancholy." *Past and Present* 191, no. 1 (2006): 83–84.

———. *The Worlds of Renaissance Melancholy: Robert Burton in Context.* Cambridge: Cambridge University Press, 2006.

Guarnieri, Gino. *L'ordine di Santo Stefano nei suoi aspetti organizzativi interni sotto il Gran Magistero Mediceo*, vol. 1. Pisa: Giardini, 1966.

Halbwachs, Maurice. *On Collective Memory.* Translated and edited by Lewis A. Coser. Chicago: University of Chicago Press, 1992.

Healy, Róisín. "Suicide in Early Modern and Modern Europe." *Historical Journal* 49, no. 3 (September 2006): 903–19.

Hodgkin, Katherine. *Madness in Seventeenth-Century Autobiography.* New York: Palgrave Macmillan, 2007.

Innocenti, Luca degl', Brian Richardson, and Chiara Sbordoni, eds. *Interactions Between Orality and Writing in Early Modern Italian Culture.* London: Routledge, 2016.

Kirshner, Julius. *Marriage, Dowry, and Citizenship in Late Medieval and Renaissance Italy.* Toronto: University of Toronto Press, 2015.

Klapisch-Zuber, Christiane. *Women, Family, and Ritual in Renaissance Italy*. Chicago: University of Chicago Press,1985.

Kounine, Laura. "Emotions, Mind, and Body on Trial: A Cross-Cultural Perspective." *Journal of Social History* 51, no. 2 (2017): 219–30.

Kuehn, Thomas. "Fama as a Legal Status in Renaissance Florence." In Fenster and Smail, *Fama*, 27–46.

——. *Heirs, Kin, and Creditors in Renaissance Florence*. Cambridge: Cambridge University Press, 2008.

——. *Law, Family, and Women: Toward a Legal Anthropology of Renaissance Italy*. Chicago: University of Chicago Press, 1994.

Lemmings, David. "Law." In *Early Modern Emotions. An Introduction*, edited by Susan Broomhall, 192–95. London: Routledge, 2017.

Lockwood, Dean Putnam. *Ugo Benzi: Medieval Philosopher and Physician*. Chicago: University of Chicago Press, 1951.

Maclean, Ian. "Evidence, Logic, the Rule and the Exception in Renaissance Law and Medicine." *Early Science and Medicine* 5, no. 3 (2000): 227–57.

——. *Interpretation and Meaning in the Renaissance: The Case of Law*. Cambridge: Cambridge University Press, 1992.

——. *Logic, Signs and Nature in the Renaissance: The Case of Learned Medicine*. Cambridge: Cambridge University Press, 2002.

Magnusson, Sigurdur Gylfi, and István Sijártó. *What Is Microhistory? Theory and Practice*. London: Routledge, 2013.

Manfroni, Camillo. "La legazione del Cardinale Caetani in Francia (1589–90) con nuovi documenti della collezione Taggiasco e dell'Archivio Vaticano." *Rivista Storica Italiana* 10, no. 2 (1893): 193–270.

Maroney, Terry A. "Law and Emotion: A Proposed Taxonomy of an Emerging Field." *Law and Human Behavior* 30, no. 2 (April 2006): 119–42.

Matt, Susan. *Keeping up with the Joneses: Envy in American Consumer Society, 1890–1930*. Philadelphia: University of Pennsylvania Press, 2003.

Mazzetti, Serafino. *Repertorio dei professori dell'università e dell'istituto delle scienze di Bologna*. Bologna, 1848.

Mellyn, Elizabeth W. *Mad Tuscans and Their Families: A History of Mental Disorder in Early Modern Italy*. Philadelphia: University of Pennsylvania Press, 2014.

Midelfort, Erik. *A History of Madness in Sixteenth-Century Germany*. Stanford: Stanford University Press, 1999.

Milani, Giuliano. "Lucio II." In *Enciclopedia dei papi*. Rome: Istituto dell'Enciclopedia Italiana, 2000. https://www.treccani.it/enciclopedia/lucio-ii_%28 Enciclopedia-dei-Papi%29.

Minois, George. *History of Suicide: Voluntary Death in Western Culture*. Translated by Lydia G. Cochrane. Baltimore: Johns Hopkins University Press, 1999.

Montanari, Valerio. *Cronaca e storia bolognese del primo Cinquecento nel memoriale di Ser Eliseo Mamelini*. Bologna: Atesa Edizioni, 1979.

Niccoli, Ottavia. "Manoscritti, oralità, stampe popolari: Viaggi dei testi profetici nell'Italia del Rinascimento." *Italian Studies* 66, no. 2 (July 2011): 177–92.

———. *Perdonare: Idee, pratiche, rituali in Italia tra Cinque e Seicento*. Bari: Laterza, 2007.

———. "Voci, scritture, stampe per la battaglia di Ravenna." In *1512: La battaglia di Ravenna, l'Italia, l'Europa*, edited by Dante Bolognesi, 223–35. Ravenna: Longo Edizioni, 2014.

Nussbaum, Martha. *From Disgust to Humanity: Sexual Orientation and Constitutional Law*. Oxford: Oxford University Press, 2010.

Ortalli, Gherardo. "La perizia medica a Bologna nei secoli xiii e xiv: Normativa e pratica di un istituto giudiziario." *Atti e memorie della deputazione di storia patria per le provincie di Romagna* 17–19 (1969): 223–59.

Paoletti, Italo. *Girolamo Mercuriale e il suo tempo*. Lanciano: Cooperativa Editoriale Tipografica, 1963.

Park, Katharine. *Doctors and Medicine in Early Renaissance Florence*. Princeton: Princeton University Press, 1985.

Pastore, Alessandro. *Crimine e giustizia in tempo di peste nell'Europa moderna*. Bari: Laterza, 1991.

———. "Maladies vraies et maladies simulées: Les opinions des juristes et des médecins (XVIe–XVIIe siècles)." *Équinoxe* 22 (Fall 1999): 11–26.

———. *Il medico in tribunale: La perizia medica nella procedura penale d'antico regime (secoli XVI–XVIII)*. Bellinzona: Edizioni Casagrande, 1998.

———. *Veleno: Credenze, crimini, saperi nell'Italia moderna*. Bologna: Il Mulino, 2010.

Pezzarossa, Fulvio. "Alcune osservazioni sulle scritture storiche e di memoria nella Bologna tra Medioevo e Età moderna." In Bastia and Bolognani, *La memoria e la città*, 495–522.

———. "'Cose che non debbono assolutamente vedere la luce': Società e storiografia a Bologna in età senatoria." In *Fra Olimpo e Parnaso: Società gerarchica e artificio letterario*, edited by Fulvio Pezzarossa, 37–89. Bologna: CLUEB, 2008.

———. "Una prima verifica dei rapporti fra strumenti culturali e ruoli sociali: La memorialistica e i ceti bolognesi nei secoli XIV–XVII." In *Sapere e/è potere: Discipline, dispute e professioni nell'Università medievale e moderna; Il caso Bolognese a confronto; Atti del quarto convegno, Bologna, 13–15 Aprile 1989*, edited by Angela De Benedictis, 3:111–34. Bologna: Istituto per la Storia di Bologna, 1990.

Pomata, Gianna. "Observation Rising: Birth of an Epistemic Genre, 1500–1650." In *Histories of Scientific Observation*, edited by Lorraine Daston and Elizabeth Lunbeck, 45–80. Chicago: University of Chicago Press, 2011.

———. "Sharing Cases: The *Observationes* in Early Modern Medicine." *Early Science and Medicine* 15, no. 3 (2010): 193–236.

Quaquarelli, Leonardo, ed. *Memoria Urbis: I. Censimento delle cronache bolognesi del Medioevo e del Rinascimento*. Bologna: Il Nove, 1993.

———. *Per singulare memoria: Retoriche a margine e identità municipale nel Quattrocento Bolognese*. Bologna: CLUEB, 2001.

Raule, Angelo. "La chiesa di San Giovanni in Monte." In Angelo Raule, Giuseppe Rivani, and Mario Maragi, *La Chiesa Parrocchiale di San Giovanni in Monte in Bologna*, 9–18. Bologna: Cassa di Risparmio di Bologna, 1965.

Reinhardt, Nicole. "Quanto è differente Bologna? La città tra amici, padroni e miti all'inizio del Seicento." *Dimensioni e problemi della ricerca storica* 2 (2001): 107–46.

Remer, Gary. "Rhetoric, Emotional Manipulation, and Political Morality: The Modern Relevance of Cicero vis-à-vis Aristotle." *Rhetorica* 31, no. 4 (2013): 402–43.

Richardson, Brian. *Manuscript Culture in Renaissance Italy.* Cambridge: Cambridge University Press, 2009.

Robisheau, Thomas, Thomas Cohen and István Sijártó, eds. "Virtue, Identity, and Agency: Ethical Formation from Medieval to Early Modern." *Journal of Medieval and Early Modern Studies* 42, no. 1 (2017).

Romanello, Marina. "Duglioli Elena." In *Dizionario Biografico degli Italiani*, vol. 41.

Roscioni, Lisa. *Il governo della follia: Ospedali, medici e pazzi nell'età moderna.* Milan: Mondadori, 2003.

Rose, Colin. *A Renaissance of Violence: Homicide in Early Modern Italy.* Cambridge: Cambridge University Press, 2019.

———. "Violence and the Centralization of Criminal Justice in Early Modern Bologna." In *Violence and Justice in Bologna, 1250–1700*, edited by Sarah Rubin Blanshei, 101–22. Lenhan: Lexington Books, 2018.

Rosenwein, Barbara H. "Problems and Methods in the History of Emotions." *Passions in Context* 1, no. 1 (2010): 1–31.

———. "Worrying About Emotions." *American Historical Review* 107, no. 3 (2002): 821–45.

Rossi, Guido. *Consilium Sapientis Iudiciale: Studi e ricerche per la storia del processo romano-canonico I (secoli xii–xiii).* Milan: Giuffré, 1958.

Ruggiero, Guido. "The Cooperation of Physicians and the State in the Control of Violence in Renaissance Venice." *Journal of the History of Medicine and Allied Sciences* 33, no. 2 (1978): 156–66.

Sacco, Filippo. *Statuta civilia, et criminalia civitatis Bononiae.* Vol. 1. Bologna, 1735.

Salterini, Claudia, ed. *L'archivio dei Riformatori dello Studio.* Bologna: Istituto per la Storia dell' Università, 1997.

Santarelli, Umberto. *L'esperienza giuridica basso-medievale: Lezioni introduttive.* Turin: Giappichelli, 1991.

Savoia, Paolo. *Cosmesi e chirurgia: Bellezza, dolore e medicina nell'Italia moderna.* Milan: Editrice Bibliografica, 2017.

Sbriccoli, Mario. "Giustizia criminale." In *Lo Stato moderno in Europa: Istituzioni e diritto*, edited by Maurizio Fioravanti. Bari: Laterza, 2015.

———. "Giustizia negoziata, giustizia egemonica: Riflessioni su una nuova fase degli studi di storia della giustizia criminale." *In Criminalità e giustizia in Germania e Italia: Pratiche giudiziarie e linguaggi giuridici tra tardo medioevo ed età moderna*, edited by Marco Bellabarba, Gerd Schwerhoff, and Andrea Zorzi, 345–64. Bologna: Il Mulino, 2001.

Seneca, Federico. "Un fallito tentativo di Girolamo Mercuriale di tornare nell'Ateneo patavino." In *Rapporti tra le Università di Padova e di Bologna*, edited by Lucia Rossetti, 161–69. Trieste: Edizioni Lint, 1988.

Simili, Alessandro. "The Beginning of Forensic Medicine in Bologna with Two Unpublished Documents." In *International Symposium on Society, Medicine and Law,*

Jerusalem, March 1972, edited by Hans Karplus, 91–100. Amsterdam: Elsevier, 1973.

———. "Gerolamo Mercuriale lettore e medico di Bologna." *Rivista di storia delle scienze mediche e naturali* 23 (1941): 161–91.

———. *Gerolamo Mercuriale lettore e medico a Bologna. Nota II: Il soggiorno e gli insegnamenti*. Bologna: Azzoguidi-Soc. Tip. Editoriale, 1966.

———. "Gerolamo Mercuriale lettore e medico a Bologna. Nota III: La partenza." *Minerva medica* 57, no. 72 (1966): 1–36.

———. "Gerolamo Mercuriale nell'ombra e nella luce del suo tempo." *Il Policlinico (Sezione Pratica)* 48 (1941): 170–80.

Sinisi, Lorenzo. "Mascardi, Giuseppe." In *Dizionario Biografico degli Italiani*, vol. 71.

Siraisi, Nancy. "Anatomizing the Past: Physicians and History in Renaissance Culture." *Renaissance Quarterly* 53, no. 1 (2000): 1–30.

———. *Avicenna in Renaissance Italy: The Canon and Medical Teaching in Italian Universities After 1500*. Princeton: Princeton University Press, 1987.

———. "History, Antiquarianism, and Medicine: The Case of Girolamo Mercuriale." *Journal of the History of Ideas* 64, no. 2 (2003): 231–51.

———. *Medicine and the Italian Universities, 1250–1600*. Leiden: Brill, 2001.

———. *Medieval and Early Renaissance Medicine: An Introduction to Knowledge and Practice*. Chicago: University of Chicago Press, 1990.

———. "Psychology in Some Sixteenth-and Seventeenth-Century Works on Medicine." In *Psychology and the Other Disciplines: A Case of Cross-Disciplinary Interaction (1250–1750)*, edited by Paul J. J. M. Bakker, Sander W. Boer, and Cees Leijenhorst, 325–43. Leiden: Brill, 2012.

———. *Taddeo Alderotti and his Pupils: Two Generations of Italian Medical Learning*. Princeton: Princeton University Press, 1981.

Smail, Daniel Lord. *The Consumption of Justice. Emotions, Publicity, and Legal Culture in Marseille, 1264–1423*. Ithaca: Cornell University Press, 2003.

Snyder, Jon R. *Dissimulation and the Culture of Secrecy in Early Modern Europe*. Berkeley: University of California Press, 2009.

Spinelli, Salvatore, ed. *La relazione ai deputati dell'Ospedale grande di Milano [di Gian Giacomo Gilino]: Ristampa dell'edizione in volgare del 4 novembre 1508*, edited by Salvatore Spinelli, 30–34. Milan: Cordani, 1937.

Strange, Carolyn, and Robert Cribb. Introduction to *Honour, Violence and Emotions in History*, edited by Carolyn Strange, Robert Cribb, and Cristopher E. Fort, 1–22. London: Bloomsbury, 2014.

Strocchia, Sharon. "Women on the Edge: Madness, Possession, and Suicide in Early Modern Convents." *Journal of Medieval and Early Modern Studies* 45, no. 1 (2015): 53–77.

Tamassia, Nino. *La famiglia italiana nei secoli decimoquinto e decimosesto*. Milan: R. Sandron, 1911.

Terpstra, Nicholas. *The Art of Executing Well: Rituals of Execution in Renaissance Italy*. Kirksville: Truman State University Press, 2008.

———. "Confraternal Prison Charity and Political Consolidation in Sixteenth-Century Bologna." *Journal of Modern History* 66, no. 2 (June 1994): 217–48.

————. "Piety and Punishment: The Lay *Conforteria* and Civic Justice in Sixteenth-Century Bologna." *Sixteenth Century Journal* 22, no. 4 (1991): 679–94.

Trivellato, Francesca. *The Familiarity of Strangers: The Sephardic Diaspora, Livorno, and Cross-Cultural Trade in the Early Modern Period*. New Haven: Yale University Press, 2009.

Turner, Wendy J., ed. *Madness in Medieval Law and Custom*. Leiden: Brill, 2010.

Valsecchi, Chiara. "Menochio, Giacomo." In *Dizionario Biografico degli Italiani*, vol. 73.

Verardi Ventura, Sandra. "L'ordinamento bolognese dei secoli XVI–XVII: Introduzione all'edizione dei ms. B.1114 della Biblioteca dell'Archiginnasio; Lo stato, il governo et i magistrati del cavalier Ciro Spontone." *L'Archiginnasio. Bollettino della Biblioteca comunale di Bologna* 74 (1979): 181–425.

Villari, Rosario. "Elogio della dissimulazione." In *Elogio della dissimulazione: La lotta politica nel Seicento*, 3–48. Bari: Laterza, 1987.

Wear, Andrew. "Galen in the Renaissance." In *Galen: Problems and Prospects. A Collection of Papers Submitted at the 1979 Cambridge Conference*, edited by Vivian Nutton, 229–62. London: Wellcome Institute for the History of Medicine, 1982.

————. "Medicine in Early Modern Europe, 1500–1700." In *The Western Medical Tradition, 800 BC to AD 1800*, edited by Lawrence I. Conrad, Michael Neve, Vivian Nutton, Roy Porter, Andrew Wear, 215–362. Cambridge: Cambridge University Press, 1995.

Welch, Evelyn. "Art on the Edge: Hair and Hands in Renaissance Italy." *Renaissance Studies* 23, no. 3 (June 2009): 241–68.

Wiener, Richard L., Brian H. Bornstein, and Amy Voss. "Emotion and the Law: A Framework for Inquiry." *Law and Human Behavior* 30, no. 2 (April 2006): 231–48.

Yanagisako, Sylvia Junko. *Producing Culture and Capital: Family Firms in Italy*. Princeton: Princeton University Press, 2002.

Zagorin, Perez. *Ways of Lying: Dissimulation, Persecution, and Conformity in Early Modern Europe*. Cambridge, MA: Harvard University Press, 1990.

Zanardi, Zita. *Bononia manifesta: Bandi, editti, costituzioni e provvedimenti diversi stampati nel XVI secolo per Bologna e il suo territorio*. Florence: Olschki, 1996.

Zarri, Gabriella, ed. "L'altra Cecilia: Elena Duglioli Dall'Olio." In *Indagini per un dipinto: La Santa Cecilia di Raffaello*, edited by Carla Bernardini, 83–118. Bologna: Edizioni Alfa, 1983.

————. *Finzione e santità tra medioevo ed età moderna*. Turin: Rosenberg & Sellier, 1991.